A HISTORY OF THE JEWS IN BAGHDAD

BY

THE LATE

DAVID SOLOMON SASSOON ע"ה

SIMON WALLENBERG

2006

HACHAMIM AND RABBIS OF BAGHDAD, 1910

[Frontispiece

ISBN 1-84356-002-X
Second Edition

First Edition Published 1949

British Library Catalog Number:

Published by The Simon Wallenberg Press

Printed in the United Kingdom

To the Memory
of those pious men and
women who lived in Baghdad
and worked for the welfare
of their community.
The memory of the
righteous is for
blessing

CONTENTS

PAGE

NOTE BY THE PUBLISHER iv

AUTHOR'S PREFACE vi

I. EARLIEST TIMES 1

II. TALMUDIC AGE 4

III. GEONIC AGE 6

IV. THE EXILARCHS IN BAGHDAD 16

V. SOME FAMILIES AND NAMES PROMINENT IN THE TENTH CENTURY 28

VI. BAGHDAD UNDER R. SHERIRA AND R. HAI 41

VII. R. SHERIRA AND HIS SON R. HAI, AND R. SAMUEL BEN HOFNI 46

VIII. THE GEONIM OF BAGHDAD 59

IX. SAMUEL B. 'ALI GAON 63

X. THE SUCCESSORS TO SAMUEL B. 'ALI 72

XI. INTELLECTUAL LIFE IN BAGHDAD IN THE TWELFTH CENTURY 82

XII. THE POLITICAL CONDITIONS IN BAGHDAD DURING THE PERIOD OF THE LAST GEONIM 89

XIII. JEWS IN THE SURROUNDINGS OF BAGHDAD 95

XIV. THE FOURTEENTH AND FIFTEENTH CENTURIES 100

XV. THE ADMINISTRATION OF THE BAGHDAD COMMUNITY 102

XVI. THE MIZRAHI FAMILY 106

XVII. MOSES B. BENJAMIN AND HIS CONTEMPORARIES 110

XVIII. SADKAH B. SE'ADYAH HUSEIN 113

XIX. ISAAC PASHA 120

XX. THE NESIIM OF BAGHDAD 122

XXI. SALEH B. JOSEPH MASLIAH 128

		PAGE
XXII.	SASON B. MORDECAI SHINDOOKH	132
XXIII.	MOSES B. HAYYIM B. MOSES B. 'ABDALLAH	136
XXIV.	'ABDALLAH B. ABRAHAM SOMEKH	141
XXV.	ELIJAH B. SLIMAN MANI	145
XXVI.	HAKHAM JOSEPH HAYYIM	149
XXVII.	THE OFFICE OF THE HAKHAM BASHI	157
XXVIII.	SYNAGOGUES, SCHOOLS AND CHARITIES	165
XXIX.	THE LITURGY OF THE BAGHDAD JEWS	176
XXX.	CUSTOMS AND USAGES	181
XXXI.	SUPERSTITIONS AND PROVERBS	190
XXXII.	PRINTERS	200
XXXIII.	SETTLEMENTS OF BAGHDAD JEWS IN THE FAR EAST	203

ADDITIONAL NOTES 218

INDEX 219

LIST OF ILLUSTRATIONS

Frontispiece: GROUP OF ḤAKHAMIM OF BAGHDAD IN 1910

Standing, from right to left: Ezekiel Ezra Eliah Bassa; Meir, Scribe to the Beth Din; Simeon Mordecai; Sason Khdoori; Yehuda Moshe Ftayya; Hayyim Muallam Ezekiel. Seated, from right to left: Shemuel Abraham Mjalled; Ezra Kohen; Moshe Shelomoh David Shamash; Abraham Hillel; Sason Eliyyahu Moshe Ha-Levy; Isaac Abraham Mjalled.

I. HAKHAM JOSEPH HAYIM *Facing page* 149

II. BURIAL GROUND, BAGHDAD 156

III. NEW SYNAGOGUE, BAGHDAD 165

IV. GRAVE OF JOSHUAH THE HIGH PRIEST, BAGHDAD 180

V. CATAFALQUE AT EL-KIFIL 181

ב"ה

NOTE BY THE PUBLISHER

MY late Father נ"ע from his earliest youth made it one of his aims in life to collect historical material bearing on the Jews of the East in general and on the Jews of Baghdad in particular. The history of the Jews of Baghdad and the Far East has till this day not been written and the records and documents they have left are few and difficult to find. With untiring zeal my father worked, although his time was seriously limited by family responsibilities and varied communal work. By his unflagging energy he succeeded in collecting numberless documents relating to this almost completely forsaken field of Jewish History. If the time at his disposal would have permitted he could, with the books and with the documents he had collected and was sorting and filing up to his last days, have produced a number of monographs on these subjects and most probably a large volume giving a full and accurate account of the history of the Jews of India and China. But the causes which retarded him were many and insurmountable. During the last eight years or so of his life, his spare time was almost entirely taken up with the work of relief for our persecuted brethren in Germany, which he undertook together with my dear Mother תבדל מב"ח, לחיים טובים with selfless devotion. The present work was designed originally to fit into a popular series of small histories on various Jewish Communities. Had my Father not been approached to write a short history when he was and had he waited until such time as he could have given the subject a fuller treatment, he might never have accomplished the task, for after the completion of this work in 1932 he never found the time (as a number of his letters show) to go over it again comprehensively or to make all the additions which he had in mind, owing to the causes above mentioned. We are, therefore, fortunate in having before us a short account of The History of the Jews of Baghdad from his pen. This work marks a most important milestone in Jewish history in that, as has been said, a history of the Jews in Baghdad as such has never before been undertaken. It will form a foundation stone for future writers who, by additions and expansions, may build securely upon it.

The reader will bear in mind that this work was completed in 1932. References to material which has appeared since then in books or periodicals will, therefore, not be found to have been incorporated. There are a few exceptions to this rule where my Father did make some additions and in a small number of instances I also have added some references to later publications, but have usually differentiated my additions by square brackets.

I should like to record here the gratitude I feel to the late Mrs. Melanie Becker ז"ל for having greatly helped me in carefully copying out my late Father's MS., to my dear Sister, Flora מב"ת for having gone over the MS. with me, and to my good friend Mr. Meir Benayahu הי"ו for his assistance in compiling the Index.

If this work, besides forming a record of the past, stirs the interest of Jewish historians on the one hand, inducing them to give greater attention to the new vistas of Jewish history opened up, and on the other hand intensifies the historical consciousness of the many Jewish communities which have sprung from the mother tree, Baghdad, inspiring them with a fresh desire to preserve the continuity of their noble traditions, then the hopes and aspirations of my revered and saintly Father in writing it, will have been in a goodly measure fulfilled.

SOLOMON D. SASSOON

Letchworth, 6th Elul 5709
31st August, 1949.

PREFACE

THE aim of this work is to give a concise and fairly popular account of the history of the Jews in the place of my ancestors. For many years I had entertained the desire to compile such a record and directed my studies with that end in view. I am therefore grateful that it has been granted to me to realize this cherished hope in the present monograph.

The material employed has been derived from unpublished as well as from published matter. The number of footnotes has been minimized to suit a book of this size and character. Where references have been omitted, the historical evidence will be found in my work *Ohel Dawid, Descriptive Catalogue of the Hebrew and Samaritan Manuscripts in the Sassoon Library*, London (Oxford, 1932), which is provided with adequate indexes for the guidance of the reader. This, I believe, is the first attempt which has been made to collect and group together various data about the Jews in Baghdad in order to describe their literature, their spiritual and lay leaders, their synagogues and shrines, schools and charities. The History of the Jews in Baghdad extends from the year of the foundation of the city, 762 C.E., down to the present day. In such a long interval of thirteen centuries, there are, of course, periods of greater and lesser importance. Again centuries passed of which we are left without records altogether. This apparent silence does not mean that the continuity of the Jewish settlement in Baghdad was broken, but is evidence of the loss of literary records. It is to be hoped that in the course of time the many gaps in our present knowledge of the history of the Jewish community in Baghdad will be filled by fresh discoveries of instructive material. Meanwhile I wish that those illustrious and saintly men and women who of old lived and suffered within the community of Baghdad may, by the recounting of their deeds and ideals, speak through these pages to their posterity—the children of the present age. May their blessed memory endure for all time.

CHAPTER I

EARLIEST TIMES

TEACHERS of the third century C.E. set forth in their homilies interesting views about the exile of the Jews to Babylonia, which throw light on their appreciation of the second homeland of the Jews. R. Ḥiyya, himself a native of Babylonia, expresses the opinion that the Holy One, blessed be He, exiled Israel to Babylon because they would not have been able to survive the severe decrees of Rome. Another native of Babylon, R. Eleazar b. Pedath, saw the cause of the Babylonian exile in a topographical fact, namely, that Babylonia is a low lying land and in that it resembles the nether world and from such a land the Jews would soon be redeemed. A third sage, R. Ḥanina bar Ḥamma, suggests the reason that the language of Baylonia is akin to that of the Torah. A fourth, R. Yoḥanan bar Nappaḥa, says: God sent the children of Israel back to their mother's home.[1] It is remarkable how these Rabbis looking at the Jewish settlement between the two rivers from various aspects, could not help seeing in the Babylonian exile a providential act of the God of Israel. The way which their ancestor Abraham travelled from the south of Babylonia to the south of Palestine was reversed by the multitudes of his descendants from Samaria and Jerusalem respectively, who returned to the plains of Mesopotamia. Whether the exiles settled in or about the vicinity of Baghdad is doubtful, although it is not impossible that they did so. Archæological evidence tends to the conclusion that the seventh and sixth centuries B.C.E. saw this part of the country inhabited. In a list of urban and rural settlements,

[1] *Pesaḥim* 87b, where the text reads Aram, meaning Rome.

which was compiled by government officials in the reign of the Assyrian king Ashur-bani-pal, or Sardanapalus, we find a name which sounds and reads very much like our Baghdad.[1] In 1848, during an unusually dry season, Sir Henry Rawlinson found on the western bank of the Tigris, bricks stamped with the names and titles of Nebuchadnezzar (604-561 B.C.E.). Such bricks are very frequently found in buildings all over the country. I myself possess one which was presented to a friend of mine by Dr. Koldeway, the chief of the German excavation party in 1902. According to an old translation, kindly supplied by Sir (then Dr.) E. A. W. Budge, the inscription reads: "Nebuchadnezzar King of Babylon, Restorer of E-sagili and E-zida, son of Nabopolassar, King of Babylon, I am". It is quite likely, therefore, that Baghdad existed at the time of the destruction of the first Temple of Jerusalem, when the unfortunate exiles, sighing under the rod of Nebuchadnezzar's sergeants and taskmasters, halted in this place, hung their harps on the willows of the brook, and wept bitterly at the remembrance of Zion. However that may be, we lack much information about the place at that time, generally, and about the history of the Jews particularly. This is not surprising considering the eventful period we are speaking of, for at this time the world was undergoing one of the greatest changes in the history of empires. The more than a thousand-year old empire of Babylonia was tumbling down, to be crushed for ever, while from the unexplored East a new power arose which till then had been ignored or unknown. With the change of empires, new experiences, bad and good, new habits, useful and baleful, must have been the lot of the Jewish exiles in the second homeland. The wealthy family of Murashu which flourished in the south at Nippur, the old temple city, may have continued its prosperous activity as bankers and financiers,

[1] G. Le Strange, *Baghdad During the Abbasid Caliphate from Contemporary Arabic and Persian Sources*, Oxford, 1900, p. 9; v. also Jacob Obermayer, *Die Landschaft Babylonien*, Frankfort/M., 1929, p. 148.

exporters and importers, under the Persian rule in the same way as under the Babylonian kings.[1] However useful and interesting more exact information about the wealth and business activity of the Jews, their numbers and strength, social position and political influence at this period might be, for us who look back from a distance of twenty-five centuries, the culminating point of interest is the wonderful turn in the history of our people which occurred under the Persian ruler Cyrus. Palestine was restored to the children of Jacob and the Babylonian captivity ended, though all the Jews did not evacuate Babylon and return to the land of their fathers. Only a small minority availed itself of the permission given to return and build the Temple and city of Jerusalem. The greater part, surely the wealthier members and the more influential families were reluctant to give up their homes and associations and start on new adventures. Thereafter during the whole period Jews lived in great numbers all over Babylonia, south as well as north, under their Persian rulers. The paucity of data in connection with this period is most probably due not to the passivity of the Babylonian Jews, but to the loss of historical sources. This applies to the Babylonian Jews generally, and especially to the Jews of Baghdad.

[1] S. Daiches, *The Jews in Babylonia in the Time of Ezra and Nehemiah*, London, 1910. The Jewish origin of the numerous correspondents in the Murashu documents is an assertion partly assumed and partly based on the Hebrew and Jewish names borne by the persons mentioned in them.

CHAPTER II

TALMUDIC AGE

OUR sources are richer when we come to the Talmudic age. We can point to Jewish scholars hailing from Babylon, like Hillel ha-Babli, Naḥum ha-Madi, Nathan ha-Babli, etc. On the other hand Palestinian scholars emigrated to Babylonia, like Judah b. Bathira, Ḥananiah the nephew of R. Joshua b. Ḥananiah, etc. In earlier times Palestinians used to inform the communities in Babylon by signals and later by special messengers about the fixing of the calendar, while Babylonian pilgrims trod the long way from Ihi Deḳira, the modern Hit, to Jerusalem in order to appear before the Lord. Jews of Neharde'a are known to us by name, Anilai and Ḥanilai who fought the Romans and suffered martyrdom.[1] Some scholars credit Babylonia with great activity in all branches of Jewish learning, and visualize flourishing centres of study in Babylonia before the return of Rab to his native country from Palestine. There is certainly some tangible evidence for this assumption.[2] Nevertheless a new impetus in religious and scholarly life can be observed from the time when Abba Arikha, called Rab, established his school in Sura (about 219) at the confluence of Nahr Sura and the Euphrates, and Samuel directed the affairs of the Jewish Academy at Neharde'a which stood at the junction of Nahr Malka and the Euphrates. In this period we meet a scholar, R. Ḥana, whose surname, distinguishing him from others of the same name, was Bagdathaa, i.e. a native of Bagdath. He occurs at least ten times in the Talmud.[3] In

[1] Josephus, *Antiquities*, Book XVIII, ch. 9.

[2] See *Iggereth Rab Sherira Gaon*, ed. B. M. Lewin, Haifa, 1921, p. 73, and Halevy *Doroth Harishonim* II pp. 162 ff.

[3] *Berakhoth* 54b; *Shabbath* 147b; *'Erubin* 81b; *Kethubboth* 7b, and 10b in three connections; *Yebamoth* 67a; *Baba Bathra* 142b; *Zebaḥim* 9a and 92a.

two of these passages Samuel addresses him, a fact which establishes the period when he flourished, namely, before 245, and that a Jewish community already existed in Bagdath at the time. From another report we learn that he visited the Rabbanan and the leader of the school in Pumbaditha, R. Judah bar Ezekiel, after the latter's recovery from a severe illness, which shows that after the death of Samuel this Baghdad scholar took a leading part in religious affairs. The commentators, Rashi and Samuel b. Meir, his grandson, identify Bagdath with our Baghdad. Their view goes back to Geonic origin and there is no need to place Rab Ḥana of Bagdath in Susiana in Persia or in Bagadaonia, as the editor of the 'Arukh, Dr. Kohut, suggests.[1]

The etymology of the name Baghdad gave rise to various fanciful suggestions. One is that Baghdad is composed of two Persian words, Bag, meaning garden, and Dad, the name of the owner of the garden. Another suggestion is that Bag is the name of an idol, and that Dad stands for gift. Baghdad on this supposition means simply "the gift of Bag". This interpretation is accepted by Obermayer.[2] G. Le Strange, however, sees in the translation "founded by God" the true etymology of the name.[3] In Talmudic sources, as we saw, the name is called Bagdath. In later sources Baghdad is often substituted by Babel,[4] yet this indentification cannot be older than the Geonic period, when Baghdad was at the zenith of its influence and importance.

[1] A. Kohut, *'Aruch Completum*, Vienna, 1926, p. 10.
[2] Obermayer, p. 148.
[3] Le Strange, pp. 10-11.
[4] *Eldad ha-Dani*, ed. D. H. Muller, Vienna, 1892, p. 11; Israel Friedländer, *Nathan ha-Babli*, p. 5; *Japheth b. 'Ali* on Daniel, ed. Margoliouth p. 136, line 21, and p. 144 line 16; Ibn Ezra's commentary on Daniel, ed. Matthews, p. 14. It should be noted that Byzantine authors call Baghdad by the name of Babel, see Erwin Rhode in *Byzantinische Zeitschrift*, V, p. 5.

CHAPTER III

GEONIC AGE

VERY few countries in the world have experienced such, and so many, radical changes of empires and rulers as Babylon. Long before the most important European cities were founded, the land between the two rivers saw the rise and fall, the growth and decline of dynasties and nations. Sumer and Akkad, Babylonia and Assyria, Parthians and Medians, Persians and Sassanides are more than mere names. They are indices of changing fortunes and misfortunes, peaceful developments and ruinous battles, material prosperity and intellectual expansion, religious activities and political upheavals during thousands of years. These vicissitudes considerably influenced the fate of the Jewish communities in Babylon. We hear of great persecutions at the close of the Persian age and of disturbances which caused the discontinuation of the well established schools in Babylonia. Our material does not enable us to ascertain the rôle which Baghdad played in history before the Moslem conquest. In the earliest years of the Hijrah the Market of Baghdad was raided by a body of troops dispatched by Khalid, the general of the Arab army, during the Caliphate of Abu Bakr. Suḳ Baghdad flourished during the last period of the Sassanides, and was held at the Ṣarat Point. The name survived the Persian Empire and occurs, as we will see later on, also in Jewish documents. There is a report that "the raiders surprised the town and the Moslems filled their hands with gold and silver, obtaining also the wherewithal to carry away their booty".[1] This happened in the year 634. Baghdad disappears again from history. However, we know that even before the foundation of Baghdad by the Caliph Manṣur, Nestorian monks lived there.

[1] Le Strange, p. 12.

We also know that before that event, a scholar hailing from Baghdad, occupied the high dignity of Gaon in Sura. The Gaon Sherira in his famous letter tells us that Mar Samuel Rosh Kallah bar Rab Mar, who died in the year 748, was followed by Rab Naṭronai Kahana b. Rab Amunah (Aḥnai), a native of Baghdad. Sherira mentions as the special locality of the Gaon's birthplace Tutira Bara.[1] This place may be identical with the Jew's Bridge, or Ḳanṭarah el-Yahud, mentioned by Arabic writers.[2] At that time Baghdad was a flourishing city divided into many quarters.

There are no statistics of the Jewish population in 'Irak or in Baghdad. Two indications, however, one supplied by R. Sherira Gaon and the other found in a Genizah fragment, help us to gain an approximate idea of the considerable number of Jews in Babylonia and Baghdad during the seventh and eighth centuries. R. Sherira relates that when Rab Isaac Gaon, in the year 655, headed a procession into the presence of the fourth Caliph, 'Ali, he was followed by 90,000 Babylonian Jews. The number of Jews who gathered before Peroz-Shabur allows some suggestion as to the total of Babylonian Jewry, namely that it may have amounted to about a million Jews.[3] Another confirmation of the dense Jewish population inhabiting 'Iraḳ in these centuries can be seen in the fact that Babylonian Jews emigrated in such large numbers to Egypt that they established a separate community in Fusṭaṭ under the name of Kanisat el-'Iraḳiyyin, or el-Bablim. The members of this community played an important part during many centuries in the life of Eastern Jewry. In the year 750 Abi 'Ali Ḥasan el-Bagdadi was the leader of this Babylonian community in far distant Egypt.[4]

The same century saw another Baghdadian on the Geonic

[1] Iggereth, p. 103.
[2] Le Strange, p. 150.
[3] *Iggereth*, p. 101.
[4] *J.Q.R.*, XVII, pp. 426-430; *J.Q.R.*, *N.S.*, VII, p.477; ibid., XI, p. 433.

seat of Pumbaditha, namely R. Isaiah ha-Levy b. Rab Abba, who hailed from Kalwadi, a town in the close vicinity of Baghdad.[1] This place was situated on the eastern side of the river Tigris, and became later a suburb of Baghdad. He ruled only two years, from 796 to 798. The chief importance of Baghdad begins with the foundation of that city by Mansur. The latter, the second 'Abbasid Caliph, encamped here the first time in the year 762. Baghdad was selected for special reasons as the metropolis of the 'Abbasid Empire.

Henceforth Baghdad became the centre of gravity of the Moslem dominion. This new development in political history naturally reacted on the fate of the Jews. The first great change was that the Exilarchs, who up till then had resided in Neharde'a, Sura and Pumbaditha the seats of the academies, removed their courts from the Residencies of the Geonim to the metropolis. Being mainly political representatives of the Jewish Diaspora in Babylonia, their proper place was more under the shadow of the temporal rulers than in the vicinity of the spiritual guides and elected leaders of the Jewish communities. This change of abode, however, did not sever the connection between the lay and religious leaders of Babylonian Jewry. We hear that the Geonim of the two great academies on the Euphrates, situated as they were, one in the south and one in the north, undertook the longer or shorter journey to the capital soon after the festival of Tabernacles in order to celebrate the third Sabbath of the Annual Cycle in the company of the leading dignitaries and distinguished scholars. The origin and the name of this celebration is not given. Maybe it is to be considered as a continuation of the Shabbatta de Righla, well known in Talmudic times.[2] Yet, while the latter was held at the opening of the Kallah meetings in the months of Elul and Nisan, these new meetings took place at the beginning of the year. It is quite likely that

[1] *Iggereth*, p. 109.
[2] *Sanhedrin* 7b; *Bekhoroth* 60a, Rashi, s.v. בריגלא.

the removal of the Exilarch from the seat of the Academy to the metropolis of the Empire caused this change of date. There is very scanty material about these celebrations in the Talmudic age, yet a native of Babylonia, an eye witness of those most memorable yearly festivities furnishes a very vivid and reliable picture for the Geonic period. R. Nathan ha-Babli depicts the service in the synagogue attended by the Exilarch, who was accompanied and assisted by the two Geonim of Sura and Pumbaditha, all taking actual part in the service and the reading of the Law. The names of the Exilarch and the two Geonim were especially mentioned in an appropriate prayer for the occasion.[1] Such a prayer, a fragment of which has been discovered in the Genizah, and the sermon delivered, of which a fragment is still preserved in one of the recensions of the *Tanḥuma*, must have made a lasting impression on all who had the privilege of being present. The purpose of they seearly gatherings, apart from the spiritual side, was to renew the relations between the Exilarch and the Academies, to settle the financial affairs between the two Academies, to solve political questions which arose between Babylonian Jewry and the government, to define the administration and organization of communal life, and, finally, to advert to the relations between the Jews of Babylonia and the Jews abroad. The questions and affairs varied in volume and in value according to the importance and ability of the leading men.

There were other occasions also when the Geonim had to leave their academies and repair to the metropolis. Such an occasion was the election of a new Exilarch, as described by the same reliable eye witness, R. Nathan ha-Babli, and preserved in the Yoḥasin (Chronology) of R. Abraham Zacut. We learn that the two Geonim, the prominent members of the Academies and the lay heads of the community gathered at the residence of one of the most important members of the Baghdad

[1] *Ginze Ḳedem* II (5682) pp. 46-48, and for corrections, see S. Assaf, *Ha-Tor* 5684, No. 6 and No. 18; *MGWJ*, LXVIII (1924), pp. 150-160.

community, where they elected a descendant of David to the Exilarchate. The reporter mentions the name of Naṭira, about whom some additional information will be given later. The report permits us to have a glance at the position held by the Exilarch inside and outside the community. The installation service and the annual Sabbath service, together with the festivities and banquets connected with the religious ceremonies, were of considerable importance in the communal life of the Baghdad Jews. Great honour was shown to the Exilarch by his coreligionists when he appeared in the streets of Baghdad on his way to be received in audience by the Caliph or his Viziers and ministers. Also, minor and major officials of gentile origin treated him with honour and respect.

During the Geonic period, not only the Exilarch but sometimes the Geonim themselves either removed to Baghdad or held important meetings in that place. R. Sherira Gaon reports such a meeting about the year 816. R. Abraham b. Rab Sherira was the elected Gaon for Pumbaditha. Unfortunately a family strife broke out between Daniel and David, the sons of the Exilarch, and the Gaon. As a consequence, the Ab Beth Din of the Academy, R. Joseph bar Mar Rab Ḥiyyah, was appointed in the place of the officiating Gaon. Ultimately peace was restored, and Rab Abraham and Rab Joseph both preserved the title of Gaon. When they met in the same Academy it was R. Abraham's privilege to deliver the lecture, and R. Joseph listened as any ordinary member of the gathering. Once they met in Baghdad—according to one version at the Synagogue of Barna Shala, in Great Baghdad.[1] When the messenger of the community announced: "Listen to the words of the Heads of the Academy!" the whole congregation burst out in tears and refused to pay attention. The co-

[1] The readings of the two versions in *Iggereth*, p 111, are not satisfactory. I take the right reading to be Babla Rabbathi, a name still used for Baghdad, see, however, Mann in *J.Q.R.*, *N.S.*, VII, p. 465 f, who asserts on this very doubtful text that the Kallah meetings of the Academy were removed from the seat of the Geonate to Baghdad as early as 814-816.

Gaon himself, greatly moved, arose and resigned from the Geonate. He returned to his previous office and succeeded his colleague R. Abraham b. Sherira in the year 828.

Some interesting details about the sojourn of the Exilarchs in Baghdad are reported by Nathan ha-Babli. We hear that the Exilarch 'Uḳba resided in Baghdad before he was forced to leave the capital owing to his interference in the strife which broke out between the Gaon Kohen Ṣedeḳ and R. Joseph of Pumbaditha, and left for a place called Ḳarmisin which was to the east of Baghdad, a distance of five days' journey. Near that place was the residence of the Caliph from whom he received the right to be reinstated in his dignity. Yet his opponents by a counter move caused the Caliph to withdraw his permission and Mar 'Uḳba was forced to seek a new home abroad, in Africa.[1] The successor to Mar 'Uḳba, his nephew, David b. Zakkai, also resided in Baghdad. The locality where he was born was a place called Ḳaṣr, south of Baghdad.[2]

The first Gaon who resided in Baghdad was Hai b. David. He acted for many years as Dayyan in Baghdad. Later, from the year 889, he held the dignity of a Gaon for a period of seven-and-a-half years. His name is closely connected with a liturgical practice of the Jews in Baghdad, which differs from all other rites known to us. The liturgy of Baghdad requires a special chapter, and will be dealt with in the course of this work. We may mention, however, that the Baghdadians recited a composition of the 'Abodah not only during the additional (Musaf) service of the Day of Atonement, but also in the morning service. R. Abraham b. Nathan also speaks of many Geonim who resided in Baghdad, and whose names have not come down to us.[3] In the first half of the tenth century we

[1] *Seder 'Olam Zuṭa*, see A. Neubauer, *Mediæval Jewish Chronicles*, Oxford, 1893 II, p. 78 f.

[2] Ibid., p. 79.

[3] See *Ha-Manhigh* Berlin, 1855, p. 61, where the name of this Gaon is not mentioned; see, however, *Sha'are Simḥah*, ed. Bamberger, Fürth, 1861, pt. I, p. 63 f, from which R. Abraham b. Nathan of Lunel, author of *Ha-Manhigh*, copied the whole paragraph, where the Gaon's name is mentioned.

find a very influential family in Baghdad, namely, that of Naṭira, the members of which played an important part and exercised great influence in communal, commercial and political life. Their residence, as we have already seen, is mentioned by Nathan ha-Babli as the meeting-place of the electors of the Exilarch when a vacancy had to be filled.[1] The names of Bene Naṭira are mentioned in connection with the unfortunate strife between the Exilarch and the Gaon Se'adyah, which divided Babylonian Jewry into two camps. Many wealthy families of Baghdad supported the righteous cause of the Gaon. They were headed by Bene Naṭira, whose influence and power, wealth and connections were not at all less than those of the Exilarch, who was in great fear of them.[2] Genizah documents bear out these reports.[3]

The last of the great Geonim, R. Sherira and his son R. Hai, resided and taught at Baghdad. It seems that ultimately both Academies followed the Exilarch from their provincial residences to Baghdad and removed their seats of learning from Sura and Pumbaditha to the metropolis. At what period this change of locality took place, cannot be ascertained. Nor can it be decided whether thereafter the provincial Academies ceased to function altogether or still kept open their doors for scholars and teachers. Rab Hai Gaon himself, in the Responsum quoted earlier in this chapter,[4] informs us that R. Hai Gaon b. David was the first of the Geonim who dwelt in Baghdad, and many Geonim after him took up their residence in this place. The two Geonim, Sherira and his son, issued many documents in Baghdad, and a number of Responsa were dispatched from this place. R. Hai Gaon especially likes to point out Baghdadian customs and usages in his Responsa sent to oversea countries. Two instances may be pointed out here.

[1] *Yoḥasin*, Cracow, 1580, f. 122 b; comp. Neubauer, *Mediæval Jewish Chronicles*, II, p. 83 f.
[2] *Yoḥasin*, f. 121 b.
[3] See below ch. V.
[4] See above, p. 11, note 3.

In one of the Responsa he says: "In Baghdad they erect their tabernacles within the synagogues."[1] In another, we are told that the Baghdad Jews used to provide a temporary grave for their dead, and after a time they carried them many parsangs to the wilderness on the western side of Persia. Further he says that in the case of the death of a noble lady her body would be sent to Piri Shabur.[2]

Besides the Geonate there was a court attached to the Exilarchate. Such an office is mentioned in a document issued by the Baba de Merwatha of the Exilarch David, a contemporary of R. Se'adyah Gaon. The document refers to two Jewish litigants from Baghdad, both having non-Jewish names of Persian origin: Bahbood bar Naṭer and Ḥasan bar Barikhan.[3]

Very little is known about the officials of the Exilarch's Court. The Gaon Hai b. David may have acted as Chief Justice. Apart from him there are only two or three names kept alive in Geonic writings, which could be mentioned in this connection. R. Ṣemaḥ b. Solomon, who is described as the Lord Chief Justice of the Court of the Exilarch Ḥisdai b. Naṭronai, is one of them (about 880).[4] He may have been a contemporary of the Gaon Hai b. David, and in the course of time may have become a Gaon, although only the former is mentioned by R. Sherira.[5] Since but few names of scholars and dignitaries of the Geonic period are preserved, it is no wonder that we do not possess a list of judges who served at the Court in Baghdad[6].

Among the prominent Baghdadians of the Geonic period,

[1] *Sha'are Simḥah*, pt. I, p. 89.
[2] Ibid., pt. II, pp. 73-74.
[3] Harkavy, *Teshuboth ha-Geonim* Berlin, 1887, p. 276.
[4] See *Halakhoth Gedoloth*, ed. Hildesheimer, Berlin, 1888-92, p. 86; p. 145 (the sentence is missing in the *Aramaic Halakhoth Pesuḳoth*, MS., Sassoon, 263, p. 15, *Ohel Dawid* pp. 123-155) and p. 190. P. 188, a Responsum is signed by him: Ṣemaḥ b. Solomon Resh Methibta.
[5] *Iggereth*, p. 114.
[6] For the meaning of the title Dayyana di Baba, see Rapoport, *'Erech Millin* s.v. Ab Beth Din; Reifmann, *Keneseth ha-Gedolah*, III, p. 92; Weiss, *Dor Dor we-Doreshaw* (1904), IV, p. 12; Harkavy, *Ẕikhron ha-Gaon Rab Shemuel ben Hofni wu-Sefaraw*, Petersburg, 1880, p. 7; *Meassef Niddaḥim* p. 223; *Teshuboth ha-Geonim*, p. 389; A. Epstein, *Ha-Goren*, III, p. 80.

some scholars with the names R. Nissi, or R. Nissim should be referred to. There is first of all R. Nissi b. R. Samuel, secondly, R. Nissim a contemporary of R. Meborakh b. R. David of Baghdad, and thirdly R. Nissi of Naharwan Resh Kallah. Finally a Baghdadian Rosh Yeshibah by the name of R. Nissim is recorded as the author of some liturgical pieces. The dates of these four Baghdadian scholars or dignitaries are quite uncertain. The first, whose commentary is quoted by R. Jonah ibn Janaḥ, was surely a contemporary of the Geonim. He must have lived before the Gaon 'Amram, since his name is expressly quoted in the Siddur of Rab 'Amram. He may have been the son of R. Samuel Resh Kallah I, who was the teacher of R. Aḥa, the author of the Sheiltoth, or the son of Rab Samuel II, the great-great-grandfather of R. Sherira Gaon. R. Nissim, the contemporary of R. Meborakh b. David, was invited by this Baghdadian scholar on the Shabbatta de-Righla, which was a special Sabbath service held on the third Saturday after the High Festival held in Baghdad, in the presence of the Exilarch and the two Geonim. R. Nissim from Naharwan, a suburb of Baghdad, played a part in the election of the Gaon during the time of the Exilarch David b. Zakkai, who offered him the Geonate of Sura, which, however, he modestly refused. About the last Nissim, the liturgical writer, more will be said in Chapter XXVIII. Here reference may be made to a later Baghdadian, Joseph b. Jaber, a correspondent of Maimonides. In a letter addressed to him by Maimonides, mention is made of a liturgical work by a Baghdadian scholar, the prayer book of Ibn el-Jasus. This Ibn Jasus is called a pupil of Rabbenu Nissim. His prayer book or his treatise on the prayer book, contained the old Babylonian liturgy of the Geonic period, which is now entirely lost.

Besides the above references to Baghdad, there are other instances in which Baghdadian conditions or peculiarities are quoted. In one of these Responsa the city of Baghdad is especially pointed out as a seat of justice. The Gaon writes:

"In this city, where we now are, namely in Baghdad, no witness is accepted at the non-Jewish courts unless he is intelligent, grown up, wealthy and free from any suspicion of robbery, falsehood and untruth; and he must also be observant in his religion so as to belong to those who are known as El-Mu'addilin' ".[1] This Responsum is an eloquent witness to the mutual high esteem in which Jews and Moslems held each other.

Another interesting Responsum throws light on the commercial relations between the old capital of the Moslems, Baṣrah, and the new metropolis of the 'Abbasids, and surely that was not the first business transaction between the Jews of the two cities.[2] In the following centuries too, there was a close connection between the two communities.[3]

A special reference to the change of domicile and its influence on religious practice is clearly stated in a Responsum of the Geonim, which reads: "All these things were in vogue in the time of our predecessors when they lived in Neharde'a, Sura and Pumbaditha, but now that we have fixed our abode in the big city of Baghdad, the custom has been changed".[4] The name of the Geonic author of this epistle has not been preserved, but the passage fully agrees with the words quoted earlier in this chapter. They confirm the theory that the removal of the Academies and their establishment in Baghdad must have taken place some generations before R. Hai Gaon. This explains the item which is to be found in an ancient bookseller's catalogue in which Geonic Responsa coming from Baghdad and sent by R. Hai Gaon are specially singled out.[5]

[1] *Teshuboth ha-Geonim*, p. 140.
[2] Ibid., p. 269.
[3] For further particulars, see Sassoon, *The History of the Jews in Basra* *J.Q.R.*, *N.S.*, XVII, p. 407 ff.
[4] L. Ginzberg *Geonica*, New York, 1909, II, p. 206.
[5] *Zeitschrift für hebräische Bibliographie* XII, pp. 119-120.

CHAPTER IV

THE EXILARCHS IN BAGHDAD

THE first important consequence which followed the selection of Baghdad as a metropolis of the 'Abbasid Empire was a change in the residence of the political as well as of the spiritual leaders of contemporary Jewry. The Jews of Babylonia for centuries could boast of having in their midst the leading family of Israel which could trace its pedigree to King David. These descendants of the ancient kings of Judah were known by the name of Rashe Galuyyoth, that is, the Heads of the Exile or Exilarchs. For many centuries they resided in the midst of their brethren, in the vicinity of the Academies and in close companionship with the leading scholars of Mesopotamia. This situation remained unchanged till the advent of the Arab conquest. With the choice of Baghdad as the capital, the Exilarchs, as already mentioned, moved from their previous homes to Baghdad. The exact date of their removal cannot be fixed, but it followed soon after the foundation of the new city. In the early ninth century, about the year 825, they were already in Baghdad. In that year we find the Caliph ordering his Moslem authorities that in future they shall have no right to interfere in the internal affairs of the non-Moslem religious communities. Jews, Christians and Magi are invested with the right to select from their midst ten persons who shall be entrusted with the election of their spiritual or communal leader.[1] The considerable trouble which arose over the succession of the Bishop of Baghdad was the cause of this new regulation. It is interesting to learn that as early as the

[1] See Felix Lazarus, *Neue Beiträge zur Geschichte des Exilarchats*, *M.G.W.J.*, LXXVIII, p. 279 ff, where the sources are given.

ninth century the Jews had a representative body of ten men who met occasionally when a vacancy in the Exilarchate occurred. As in the Catholic Church, so in the Jewish community the succession of the Exilarchs gave rise to dissension and political strife. This unhappy state of affairs reflected adversely on the mutual relations between the Geonate and the Exilarchate. Since these events took place within the Jewish community of Baghdad, it is necessary to recount their story here. I shall therefore touch upon the quarrel which took place in 825 between the Exilarch David b. Judah and his brother Daniel over the succession; narrate the strife between the Gaon Kohen Ṣedeḳ and the Exilarch 'Uḳba, and then describe the unfortunate proceedings of the Exilarch David b. Zakkai against the Gaon Se'adyah.

The first event appears clearer now in the light of the new information supplied by the Genizah fragments. To Graetz it seemed quite unbelievable that the Exilarch should have turned for support to the authorities of Tiberias, but according to our present knowledge, it looks quite natural. R. Sherira reports that in the days of the Gaon Abraham b. Sherira, who ruled between 816 and 828, there broke out a quarrel between Daniel and David, the sons of Judah, both of whom endeavoured to become Exilarchs.[1] This short report is supplemented by a letter written about the year 1170 by the Gaon Samuel b. 'Ali, about whose activity more will be said later. He writes: "In the days of David b. Judah the Exilarch, the members of this family were removed from the service of the King; afterwards they tried to join the learned men and the Academies, but were not received until they had accepted the conditions of the Academy which supported them. These conditions were confirmed in the handwriting of every succeeding Exilarch. Such documents are still preserved in our archives".[2] These documents were signed by the elected Exilarchs before

[1] Neubauer, I, p. 38.
[2] *Tarbiz*, I, No. 2, p. 67, see also ibid., I No 1, p. 127; *Lazarus* p. 283.

their installation. The decline of the Exilarchate in these days was due to the quarrels between the two brothers, which caused them to lose their political influence, and in order to save some of their lost dignity, they were compelled to submit to the conditions imposed upon them by the Geonim. The story of this disagreement, which is indicated in a general way by R. Sherira, was apparently fully known to Samuel b. 'Ali in the second half of the twelfth century; to us, however, the details are unknown, but the outcome is quite clear. Another innovation which is recorded to have taken place in the days of this Exilarch is that henceforth the Geonim would celebrate the Shabbatta de-Righla not in the Exilarch's place, but in their own seat of authority, so that the Exilarch had to repair to the place chosen by the Geonim.[1]

One should have thought that the humiliating experience of the Exilarch David b. Judah might have put an end to the quarrels between the Exilarchate and the Geonate. Yet, the agreements signed seemed to have been a new source of discord which disturbed the peace of the community. The result was the strife between Kohen Ṣedeḳ Gaon and 'Uḳba the Exilarch. Probably one of the conditions laid down between the contracting party was the allocation of funds collected in or sent from communities abroad. At this time the Exilarch 'Uḳba rightly or wrongly claimed the right to withhold from the Gaon the money sent by the Jews of Khorasan. The reason for his doing so was that the members of the prominent families in Baghdad supported the Gaon against the Exilarch. One may advance the theory that politically the court bankers, about whom more will be said in the next chapter, stepped into the place of the Exilarchs, who were dismissed from government service.

The conditions grew even worse under the Exilarch David b. Zakkai. He wished to invest a scholar with the dignity of the

[1] *Iggereth*, p. 93.

Sura Gaonate. The scholars in view were Se'adyah el-Fayyumi, a native of Fayyum in Egypt, who at the time held the position of Alluf ha-Yeshibah, and a certain Ṣemaḥ b. Shahin. Neither of them was entirely satisfactory to the Exilarch. The former because he was a foreigner: hitherto the Gaonate had been hereditary in a few families. The latter, though probably of Gaonic descent, did not possess the high scholarly qualifications needed for the presidency of the Academy. As a way out of the difficulty, the post was offered to Ṛ. Nissi Naharwani, a blind man, who was generally respected for his extraordinary piety. Besides, he possessed the great merit of having made peace between the Exilarch David b. Zakkai and his opponent, the Gaon Kohen Sedek of Pumbaditha. Naharwani, however, declined this offer and hesitated to name a suitable candidate for the office. The result was that Ṣemaḥ became Gaon in spite of the fact that Se'adyah was the worthier of the two. A characterization of Se'adyah by Nissi may be quoted here. "It is true that Se'adyah is a great man, of extraordinary learning; but he is absolutely fearless, and by reason of his great learning and wisdom, eloquence and piety, he does not consider any body in the world." Hearing these words, David b. Zakkai decided to drop the candidature of Ṣemaḥ and appointed Se'adyah in his place. This event took place in the month of Iyyar, 928, when Se'adyah reached the age of thirty-six.

Soon after the election, friction broke out between the Gaon and the Exilarch. The struggle was fought with the greatest bitterness on both sides and had far reaching consequences for Babylonian Jewry. The rupture was caused by litigation between some heirs to a fortune. The Exilarch decided the case in a way by which he would profit to a great extent. Naturally a man of Se'adyah's character would not remain silent in the face of such injustice. This was only one incident which alienated the Gaon from the Exilarch. The administration of the Exilarchs in general, and that of David b. Zakkai in particular, show that such a case was by no means exceptional, and that enmity and hostility could not have been avoided. The special case which provoked the Gaon to open opposition to the Exilarch was typical of the man and conditions alike. The decision given by the Exilarch in his court would have put one tenth of the disputed amount into his own coffers, but the verdict of the Exilarch was not legal unless confirmed and signed by the two Geonim. Se'adyah examined the decree and found it impossible to attach his signature to such a document, the illegality of which was clear on the face of it. To avoid unpleasantness, Se'adyah advised the litigants to secure first the signature of his colleague, the Gaon Kohen Ṣedeḳ of Pumbaditha. The purpose of this advice must have been the hope of Se'adyah that his colleague would also refuse to sign this document. But he was mistaken, for Kohen Ṣedeḳ raised no objection in confirming the Exilarch's decision. When the matter came back to Se'adyah, he evaded the difficulty by pleading that his signature was no more needed and was superfluous. This argument raised suspicions in the minds of the litigants, who realized that Se'adyah's argument was merely an excuse, and urged him to tell them the real reason for his hesitation to sign the document. The truth was revealed. Se'adyah clearly pointed out the illegality of the Exilarch's decision and refused his signature. The parties thereupon returned to the Exilarch, who became enraged when the Gaon's attitude was made known to him. He at once sent the following message with his son Judah to the Gaon: "Go and tell him in my name that he shall at once endorse the document". When Judah came with this message to the Gaon, Se'adyah quoted to him the following words: "Tell your father that it is written in the Torah 'Ye shall not respect persons in judgment' ". One can imagine how infuriated the Head of the Captivity became when these words were repeated to him. He sent his son over and over again to the Gaon and commanded him: "Sign at once and do not persist in your folly". Instead of delivering this order, the son, who was apparently wiser than the infuriated father, implored the Gaon to yield. Thus the son tried to avoid a rupture between the Exilarch and the Gaon, yet the breach between them had already become too wide, for Se'adyah was not a man to remain silent or to connive in illegal practices. Without avail David b. Zakkai tried repeatedly to persuade or to intimidate Se'adyah to revoke his opposition. The princely messenger, Judah, the go-between, became weary, and when his last effort failed, he forgot himself and in a moment of exasperation he raised his hand against the Gaon and threatened to strike him if he did not sign the document immediately. Thereupon he was seized by the Gaon's attendants and thrust out of the room. Judah returned to his father, who on learning what had happened, excommunicated the Gaon and declared his office vacant. A young and insignificant Rabbi, Joseph b. Jacob, called also Bar Saṭia, was selected to fill his place. Se'adyah, unabashed by the high-handed manner of his enemy, deposed David b. Zakkai from the Exilarchate and put him under ban. The new Exilarch put into office by Se'adyah was called Joshiah Ḥasan, who was either a brother or a nephew of David b. Zakkai. The matter did not rest here, but soon assumed greater dimensions. Parties developed and Babylonian Jewry became divided into two camps, one faction supporting David b. Zakkai, and the other Se'adyah. With the latter sided the wealthiest and the most learned men in Babylonia, including naturally the most prominent members of the Baghdad community. Who were the supporters of the Exilarch? First of all the members of his own family, secondly the Gaon of Pumbaditha, Kohen Ṣedeḳ. The conduct of the latter in siding with the Exilarch and opposing his colleagues was due to his desire to close the gates of the Sura Academy in order that the Academy of Pumbaditha would be the only one invested with authority and power. He was guilty of aiding the Exilarch in the composition of the "Letter of Excommunication" which was issued by the Exilarch against Se'adyah. The scholars of

Pumbaditha followed their master's lead, some of them blindly, the others against their will.

Next to the Exilarch, Se'adyah encountered the hostility of another man, Aaron b. Joseph ibn Sarjadah of Baghdad. This was also an influential opponent whose activities contributed a great deal to the unhappiness of the Gaon. Aaron was a man of learning and of considerable wealth. Greater than his riches and learning were his violent temper and tyranny. His hostility to Se'adyah was due to the fact that he was not elected to, nor even considered eligible as a candidate for the vacant Gaonate of Sura. He boasted of being able to answer any question submitted to him and thought himself an equal of Se'adyah, yet Se'adyah's learning and brilliancy put him into the shade. The vainglorious and ambitious Aaron therefore bore a grudge against his stronger rival, and waited for an opportunity to rise against Se'adyah. This arrived when the strife between Se'adyah and David b. Zakkai began and spread in the community. Naturally, Aaron at once joined the party of David b. Zakkai.

We turn now to the weapons applied by these two parties against each other. We have seen mutual excommunications and depositions, which were followed by counter appointments to the alleged vacant positions. For a long time pens were busy writing abusive proclamations and wild circular letters, some of which are still extant. A contemporary Karaite has preserved a few lines from a scandalous letter written by Aaron Sarjadah, which is a sad example of the demoralized and demoralizing spirit that invaded the ranks of Se'adyah's opponents. We know that Se'adyah (and this applies also to his adherents) did not spare his enemies. His Sefer ha-Galui is a forceful reply to some of the charges levelled against him by the whole band of his enemies. Unfortunately the fight between the Gaon and Exilarch was not confined to a literary feud. Since both, in spite of excommunication and deposition, remained in office, the situation became more and more untenable and led to acts of violence. This resulted in the intervention of the government. Each party accused the other of having brought about this deplorable state of affairs. In the Exilarch's Letter of Excommunication Se'adyah is blamed for having invoked the assistance of the government and bringing about the imprisonment of some of his assailants. Indeed, we know from such a partial witness as Aaron ibn Sarjadah that the Gaon was actually assaulted and beaten by his enemies. Nevertheless, it is by no means certain that the interference of the government was not the result of the activities and machinations engineered by the Exilarch and his party, who may have endeavoured to carry out the deposition of the Gaon with the help of the government. In October, 932, the Caliph el-Muḳtadir was killed, and a very poor man, El-Ḳahir became his successor. That was a good opportunity to bring this tragic affair to a climax. The Exilarch and Sarjadah resorted to bribes, and this time with great success. The Caliph did not care in the least about the party's right or wrong. His chief concern was as to which of them was willing and able to supply the larger sum of money. Since the Exilarch and Sarjadah and their followers were the wealthier of the two parties, and backed by external forces, the result was certain. Se'adyah was driven from Sura and settled as a private scholar in Baghdad. Joshiah Ḥasan, the rival Exilarch, was exiled to Khorasan, where he remained until his death.

Se'adyah was defeated, but his spirit was not broken. In his retirement he devoted himself to the writing of an original work which brought him more glory than any great title in the world—his best work, Kitab el-Imanat wul-I'tiḳadat, or in Hebrew Sefer ha-Emunoth weha-De'oth (the Book of Religious Beliefs and Philosophic Doctrines). If the soil of Baghdad had brought forth no other literary fruit than this marvellous work of thought and religion, it would deserve a prominent place in the history of our faith. The book shows no traces whatsoever of being the literary production of a defeated and disappointed recluse. It is written with a vigour and freshness worthy of this great man, who rightly adorns the long assembly of Jewish thinkers and sages. Had he not written anything else in his life, this book would have entitled him to eternal glory and gratitude. Quite different is his Sefer ha-Galui, composed a few years later, in which his struggles and trials, hopes and disappointments are depicted. In devotional entreaties he prays God for deliverance from his enemies, adding that selfishness is far from him and that salvation, if granted him from Heaven, may serve as a living example to innocent sufferers, so that they may not lose their hope and trust in the Almighty. His words are: "If they had to endure similar insults and injuries at the hands of the wicked, they might remain firm and pray to God rather than lose heart and surrender". Since the work is not preserved in its complete form, it is difficult to judge what he meant by his "deliverance". It must be placed to the credit of the Baghdadian Jews that there were in their midst men who morally and materially supported the Gaon in different ways, although he had been deprived of office and livelihood. In Baghdad as well as outside its gates there must have been numerous admirers of the Gaon, who effectively showed their sympathy for their teacher and spiritual leader, and their contempt for the high-handed manner of the Exilarch and his party.

Just as one litigation deprived Se'adyah of his Gaonate of Sura, so another litigation paved the way for his return. Two litigants decided to have their case judged by a court of arbitration. The one chose Se'adyah, the other nominated the Exilarch. This was considered a personal insult by the Exilarch. The litigant was commanded to withdraw his nominee, but he refused to agree to such an order. This was followed by serious consequences to the litigant, for he was seized and given a severe beating. The poor man left the Exilarch's mansion wounded and his garment torn to shreds, crying aloud in the streets and complaining of the treatment he had been subjected to. Great indignation followed this deplorable incident and put an end to the patience with which the tyranny of the Exilarch was borne by the people.

The Jews of Baghdad could no longer stand the violence and lawlessness of the Exilarch. They sent their representatives to Bishr b. Aaron b. 'Amram, one of the chief men in the community, whereupon Bishr, the chief speaker, adjourned the meeting and repaired to Se'adyah's house. Here he called upon Se'adyah to follow with his friends to one of Bishr's houses which was situated opposite the meeting place. After this Bishr addressed Se'adyah with a speech similar to one which he had made to David b. Zakkai, admonishing him to conclude peace. Se'adyah naturally offered his hand without hesitation and without condition, to make peace. Thereupon the leading members of both parties formed themselves into two divisions, the one conducting the Exilarch, the other Se'adyah, and each proceeded toward the other until they met. Thus the two men, who for six years fought one another so bitterly, embraced and kissed. This was the beginning of a sincere peace and a lasting friendship.

One of the happiest men in Baghdad on this day was Bishr. We know that Bishr accomplished this reconciliation between the two great leaders in Eastern Jewry, perhaps the greatest deed of his life, on the Fast of Esther (27th February, 936). Bishr was so overjoyed, that he requested the whole assembly to stay with him over the reading of the Meghillah and spend with him a joyful Purim night. The Exilarch as well as Se'adyah declined this invitation, but each invited the other for dining and for spending the two days of Purim happily together. The matter had to be settled by the casting of lots, which decided in favour of the Exilarch. This was the end of enmity and the beginning of a new life of friendship. Se'adyah was now about to be re-installed in his former office. Some embarrasment had to be overcome by establishing the future status of the Gaon R. Joseph b. Jacob who was occupying the place of Se'adyah in Sura. Fortunately, R. Joseph was willing to retire from his post on the condition that his salary should continue without reduction. With Se'adyah's return peace was restored and the whole community greeted this turn of events with gratitude. There remained only one man who was disappointed and dissatisfied with the advent of peace, and that was Sarjadah. His share in the reconciliation of the parties is nowhere indicated, although his father-in-law was the chief instrument in bringing about peace. Nor is there any suggestion made in our sources about a reconciliation between Se'adyah and Sarjadah. Sarjadah hated Se'adyah personally as a rival in learning and as a foreigner who gained such distinction in academic life. He most probably ended his life as a member of the rival Academy in Pumbaditha. The period of peace and collaboration between the Gaon and the Exilarch was spent outside Baghdad, and therefore no longer belongs to this history.[1]

We conclude this chapter with the last Exilarch who resided in Baghdad. After the death of R. Hai Gaon the members of the Pumbaditha Academy elected the Exilarch Yeḥizḳiyyahu, the grandson of David b. Zakkai, as their Gaon. Thus the Exilarchate and Gaonate became united in one person. According to Abraham ibn Daud, this union lasted only two years, for enemies of the Gaon-Exilarch intrigued with the government, in consequence of which he was put into iron fetters and tortured.[2] This information has lately been discarded for several reasons. First of all we have clear evidence that the Gaon-Exilarch was still alive seventeen years after the death of Hai Gaon, for Samuel the Naghid wrote in Nisan, 1055, a poem in his honour which will later engage our attention. Further we know that an Exilarch of the same name,

[1] The description of the quarrel between the Exilarch and the Gaon given here is based on H. Malter, *Saadia Gaon His Life and Works*, Philadelphia, 1921, pp. 107-127.

[2] Neubauer, I, p. 67.

who was the great-great-grandson of David b. Zakkai, officiated, in the year 1021, as Exilarch. His pedigree is: Yeḥizḳiyyahu b. David b. Yeḥizḳiyyahu b. Judah b. David b. Zakkai.[1] Therefore the Exilarch lived and officiated longer than two years after the demise of Hai Gaon. Abraham ibn Daud further tells us that the two sons of the Exilarch fled from Baghdad to Spain, where they found refuge with Yehosef ha-Naghid. This must have been after the death of the Naghid Samuel, for, during the lifetime of the latter, Yehosef was not styled Naghid, and it is not conceivable that the Baghdadian princes would have sought the aid of the son instead of that of the father. Assuming that the Exilarch died either immediately before or at the time of his sons' flight from their native country, we can establish now with some certainty that he died some time after the year 4818 (1057-1058), in which year Samuel the Naghid was still living.[2]

The poem of the Naghid furnishes some interesting details about the relations between the Naghid and the Exilarch-Gaon, and between Malaga and Baghdad. Samuel fully acknowledged the authority of the Baghdadian leader. He adorns him with titles as "my King", "the annointed of the community", and "the head of the whole nation". He characterizes him as a king in his splendour, he likens his learning to the learning of Moses, and praises his zeal which he manifests against heretics, saying that he burns and consumes the licentious elements in the community. Piety and justice, noble descent and vast learning are all combined in him.[3] These "licentious elements" (Pariṣim) may have brought about the downfall of the Exilarch-Gaon in Baghdad. The particulars of this event, however, are not known to us at present.

[1] *R.E.J.*, LI, pp. 53-54
[2] Sassoon, *Diwan of Shemuel Hannaghid*, Oxford, 1934, p. VIII.
[3] Ibid., p. 100, lines 24-26.

CHAPTER V

SOME FAMILIES AND NAMES PROMINENT IN THE TENTH CENTURY

In speaking of the election of the Exilarch, Nathan ha-Babli has preserved the name of Naṭira, in whose residence the meetings were held on such occasions.[1] The same writer informs us that Naṭira sided with R. Kohen Ṣedeḳ bar Joseph, Gaon of Pumbaditha, against the Exilarch 'Uḳba. Similarly, in the strife between the Exilarch David b. Zakkai and the Gaon Se'adyah, the sons of Naṭira protected the Gaon and took his part against his adversary. Next to Naṭira and his sons, R. Aaron b. 'Amram and his sons are mentioned among the leading families of Baghdad. In a letter found in the Genizah and published by Dr. L. Ginzberg,[2] a Gaon writes: "Whenever you have transactions with the government I beg of you to let us know about them, so that we may command [the help of] the prominent members [of the community] in Baghdad among whom we dwell, namely the sons of R. Naṭira and the sons of R. Aaron—may the remembrance of the departed be for blessing and the remembrance of their offspring for life—then the government will grant your request according to God's help." The date and the authorship of this interesting piece of information cannot be adduced from the fragment. Anyhow we learn that besides the Exilarchs other influential families as well interceded with the government on behalf of their fellow Jews. It is more than mere curiosity to seek for information about these families, but it is doubtful whether we can ascertain the whereabouts of the "sons of R. Aaron". Ginzberg's suggestion that the sons of

[1] See above p. 12.
[2] *Geonica*, II, p. 87 f.

Aaron Sarjadah the opponent of Se'adyah Gaon are meant, has no support whatsoever. Nor is there any proof for the suggestion advanced by Dr. Jacob Mann that this Aaron is identical with Aaron b. Abraham b. Aaron, who, together with his brother Moses, is so highly spoken of in the letter from the Pumbaditha Gaon in 953.[1] The Bene Aaron mentioned in this letter must be the descendants of Aaron the contemporary of Naṭira. If the identification is right, then Aaron had a son Abraham whose sons Aaron and Moses followed in the footsteps of their ancestors. A Ben Aaron el-Bagdadi is mentioned together with Solomon b. 'Ali b. Ṭabnai as a representative of the Academy.[2] In a similar letter, unfortunately in a fragmentary state, the Bene Aaron are mentioned together with the Alluf Ṭob, who apparently managed the financial affairs of the Academy.[3] It may be that further discoveries will supply us with material that will remove our present doubt. Aaron b. 'Amram had two sons, one of whom was the well-known Bishr the peacemaker.[4]

We are much better off when we come to the history of R. Naṭira and his family. Dr. Harkavy[5] found an Arabic fragment which formed part of a book describing the family history of Naṭira, his wealth and honour, influence and piety. Probably it belonged to the original work of Nathan ha-Babli. A brief rendering of the Arabic text will provide the most important details for the communal and political history of the Jews in Baghdad at this period. The fragment leads us into the reign of the Caliph Mu'taḍid (892-902). It relates that the Vizier Ibn Abi el-Baghl, like Haman of old, incited the Caliph

[1] *J.Q.R.*, XVIII, p. 402; *J.Q.R.*, *N.S.*, VIII, p. 342.
[2] *J.Q.R.*, *N.S.*, VIII, p.346, line 16.
[3] Ibid., p. 347 line 9.
[4] Neubauer, II, p. 82; W. Fischel, *The Origin of Banking in Mediæval Islam: A Contribution to the Economic History of the Jews of Baghdad in the Tenth-Century*, *J.R.A.S.*, 1933, p. 45, note 6; J. Mann, *Tarbiz*, V (5694), p. 152, note 20.
[5] *Festschrift zum Siebzigsten Geburstage A. Berliner's*, Frankfort/M., 1903, Hebrew division, pp. 34-43.

to sign a death warrant against all Babylonian Jews. The decree was written by the scribes but not sealed. Three wonderful dreams prevented the sealing of the cruel edict. In these the prophet Elijah appeared to the Caliph. Harkavy[1] adduces external evidence which leaves no doubt that the Caliph was greatly influenced in his actions and decisions by dreams and visions. Thus reports of El-Mas'udi about the Caliph's character fully agree with the information derived from the fragment discovered by Harkavy. At this stage Naṭira plays his rôle. Naṭira must have had earlier transactions with the Caliph, details of which are unknown owing to the fragmentary state of our source. Yet Naṭira was called by the Caliph. The latter was appeased by Naṭira's clever answers to both his questions and Biblical quotations, which had greatly troubled the Sultan's mind. As a result of this audience the baleful letters were destroyed and their author, ibn Ạbi el-Baghl, was thrown into a dungeon where he perished. Naṭira in his turn was offered the wealth and property, the palace and the slaves of the fallen Vizier, but refused the king's bounty and did not avail himself even of the royal exemption from taxes. The Jews then lived under Mu'taḍid in peace and happiness. We are told that they wore black like the members of the 'Abbasid family. Only once was the peace disturbed by the fanatic Ṣufis, who instigated a riotous attack upon the Jews. The chief agitators were soon caught, and found their resting place in the waters of the Tigris. During the whole reign of the Caliph the relations of Naṭira with the ruler did not undergo any change. Naṭira held his dignity and influence also under the rule of Mu'taḍid's sons, namely Muḳtafi (902-908) and Muḳtadir (902-932). Naṭira died about 916. His position and his influence were inherited by his sons Sahl and Isaac. It may be mentioned here that Naṭira's father-in-law, Joseph b. Phinehas, is also mentioned by Nathan ha-Babli as one of the notables of the Baghdad community.

Sahl, the son of Naṭira, surpassed his father in learn-

[1] Ibid., p. 41.

ing. He had wide knowledge of the Bible, Mishnah and Talmud. He was well versed in Arabic writing and grammar and theology. No wonder, since he had the privilege of sitting at the feet of a man like R. Se'adyah Gaon! Greater than his learning, if we may trust the eulogy of our anonymous writer, must have been the man himself. No words of praise suffice to convey an idea of his unselfishness, his helpfulness, his charity and piety. The last mentioned characteristic is evidenced by his strict adherence to, and observance of, the Jewish Law. He had a synagogue in his house where he worshipped every Sabbath. We do not know whether it is an exaggeration or whether we may take the report literally, that from 200 to 400 poor people took their Sabbath meal with him. Besides, he provided the indigent of the city with meat and bread for the Sabbath. It is especially emphasized that the host himself waited on his guests and fanned them with a fan. His charity was not limited to Jews, but was shared by Moslems as well, who received money and raiment at regular intervals. We are told that his father used to send gifts to Kufa, where the descendants of 'Ali and the sons of Hashim lived. The part of the description dealing with the second brother, Isaac, is not preserved. We gather that he was twenty-seven years old when our writer wrote his report. He also tells us that Sahl had a son, Naṭira, who was at that time eight years old.

At this time or somewhat later, the great struggle about the calendar excited the Jews of Baghdad as well as those of the Eastern world. Palestinian and Babylonian Jewries were divided into two sections. A non-Jewish writer, a Syrian, Elijah of Nisibis, records that in the year 309 of the Hijrah (921) a great quarrel arose between the Western and Eastern communities with regard to the calendar.[1] The strife greatly

[1] See F. Baethgen, *Fragmente syrischer und arabischer Historiker*, Leipzig, 1884, p. 84; A. Epstein, *R.E.J.*, XLII, pp. 178-179; Poznanski, *J.Q.R.*, X, p. 160; *Bornstein in Sefer ha-Yobel for Nahum Sokolow*, Warsaw, 1904, p. 21, note 4. For a full treatment of the subject, see H. Malter *Saadia Gaon His Life and Works*, Philadelphia, 1921, pp. 69-88, and for bibliography, pp. 409-419.

affected Baghdad Jewry as a whole and its leaders particularly. The leader of the Western party was the Gaon of Palestine, known only by his father's name and not by his own as Ben Meir. He wanted to fix the New Year of 4682 (921) for Thursday, while the day according to the opposing party was to be Saturday. The Palestinian Gaon undertook the long journey from Palestine to Babylon and stayed in Baghdad for a time. The situation in Babylon was not a happy one. Owing to the undue interference of the Exilarch David, there were, after the death of R. Yuhudai in the year 917, two Geonim in one Academy. The scholars of the Academy elected R. Mebasser Kahana as their chief, yet David the Exilarch favoured the candidature of Rab Kohen Ṣedeḳ Kahana. Ben Meir came as a partisan of R. Mebasser Kahana and supported him with all his influence and power, but without success. Ben Meir describes his favourite as a unique person who is without rival in learning and piety either among the Palestinian or among the Babylonian scholars. The original object of Ben Meir's journey, however, was in connection with quite a different affair. He went to Baghdad in order to seek help against the Ḳaraites and 'Ananites, the enemies of the Rabbanites. From whom could he have asked help if not from the Bene Naṭira? We have seen plainly that Ben Meir was not on friendly terms with the Exilarch, otherwise he would not have opposed the Gaon Kohen Ṣedeḳ. Further he openly relied on the enemies of David b. Zakkai, the Exilarch. At that time a greater man than Ben Meir was on his way to Baghdad, namely Rab Se'adyah Gaon. By the way it is not at all impossible to see in a badly damaged Genizah fragment, discovered and published by Dr. Schechter,[1] a part of R. Se'adyah Gaon's diary or itinerary. The diarist travelled through and stayed in Arbela, Moṣul (Ashur), and Nisibis. Another letter gives evidence of Se'adyah's sojourn in Aleppo, in which he strongly

[1] S. Schechter, *Saadyana*, pp. 133-135.

protests against Ben Meir's attempt to introduce changes in the calendar. The result would be that the majority of the Palestinian Jews would celebrate Passover on Sunday and the Babylonian Jews, excepting the followers of Ben Meir, on Tuesday.[1] At that time Se'adyah had not yet received the title of Gaon, but signed himself and was styled by others Alluf. It was after this that he was put in office by the Exilarch David b. Zakkai. It would be interesting to know what attitude the sons of Naṭira took in the election and later on in the imprisonment of the Gaon. From the panegyric on Sahl, on which this chapter is based we learn that Sahl, the elder of Naṭira's sons, was a pupil of the great Gaon. We shall not follow the course of this struggle any further as it would take us beyond our field; we shall only record that Rab Se'adyah's views ultimately prevailed. Let us return to names that stand forth in this period.

New information about two prominent Baghdadian merchant bankers is furnished from external sources by Dr. W. Fischel[2] in a very interesting study. These bankers were only partly known from Jewish sources. Their names are Aaron b. 'Amram and Joseph b. Phinehas. An Arab geographer tells us that most bankers, money changers, dyers and tanners in Syria and Egypt were Jews.[3] These "two Jewish bankers", thus designated or simply called "the merchants" acted as partners. The title "Court Bankers" was conferred on them both at the same time. Thus the Vizier contracted a loan from them in which both, and even their successors are represented, and the punishment which the Vizier threatened them with was to be borne by both Joseph b. Phinehas and Aaron b. 'Amram as well as by their heirs. This already indicates that their position was not without danger. The members of this firm were called *jahbadh* in Arabic, that is bankers. According to one historian, these two Jews were appointed during

[1] *Bornstein*, p. 25.
[2] Fischel, *J.R.A.S.*, 1933, pp.339-352, 569-603.
[3] Ibid. p. 347.

the time of the Vizier 'Ubaidallah b. Yaḥya el-Ḥaḳani. This report is remarkable from two points of view. First, the function of these two men is designated "appointment". This is one of many instances where non-Moslems, in spite of strict Muhammadan law, were admitted to state service. This leads to the second question raised by this report, namely at what date was this appointment made? The Vizier 'Ubaidallah officiated under two Caliphs, El-Mutawakkil (852-858) and El-Mu'tamid (867-875). Fischel denies that such a reform in the civil service could have taken place under these two Caliphs who manifested a negative attitude towards the admission of non-Moslems (ahl el-dhimma) to the service of the state. He therefore thinks that there is a textual error, and suggests reading Muḥammad bin 'Ubaidallah bin Yaḥya, who was the real author of this reform, and one of El-Muḳtadir's Viziers (911-912), instead of reading 'Ubaidallah bin Yaḥya.[1] The chief activities of the firm were developed during the reign of the Vizier bin el-Furat who officiated in the second and third decades of the tenth century.

The firm was engaged in financial activities and mercantile transactions. The former consisted of administration, remittance and advance of funds. All the three functions were not without hazards. The deposits entrusted to the bankers were often of obscure origin consisting of bribes and other unlawful income. Naturally the depositors were anxious to keep such matters secret. A good illustration of this fact is offered by the dealing of the Vizier Muḥassin bin el-Furat with the Jewish bankers. He deposited with them considerable sums during his term of office. After his downfall he confessed having at his credit with Aaron b. 'Amram and his son, 160,000 dinars, which sum was verified by these two bankers when summoned by the Caliph El-Muḳtadir. The money was, of course, confiscated and transferred to his Majesty's privy purse. Trans-

[1] Ibid., p. 351.

actions of this kind could by no means be pleasant for these bankers, but they were forced to enter into such dealings by the all powerful Vizier. As a proof of these facts, it may be mentioned that a legal enquiry against the Jewish bankers was set up because they had become involved by the greed of the Vizier and his unscrupulous transactions. The Vizier increased his wealth by transmitting confiscated money to his own secret account instead of to the Caliph's privy purse, or to the public exchequer. Another transaction of a somewhat similar nature brought about a legal enquiry, and the bankers were called upon to furnish a detailed report and a statement of all the funds that had been entrusted to them in connection with the enquiry carried out against the Vizier bin el-Furat.

The second of their financial functions was the transmission of money. We learn that the custom of paying debts by means of letters of credit existed in the tenth century. It would be interesting to know what share Jews had in originating this method of payment by bills. They were dispersed all over the vast Arab empire and beyond it, and thus became destined to become a link between countries and continents in commercial as well as in intellectual life. We know from Jewish sources that the gifts and contributions sent by pious individuals and communities for the upkeep of the Babylonian Academies in the Gaonic period were conveyed by such bills, and that such bills accompanied the legal and ritual questions addressed to the Babylonian Geonim. Thus the gift of the Barcelona community mentioned in Seder Rab 'Amram Gaon, and several other donations referred to in various Geonic Responsa were transmitted in this way.[1] In an Arabic letter addressed to Joseph b. Jacob b. 'Ubal by the famous Ḳairuwan scholar, Nissim b. Jacob, there is a passage in which the writer begs the addressee to forward a bill of exchange to Baghdad.[2] It is interesting to read in a Geonic Responsum that this way of

[1] *Seder Rab 'Amram Gaon*, Warsaw, 5625, p. 1a.
[2] Mann *Texts and Studies*, I, pp. 142-143.

sending money is not in strict agreement with Talmudic practice, yet owing to its general adoption and commercial convenience, the Geonic authorities found it right according to Talmudic principles to give this method legal recognition, and raised no objection against it.[1] The difficulty here again was that in a good many cases disputes may have arisen to the detriment of the bankers. The above-mentioned Vizier bin el-Furat is reported as having "opened his ink-pot and written an order to his banker Aaron b. 'Amram, telling him to pay from his account and without any further admonition 2,000 dinars to Abu'l Ḥasan 'Ali b. 'Isa, as a subvention towards payment of a fine imposed upon him. Muḥassin b. al-Furat also ordered his banker to pay this 'Ali b. 'Isa 1,000 dinars from his account that was in Aaron b. 'Amram's bank."[2] The Vizier further was in the habit of depositing unpaid *suftajas* (bills of credit) with his Jewish bankers which probably led to many troubles.

More unpleasant was the third duty of these Jewish bankers, which was in connection with the supply of funds for special objects, such as military purposes. In such situations the Viziers responsible to the Caliphs turned to their Jewish bankers. Dr. Fischel says: "We are entitled to infer from the picture the sources present of Aaron b. 'Amram and Joseph b. Phinehas, that their importance for the financial economy of El-Muḳtadir's empire lay in their capacity as privileged money-suppliers and money-lenders".[3] Thus the Vizier bin el-Furat during his first Vizierate called the Jewish banker Joseph b. Phinehas and asked him to advance money for the payment due to the officials of the province of Ahwaz for two months. The transaction was not so smooth as one would think, for the Jewish banker hesitated to grant the loan. Only after long negotiations did the Vizier succeed in contracting

[1] Harkavy, *Teshuboth ha-Geonim* p. 216, No. 423.
[2] Fischel, ibid., p. 578.
[3] Ibid., p. 579.

the loan for a month. There is another report of the transactions between the Vizier 'Ali bin 'Isa and the Jewish bankers for a loan to consolidate the public budget. The letter in which the Vizier addressed the Jewish bankers in this matter may be quoted here in full: "Do you want to avoid my inflicting penalties on you that may affect you and your heirs for ever? I shall only refrain from it in consideration of a matter that will cause you no damage whatever. At the beginning of each month I need an amount of 30,000 dinars, which must be paid within the first six days to the infantry troops. However, I am usually not in possession of such a sum, either on the first or on the second day of the month. I want you, therefore, to advance on the first of each month a loan of 150,000 dirhams, an amount that you, as you know, will get back in the course of the month from the Ahwaz revenue. For the administration of the Ahwaz revenue belongs to you, and these moneys (from Ahwaz) are a permanent advance of money to you, to which I am going to add (as security) the amount of 20,000 dinars that are payable every month by Ḥamid bin 'Abbas. This will be the compensation for the first instalment, and I shall be relieved of a heavy burden".[1] We see from here that words of threat were not lacking on the part of the Vizier. Secondly we infer that the whole province of Ahwaz, as Obermayer holds,[2] is to be identified with the ancient Ḥuzai of the Talmudic period and with the modern Persian province Khuzistan. The banker, Joseph b. Phinehas is designated as the "banker of Ahwaz" in a letter of the Vizier bin el-Furat. Comparing the reports of the two Viziers we deduce that the financial administration of the province of Khuzistan was in the hands of Joseph b. Phinehas, who probably also resided there.

A few words should be added about the mercantile transactions of this Baghdadian banking firm. They derived their wealth from trade as well as from their services to the State and the Viziers. The considerable fortune which they amassed

[1] Ibid., p. 580 f. [2] *Obermayer*, p. 204 ff.

was invested in, and utilized for, commerce and trade. Therefore these men figure in the Arabic documents under the title of "el-tujjar" (merchants). The extent of their fortune and activity can be gauged by the large sums mentioned in these reports. They placed their services so whole-heartedly at the disposal of the State that the Caliphs never dismissed one of them from their office. No wonder that they used their influence for the benefit of their community and played so important a part in the history of Babylonian Jewry in this period. Babylonian Jewry in the age of the Geonim was in close contact with all parts of the Jewish Diaspora. From Persia to Spain, from Palestine to Byzantium, Egypt and North Africa, the Jews returned to Baghdad for spiritual guidance and political help. Our Hebrew sources fully verify the important position of these bankers as revealed by the Arabic historians. Thus the name of Joseph b. Phinehas, who appears now in a fuller light, lived before these accounts were published in the report of his countryman, Nathan ha-Babli. The latter mentions the name of Joseph b. Phinehas in connection with the quarrel between the Gaon Kohen Ṣedeḳ Kahana, and the Exilarch Mar 'Uḳba who tried to seize the contributions sent from Khorasan for the upkeep of the Geonic institutions. Joseph b. Phinehas and the previously mentioned Bene Naṭira supported the righteous case of the Gaon so that the Exilarch Mar 'Uḳba was forced to leave Baghdad, and went to a place called Ḳarmisin. Later on when the Caliph granted the Exilarch permission to return to Baghdad, Naṭira and Joseph b. Phinehas "and all those who belonged to their retinue", succeeded by their intervention at the Caliph's court to have this permission cancelled.[1] Further we learn that the famous Naṭira was the son-in-law of Joseph b. Phinehas, who is also mentioned in the report of Nathan ha-Babli.

This internal Jewish strife had a greater political bearing

[1] *M. J. C.*, II, pp.78-79.

than can be gathered from the simple narrative of the Baghdadian reporter. The Exilarch who was forced to leave Baghdad and throw off the allegiance of the 'Abbasid Caliph, found a new home under the sovereignty of the Faṭimid Caliph in Ḳairuwan, where he was welcomed and respectfully treated. Recently the veracity of Nathan's report about the strife between Kohen Ṣedeḳ and the Exilarch and about the intervention of Joseph b. Phinehas came to be doubted.[1] It seems that there is a plain contradiction between the report of Nathan ha-Babli and the Letter of R. Sherira Gaon which cannot be discussed here. For our purpose, it is sufficient to establish that these bankers and merchant princes played an important, if unobtrusive part in the communal activities of Baghdad in the first decades of the tenth century.

[But not only in Commerce was Jewish activity to be found. Baghdad, in the eighth, ninth and tenth centuries was famed as a centre of culture from which knowledge of the Classical Greek scientists and philosophers radiated and in this movement the Jews played their part. They shared in the work of translating Greek authors into Arabic[2] and thus helped in the diffusion of Greek science and in its preservation, an accomplishment which was to lead many centuries later to the Renaissance in Europe. However, our knowledge of these Jews is by no means yet complete and stands in need of expansion by careful research. Nevertheless from the few sources at our disposal we know that they may be counted among the earliest writers who were active in this field. Among these scholars there were those who came from Persia, Syria and other places to Baghdad.

A few names will be mentioned here. John bar Maserjoye (eighth century) who translated the Syntagma of Aaron into Syriac presided over the medical school gathered in Baghdad.[3]

[1] *Tarbiz*, V (5694), p. 148 ff.
[2] See *Arabic Thought and its Place in History*, by De Lacy O'Leary, London, 1939, p. 105.
[3] Ibid., p. 110.

Sahl ibn Rabban al-Tabari a native of Marw (the capital of Khurusan) who lived in the same century was, according to one tradition, the translator of al-Majisti, a work by Ptolemy. He is said to have gone to Baghdad in the days of Harun ar-Rashid and to have made the translation for him.[1] A distinguished scholar and teacher in Marw, he was known there as Barbun "the surpassing".

His son 'Ali (d. 850) who became a Moslem was the author of a great medical work "Firdaws al-Hikhma".

During the tenth century there figures the name of Ishaq ibn Amran al-Israeli[2] who was trained in Baghdad and later served at the court of Ziyadet Allah III (902-903) at Kairuwan partly as a court physician, partly as a kind of lecturer on philosophy. He became a pioneer in introducing Greek Medicine to Africa whence it spread to Spain. His treatise, Kitab al-Bawl on Urine is the best mediæval work on the subject. His "Guide to Physicians" of which the Arabic Text is now lost, was translated into Hebrew as Manhig (or Musar) ha-Rofeim and became a favourite manual for Jewish Physicians.]

[1] *How Greek Science Passed to the Arabs* by De Lacy O'Leary, London, 1948, p. 158.
[2] Ibid., p. 187.

CHAPTER VI

BAGHDAD UNDER R. SHERIRA AND R. HAI

In the days of R. Sherira and R. Hai, Baghdad became the most important political and intellectual centre of world Jewry. Prior to their time we saw leading families and important scholars there; now Baghdad by far eclipsed the importance and the glory of the old Academies.

In a document issued from the Great Court (Beth Din ha-Gadol), dated Marḥeshwan, 1309 Sel. (998), at the Old Market of Baghdad on the Tigris, we make the acquaintance of some Baghdadian Jews. Although the dry legal document does not furnish us with many details about the contracting parties and their peculiar circumstances, yet the names and the places of their origin are not without interest. One of them is called 'Ali b. David el-Shami. He may have been a Palestinian or perhaps a Syrian Jew. Another is called Nahum b. Haroon el-Ba'albeki. He hailed, therefore, from Ba'albek, an ancient Jewish settlement in the valley of the Lebanon. Of other Jews mentioned in that document as parties or as witnesses, only the names are of interest, for example, Abraham b. Sahl b. Ṣagri, Ḥabib b. Isma'il, Nehemiah b. Abraham, and Se'adyah b. Shalom.[1]

In the time of R. Hai Gaon, Solomon b. Judah, the son of the Palestinian Gaon, studied in Baghdad. From a letter written by Yaḥya the son of this Palestinian Gaon, we learn that Hai Gaon lectured to his pupils on the Halakhoth Gedoloth.[2] Other visitors to the schools came from Africa, like Shemaryah b. Elḥanan and his son Elḥanan of Alexandria,[3]

[1] *J.Q.R., N.S*, VIII, p. 359.
[2] S. Poznański, *Babylonische Geonim im nachgaonaischen Zeitalter*, Berlin, 1914, p. 90.
[3] *J.Q.R.*, VI, pp. 222-223.

and a number of pupils from the south of Italy and from the Byzantine Empire. Baghdad itself gave scholars and poets to Jewish literature in this age. Baradan, a suburb of Baghdad, gave Jewish liturgy the Paiṭanim Nahum ha-Ḥazzan el-Baradani, and Joseph el-Baradani. The former is a contemporary of Hai Gaon, but the date of the latter is uncertain.[1] The Vizier, Samuel ha-Naghid, preserved the name and the fame of another Baghdadian, Samuel b. Joseph Resh Kallah, who would have been worthy, if he had stayed in his native country, to fill the vacancy which occurred through the death of R. Hai Gaon.[2]

The happy state of affairs was rudely shaken by inner and external troubles which darkened the horizon of Babylonian Jewry. On one side there was continuous strife between the Exilarch and the Gaon. The Geonim among themselves did not live in a peaceful atmosphere. Jealousy and discord went so far that they called each other by not very flattering nicknames. Character and learning were defamed and suspected. The cause lying at the root of all these troubles was the desperate and deplorable economic conditions of the time. Through lack of sympathy the regular contributions from abroad ceased and the income from the Babylonian communities was negligible. Yet the Geonim had great responsibilities. Apart from their own and their families' needs they had to provide all the dignitaries and their families with the necessities of life. No wonder that the numerous letters of the Geonim in the latter part of the tenth century are filled with bitter complaints of suffering and crying for bread for their children. It is rather touching to read in one letter that the Gaon, deprived the members of his own family of their necessities in order to assure the upkeep of the various schools. Attached to the Academies were elementary schools for Bible, Mishnah and Talmud. Teachers as well as scholars had to be supplied with

[1] Ginzberg, *Geonica*, II, pp. 58-69; Davidson, *Ginze Schechter*, 51.
[2] Sassoon, *Diwan of Shemuel Hannaghid*, p. XXXIII f.

food and raiment by the authorities, otherwise the poorer members of the community refrained from sending their sons to school. They found it more profitable to put them into business and professions, where they could earn a living sooner. To these troubles we have to add interference on the part of the government caused by Jewish informers. As a result the Geonim Sherira and Hai were imprisoned, all their property confiscated, and Sherira deprived of his dignity. Our chroniclers and poets who speak of this deplorable affair are disinclined to dwell on it and so we will also shorten and close the story without a fuller enquiry into the names and nature of the Pariṣe Yisrael.

Another aspect of conditions, spiritual as well as political, is revealed by an epistle from Hai Gaon in Baghdad, addressed to the Vizier, Samuel the Naghid of Malaga. This document purports to express R. Hai Gaon's opinion on whether philosophical studies are advisable or not. The letter is preserved in the Meirath 'Enayim of Isaac of Acre, a commentary on Nahmanides' Pentateuch commentary and published by Graetz.[1] The Responsum is also quoted by Abbamari, Solomon ibn Addereth and Isaac b. Sheshath. Graetz is doubtful whether the letter is genuine. He is inclined to decide in the negative, asserting that some of the French students, hostile to Maimonides and his writings, fabricated the document in order to array Hai Gaon's authority against secular studies. Rapoport in his biography[2] of Hai mitigates the decision of the Gaon by interpreting that a Jew should not be exclusively engaged in philosophic studies, but combined with religious studies some attention may be paid to philosophy and kindred subjects. Here is not the place to decide between the opposing interpretations as to R. Hai's attitude towards philosophy. The question of the genuineness of the letter is, however, of first rate interest for our subject, since it points

[1] *Monatsschrift*, XI (1862), pp 37-40.
[2] *Bikkure ha-'Ittim*, X (5590), p. 89, note 15.

especially to conditions prevailing in Baghdad during the lifetime of R. Hai Gaon. There are two references to Baghdad in the epistle. The first runs as follows: "You do not seem to be aware of the troubles, quarrels and follies which possessed the hearts of many people who during the rule of the king 'Aḍud el-Dawlah had been engaged in philosophic studies. Moreover doubts and controversies arose among them with reference to the principal laws of religion, till they became renegades." Such a ruler—the Caliph 'Aḍud el-Dawlah—actually is recorded as having ruled in Baghdad about the year 997. It would be greatly surprising for a mystifier or a forger in the late thirteenth century in France to recall with such exactitude the name of an Eastern king who lived two hundred years before the forger's time, and describe events happening in his days as having happened in the past. In spite of all the difficulties arising out of the style of the letter, and Samuel the Naghid's well-known attitude toward secular studies, the epistle may be used as material for the conditions prevailing among the Jews of Baghdad in the declining years of the tenth century.

There is another point in the very same letter which has an interest for the historian of the Baghdad Jews. The Gaon says: "And there arose earlier some Baghdad Jews, for whom it would have been much better if they were not Jews at all, but gentiles, for they provoked the jealousy of the nations through their philosophy. They (the gentiles) of their own will kept back from these studies, and so have we, and have restrained our fellow Jews from this occupation since we saw the great damage entailed through it." We see that the irreligious attitude shown by those Jews who had sunk themselves in the depths of secular studies, aroused the enmity and hatred of their surroundings. No doubt such Jews must have lived in Baghdad, and by their irreligious behaviour and free-thinking provoked ill-feeling among the Moslems. This coincided with anti-philosophic movements in Muhammadan circles. Consequently the Geonim also may have altered their earlier friendly attitude to secular studies, and emphasized more strongly the greater importance of religious studies.

This attitude of the Gaon towards philosophic studies is not contradicted by the spirit of his letter addressed to R. Joseph b. Berakhyah and his colleagues of the Academy in Ḳairuwan, who raised many questions about mysticism and superstition. The Gaon in his answer shows unmistakably that he is opposed to all kinds of superstitions and magic performances. It is interesting to hear that the Gaon does not favour the attitude of the people of Sura in these questions, and one could read some censure in his words. They also convey that the Baghdadians, in contrast to the people of Sura, were free from such weakness.[1] Granted further that the Gaon may be considered, as Dr. D. Kauffmann essayed to show[2] a Jewish Mutakallim, nevertheless, it can easily be understood that he did not favour a one-sided and general study of philosophical works and subjects. He perhaps tried to limit these studies to qualified persons who, firm in their faith and well satiated by knowledge of the Bible and the Talmud, could not fall into the nets of heresy and apostasy.

[1] See Eliezer Ashkenazi *Ta'am Zekenim*, Frankfort/M, 1854, pp. 54-58.
[2] *Ein Responsum des Gaons R. Hâja über Gottes Vorherwissen und die Dauer des menschlichen Lebens* (Aǵal) *in Zeitschrift der Deutschen Morgenländischen Gesellschaft*, XLIX (1895), pp. 73-84; comp. Erich Hildesheimer, *Mystik und Aggada im Urteile der Gaonen R. Scherira und R. Hai*, 1931.

CHAPTER VII

R. SHERIRA AND HIS SON R. HAI, AND R. SAMUEL BEN ḤOFNI

THE three Geonim, R. Sherira and his son R. Hai, and R. Samuel b. Ḥofni, the father-in-law of R. Hai, spent their lives in Baghdad. It would therefore be proper that this monograph should give a sketch of the biographies and a characterization of these three great luminaries of Judaism who conclude the classic period of the Geonic age. It is to the glory of Baghdad that men like Se'adyah and these three Geonim wrote and compiled their everlasting contributions to Jewish learning within her gates. The names of these men and those of their unknown assistants and colleagues attracted to Baghdad scores of young and old scholars from all Jewish settlements in Egypt, North Africa, Spain, Italy and Byzantium. Further, to Baghdad were turned the eyes of all the Jews in the Diaspora for instruction and guidance, and from the Geonim in Baghdad went forth the word of the Torah in their replies to ritual or legal questions. There was no other place in contemporary Judaism which ranked in importance with Baghdad. This was not due merely to the great institutions situated on the banks of the river, but to the personal qualities of their leaders, whose biographies will be given in the following lines.

I

R. Sherira traced his pedigree to the family of the Exilarchs. According to a tradition he descended from Rabba bar Abbahu, who was a scion of Zerubbabel, and therefore of Davidic origin. Sherira was the son of the Gaon Ḥananiah, a grandson of the Gaon Judah, and a great-grandson of R. Samuel who bore the title Resh Kallah. The forebears of Sherira were active Exilarchs, but from a certain date onwards, his ancestors withdrew from political activities connected with that dignity, and turned all their attention to study and learning, so that they excelled in scholastic life as heads or dignitaries of the Yeshibah (Academy). Sherira was born before the year 900. He joined the Academy very early in life and ascended the ladder of promotion until he was elected head of the Yeshibah in the year 968. He officiated for thirty years, till 998, when old age and political considerations forced him to resign. Sherira Gaon's fame will rest on his Letter (Iggereth Rab Sherira Gaon) which he addressed to the scholars in Ḳairuwan as a reply to their request to give them a history of the Oral Law, information about the redaction of the Mishnah and Talmud, the extent of Rabbinic literature and about the chronology of the Tannaim and Amoraim, Saburaim and Geonim. The Gaon did it with the greatest skill by using documents and writings preserved in the Geonic archives. This is not the place to enter into details about the superlative merits and value of the work; it will be sufficient to mention that Talmudic scholarship, ancient as well as modern, looks upon this Letter as the corner stone of Rabbinic research. Recently some of his commentaries on the Talmud came to light. In addition to these, other explanations of his, preserved by earlier lexicographers and Talmud commentators, were already known. Both these commentaries and explanations, however, are in such a fragmentary state that they do not convey a clear idea of the Gaon's literary importance. Whereas more light is shed on his significance in the numerous Responsa which were issued from the Academy under his presidency.

An interesting feature of his Responsa is the Aggadic element in them. Some of his commentaries on the Talmud give interesting insight into contemporary intellectual and religious life. His attitude towards the Aggadah is worth considering. According to Sherira most of the Aggadah is to be interpreted allegorically. This is an important landmark in Aggadic studies. His words were often quoted by teachers of the following generations. He says: "Things derived from the Scriptures which are current under the names of Midrash and Aggadah, are mostly not to be taken literally, and therefore not to be relied on. Yet, whatever agrees with the Scriptures and is based on logic has to be accepted."[1] The more intensive studies of Aggadic problems on the part of the Gaon was due to the hostile propaganda against the Talmud, Halakhah as well as Aggadah, on the part of the Karaites. Questions about these problems reached the Geonim from near and far, so that they had to direct individuals as well as communities in these matters. The attention of the contemporaries turned also to Kabbalistic literature which was current in those days. Thus the Gaon was asked about the nature of such mystic literary documents as the Shi'ur Ḳomah and the Hekhaloth. Sherira admits that they are ancient works ascribed to such authorities as R. 'Aḳiba and R. Ishmael, but that as they are full of mysteries they cannot be taken literally, and advises that they should not be the subject of study and research. His Responsum is of special value for the literature of the practical Ḳabbalah in the tenth century.[2] The greater part of his Responsa was issued jointly with Hai, and it is therefore difficult to establish which was the father's and which the son's.

Of greater importance for the historian are the letters written by Sherira on behalf of his Academy. These reveal his character and nobility of soul to a much larger extent than his correspondence. The Genizah has furnished a number of new documents which tell us of the sad economic plight of the Babylonian Academies under Sherira and Hai. In one of the

[1] *Ha-Eshkol*, ed. Auerbach, Halberstadt, 1868-69, II, p. 47.
[2] *Teshuboth ha-Geonim*, ed. Mussafia, Lyck, 1864, No. 29.

documents Sherira complains that they have to withhold nourishment from their children owing to lack of funds coming from abroad, and the great poverty prevailing at the seat of the Gaonate. He begs of the addressees to continue the old custom of their fathers of supporting the Geonic institutions, lest the academic institutions and the Geonic authority collapse.[1] It seems that the communities abroad desisted from sending their questions to Baghdad, which meant in the first instance a great material loss, and in the second an attempt to overthrow the Gaonic authority. The Gaon is rather strong on both points, not for selfish reasons but for the good of the community. He fears that the downfall of the Gaonic institutions, which have lasted now for more than three centuries, may spell misfortune to the study of the Torah and to religious life. A fragment of a pathetic letter written by Sherira is the best proof of the Gaon's unselfishness and his warm feeling for the Torah. He complains that the addressees for many years kept silent. Neither their religious questions nor their financial contributions reached the Geonic offices. In spite of that the Gaon prayed for the welfare of the addressees. Then he proceeds to describe the economic conditions of his surroundings: "Our old scholars sit desolate, our young students are sighing in desperation, our teachers are complaining. We feel bitterly, for it seems to us as if the whole world is going to destruction." His only hope is God and His Covenant. Complaint reached him that the wisdom and the learning of the Academy had diminished, which probably induced many communities and supporters of the Academy to discontinue their regular contributions. Sherira retorts: "Indeed it is so, behold our glory is dimmed, our learning decreased, our Midrashim are desolate, we are left a few out of many, the Mishnah school (Midrash Tannaim) is almost forsaken, for previously any lad, even if he was blind, was brought to the

[1] Schechter, *Saadyana*, No XLVI, line 12 ff.

Midrash ha-Mishnah, but nowadays no one brings his son, and we have to use tricks so that some students should enter in order that the Mishnah should not entirely be forgotten. Most parents send their sons to other occupations where they can earn a living. From generation to generation, from year to year the situation gets worse and worse." These words convey an idea of the low standard of religious studies in this period. It was mainly due to the prevailing economic plight of Babylonian Jewry. Parents, looking for the material security of their children, neglected then as in all times the Torah and turned to more profitable professions and work. It was the fault of the leaders who did not supply the scholars with the necessities of life. What shall the scholars do? asks Sherira. Can they endure starvation and thirst? Sherira says of himself and of his surroundings that they have to forego daily food in order to supply others who are even in greater need.[1]

Apart from these material difficulties, there were other troubles which darkened the life of Sherira Gaon. This Gaon inherited a bad legacy, the long standing quarrel between Sura and Pumbaditha. Strife and conflicts were frequent enough when the Geonim officiated in distant places. Now that they removed the seats of the Gaonate to Baghdad and dwelt near one another, it was natural for the situation to become worse instead of better. The result of these calamities was an accusation against the aged Gaon, who was imprisoned by the government, had all his property confiscated, and was probably put to death in a very cruel way.

II

Hai Gaon was born in the year 939.[2] At an early age he joined the Academy. He passed through all the ranks of the Geonic school. We find him as teacher occupied in spreading

[1] A. Marmorstein, *M.G.W.J.*, LXVII, pp. 257-260.
[2] Sassoon, *Diwan of Shemuel Hannaghid*, p. xviii.

knowledge among the young. His father, Sherira, writes about him and his teaching activities as follows: "Our son Hai is very diligent in teaching them (the students), and in explaining to them, and he who does not know to ask, he shows the way of raising questions, and makes this method of study popular with them."[1] At the age of forty-eight he was elevated to the dignity of Ab Beth Din and at the age of fifty he signed jointly with his father documents and Responsa issued from the Geonic offices. Ten years later, at the age of sixty, in the year 998, he became Gaon, shortly before the death of his father.

About his family life we have some information which is more than of personal interest. The strife which for many years embittered the life of Sherira Gaon, as mentioned above, was due to the claims of R. Samuel b. Ḥofni to the Gaonate of Pumbaditha. These rival claims of the two families were amicably settled by a marriage between the daughter of Samuel b. Ḥofni and the son of Sherira, Hai. By this happy solution Hai was confirmed in his position as Gaon of Pumbaditha, while his father-in-law took over the Gaonate of Sura which was vegetating since the death of Se'adyah and his son Dosa.

Hai's literary activities and scholarly influence was by far greater than that of any of the previous Geonim. His explanations and decisions have been accepted as authoritative in every country. Even greater than his learning and wisdom were his kind-heartedness, humility, and saintliness. For generations he was spoken of, in the colleges of Israel, as the father of the nation. His teachings and works were preserved by the two great scholars of Ḳairuwan, R. Ḥananel b. Ḥushiel and R. Nissim b. Jacob of Ḳairuwan, who transplanted Talmudic studies from the East to the West, from Mesopotamia to North Africa and Europe. Hai followed closely in the footsteps of his father, Sherira, and

[1] Lewin, *Iggereth Rab Sherira Gaon*, p. XXVIII.

was his spiritual as well as his political heir. Just as his father, so Hai manifests a special interest in secular studies. We find Hai in consultation with Christian clerics and Moslem scholars about Biblical and theological problems. Kabbalistic studies were also favoured by Hai and his circle. His chief works are his Talmud commentaries, which were the basis of Talmudic studies of R. Nathan b. Yeḥiel for his 'Arukh (lexicon). Although these commentaries were lost for many centuries, fragments of them were current in the Spanish as well as Italian schools through many channels. Next to his commentaries on the Talmud there are preserved Halakhic Compendia on various subjects of law and rite, some in prose, others in verse. Here we may mention his work Kitab el-Shara wul-Bai', which codifies all the details of civil law. This book, written in Arabic like all his other works, was translated by Isaac b. Reuben of Barcelona under the name of Meḳaḥ u-Memkar. There seems to have been another translation of this work, perhaps by an earlier translator. Another work by Hai, Kitab el-Iman, was also translated into Hebrew by the same Spanish Rabbi, and was called Mishpete ha-Shebu'oth. Early authorities used Hai Gaon's lexicon a great deal; however, it is no longer accessible to us. It was known as Kitab el-Ḥawi, or in Hebrew, Sefer ha-Meassef. This shows that he was interested in grammatical and lexicographical questions. He manifested great interest in Biblical studies of which many examples are preserved in the exegetical literature of the Middle Ages.

Liturgical tradition records his name among the poets of the synagogue, and ascribes to him the litany Shema' Ḳoli Asher Yishma' be-Ḳoloth, which is to be found in many rites such as those of Spain, North Africa, and Yemen, and of course, Baghdad. In all these countries the Gaon's fervent prayer is repeated up to this very day on the eve of the Day of Atonement—a worthy monument to the pious memory of the great teacher of Baghdad. Professor I. Davidson registers besides this, eleven other poems coming from the Gaon.[1] There is also a long moralistic poem under the title Musar Haskel, ascribed to Hai, which gained great popularity, as shown by the large number of manuscripts which contain it. Some rhymes are attributed to R. Hai, which describe the codified laws in his books mentioned above. Modern research, however, is sceptical about the authorship, and attributes them to a later poet named Se'adyah. Harkavy, for instance, is inclined to deprive the Gaon of a title to this poem and to Musar Haskel.[2] No reliance can be placed on the spurious Kabbalistic books current under the name of Hai Gaon, such as the work Pithron Ḥalomoth, which are devoted to the interpretation of dreams and magic prescriptions.

The importance of the Gaon lies in the first instance in the great number of scholars who sat at his feet in Baghdad and who afterwards, by founding new centres of scholarship, spread the Torah to all other Jewish settlements. He was in frequent correspondence with nearly all the prominent scholars of his age, such as Samuel the Naghid, Jacob b. Nissim of Ḳairuwan and his son Nissim, Ḥananel b. Ḥushiel, Elḥanan b. Shemariah of Fusṭaṭ, Abraham b. Moses ibn Jami' of Ḳabeṣ, Joseph b. 'Amram of Sajelmasa, Moses b. Isaac of Maghreb, Meshullam b. Ḳalonymos of Lucca, Samuel b. Abraham of Tahart, and others. Among his pupils was R. Maṣliaḥ of Sicily who acted as intermediary between the Gaon and the Naghid, and brought to the latter information about Biblical interpretations which were discussed in Baghdad. The affair which split Spanish Jewry into two camps, the one following Ḥanokh b. Moses and the other Joseph b. Isaac ibn Saṭanas, was brought for decision before the Gaon in Baghdad. Joseph ibn Satanas undertook the lengthy journey to Baghdad,

[1] I. Davidson, *Thesaurus of Medieval Hebrew Poetry*, IV, New York, 1933, p. 378. [Further see *Sinai* Vol. 1, Nos. 12-13 (which numbers are devoted completely to R. Hai), pp. 592-676, where I. Werfel reproduces 24 poems attributed to this Gaon prefacing same with a discussion.]

[2] *Ozar Yisrael*, IV, p. 97.

but the Gaon felt reluctant to receive him. Saṭanas expected that the Gaon would readily support him, because the establishment of a new religious centre in Spain actually undermined the financial position and the very existence of the Babylonian Academies. Now Saṭanas thought the Gaon would use the opportunity to put an end to the activities of the Spanish school. But he was utterly mistaken. The Gaon was not guided by selfishness; he paid due attention to the bill of excommunication issued against Saṭanas by the authorities of Cordova, and forbade Saṭanas to appear before him. Saṭanas, disappointed, left Baghdad for Damascus where he died.[1]

A medieval author, the compiler of Sefer Ḥasidim, relates of a visit paid by Hai Gaon to Jerusalem, which deserves mention here. The writer precedes his narrative with the information that the Gaon repaired year by year to Jerusalem from Baghdad. It is not the place here to investigate the veracity of this report, but it is quite likely that there is some truth in it. The visit coincided with the festival of Tabernacles. There is other evidence besides this report that the day of Hosha'na Rabbah was celebrated in the tenth and eleventh centuries on the Mount of Olives and they made seven circuits (Haḳḳafoth), which were accompanied by the singing of hymns composed by the Gaon. It is described thus: "In front of Rab Hai went priests (Kohanim) attired in silk and turbans, and behind him the people. The Gaon was between the priests and the people, leaving between either a distance of 100 cubits." It happened that a man who was guilty of murder confessed to his crime and applied to the Gaon Hai and R. Ebiathar Kohen Ṣedeḳ of Jerusalem for means of atonement. This was duly granted by the punishment of the lashes. This very man approached the Gaon Hai after the circuits, when the Gaon was laughing after his festive meal, asking him: "Rabbi, why did you walk by yourself when all of you went around the

[1] *Neubauer*, I, p. 69.

Mount of Olives?" Hai replied: "I come yearly from Baghdad in order to make the circuits on the Mount of Olives during Tabernacles. I purify myself on the day of Hosha'na Rabbah and the Prophet Elijah walks beside me. That is the reason why I keep a distance in front and behind. Elijah speaks to me (on these occasions), and I asked him: 'When will the Messiah come?' Elijah answered: 'When they will go around the Mount of Olives with the priests.' Thus I took all the priests whom I could find in order to make the circuits, perchance he (the Messiah) may be among them. And Elijah told me: 'Look at all these priests who are attired in silks and turbans walking about proudly and yet only one of them is a descendant of Aaron.' This one, the genuine priest, goes behind all of them, is despised by them, walking in shabby garments, desires no honour, is full of humility, besides being lame in one foot and blind in one eye. That is the only one who can rightly claim true descent from Aaron." Hai said in conclusion: "Should I not laugh that among all these priests there is only one who is a genuine priest, and he is a man with blemish?"[1] The source from which the pious writer drew this story is not known; yet it may reflect actual conditions and may have some historical value. Hai's relations to Palestine are now known better through the discovery of the Genizah. Thus we are told that the Palestinian Gaon, Solomon b. Judah, sent his son to Baghdad in order to complete his studies and gain experience under the guidance of the Gaon and his brother-judges. Likewise we learn that the Palestinian authorities turned for Halakhic instruction and guidance in religious practice to Hai Gaon.

All these facts point to the literal fulfilment of the high expectations of the Baghdad Jews when they acclaimed Hai's succession to his father's office by applying to him the words

[1] *Sefer Ḥasidim*, Frankfort/M., 1924 (2nd ed.), p. 169. [Further compare R. Hai Gaon's letter to the Priests of Africa, *Ginze Kedem*, Vol. 4, p. 51 *et seq.*]

of the Scriptures (I Kings 2, 12), paraphrased thus: "And Hai sat upon the throne of Sherira his father: and his kingdom was established greatly."[1]

III

Together with Sherira and Hai Baghdad can boast of the presence in her midst of a third great light in contemporary Jewry, namely Samuel b. Ḥofni Gaon. It is a rare phenomenon even in Jewish history, which is so rich in great personalities and saintly figures, that the same place should accommodate at the same time academies of learning and courts of justice headed by three such spiritual giants. Samuel descended from an ancient Geonic family. His father, Ḥofni, having served as Ab Beth Din and bearing the title Dayyan, was a member of the Academy in Sura, where his father, Kohen Ṣedeḳ, occupied the position of Gaon in the days of Se'adyah and David b. Zakkai. As a member of the Geonic family of Pumbaditha, he rightly thought that he might succeed to his grandfather's office. His learning and leadership, his piety and wisdom certainly qualified him for such a position and supported his aspirations. The non-fulfilment of his hopes was a source of strife between him and the more successful Sherira. Letters and proclamations of both parties which are still extant, breathe the spirit of bitterness and hostility. This unfortunate affair poisoned the atmosphere of scholarly as well as of social life in Baghdad.

It almost seems that the glory of Baghdad was envied, and was disturbed by personal interests. It would carry us too far to dilate here on the whole course of this strife, but it is sufficient to say that a compromise enabled the conflicting parties to arrive at an amicable settlement. The agreement between Sherira and Ḥofni was facilitated by the two important

[1] See S. Assaf, *Encyclopaedia Judaica*, *s.v.* Hai b. Sherira.

factors already mentioned. Hai, the son of Sherira, married the daughter of Samuel b. Ḥofni. This marriage was a pledge of peace between the parties. Also, the Gaonate of Sura was conferred on Samuel b. Ḥofni. This institution came into disrepute through the unfortunate attack of David b. Zakkai the Exilarch upon Se'adyah Gaon. In spite of the final restoration of Se'adyah to the Gaonate of Sura, the Academy collapsed and remained without a leader. When peace was finally concluded between Sherira and Samuel b. Ḥofni, the latter took the reins of the Academy of Sura in his hands. Samuel b. Ḥofni was a worthy successor to Se'adyah. Both in character and in learning the great ideal of Se'adyah guided him. Altogether the influence of Se'adyah and of his religious movement were strongly felt long after his death in the literary activities and in the religious development of the Geonim who succeeded him. Samuel b. Ḥofni devoted a great deal of his works to the explanation of the Bible. His Bible exegesis was rationalistic to such an extent that it provoked opposition from many quarters. Hai could not see eye to eye with him in rationalizing the Biblical accounts of the serpent in the Garden of Eden, Bileam's ass, the story of the witch of Endor, etc. It is natural that his literary activities should include works on the Talmud. Here again he closely followed the example of Se'adyah. Like Se'adyah, Samuel b. Ḥofni wrote a long introduction to the Talmud, of which, however, only some Genizah fragments and various quotations in the medieval Rabbinic literature have survived. Some scholars suggest that Samuel ha-Naghid's Mebo ha-Talmud (Introduction to the Talmud) is really a re-shaping of Shemuel b. Ḥofni's Kitab el-Madkhal ila el-Talmud. Samuel b. Ḥofni left a number of treatises which deal with certain branches or certain chapters of the law, such as a treatise codifying the laws about the Status of the Minor in religious life, the laws of Ṣiṣith and of Benedictions. It may be, however, that all these small tractates were parts of a larger volume which extended over the whole ritual law known to bibliographers by the name of Kitab el-Sharayi', that is, Book of Precepts. There are, further, a number of smaller treatises on themes taken from various branches of civil law. They also may have originally comprised one volume.

Of greater importance is the Gaon's philosophic work which is known by the title Kitab Nuskh el-Shar' wa-Uṣul el-Din wa-Faru'ah (Book about the Abrogation of the Law and the Origin of Religion and its Branches). It is to be regretted that this work was not translated into Hebrew, and consequently Jewish literature has been deprived of a precious document. For, to judge from the fragmentary information which we have, religious philosophy was well represented by the Gaon's work. A few instances will suffice to show this. He goes against the argument of philosophers who believe in the eternity of the world and deny the Divine Creation; he condemns anthropomorphic teachings; he disproves the claim of the Moslems who attribute heavenly origin to their Koran on the ground of its style and language.

Needless to say that the Gaon did not withold his views on Karaite contentions regarding calendar subjects, the celebration of the Pentecost, and others. Probably his anti-Karaite doctrines which were the target for attack by contemporary Karaite writers such as Joseph el-Baṣir were a part of his great book on the philosophy of religion. Finally, it may be mentioned that Samuel was a great student of the Hebrew language and tried his skill at poetry also. In difficult passages he did not hesitate to consult non-Jewish translations of the Bible in order to establish the truth.[1]

The Gaon left a son who succeeded him in the Gaonate of Sura. His name frequently occurs in post-Geonic Rabbinic literature, as R. Israel Kohen Gaon. He also resided and taught in Baghdad.

[1] The material on which the characterization of Samuel b. Ḥofni is based will be found in Harkavy, *Zikhron ha-Gaon Rab Shemuel ben Ḥofni wu-Sefaraw*, Petersberg, 1880.

CHAPTER VIII

THE GEONIM OF BAGHDAD

THE death of Hai Gaon which occurred on the sixth day of Passover in the year 1038[1] at Baghdad, turned the days of festivities into days of weeping and mourning. Far beyond the residence of the Gaon and of his native land his death made the greatest impression on all sections of contemporary Jewry. The two outstanding poets of the age preserved in their lamentations the feelings of general mourning on the death of Hai. Solomon ibn Gabirol commemorated this mournful event in three elegies worthy of the poet and of the Gaon.[2] Gabirol calls on the whole nation to mourn the death of the Baghdadian Gaon. All the children of the Diaspora and Palestine feel the loss of their king and their protector. The crown of their heads is removed, and the chain of dignity fallen from their necks. The loss was felt the more since there was no suitable successor who could worthily occupy the deceased Gaon's seat and replace him in learning and character. The personal relation of the poet to the Gaon finds beautiful expression in the following two lines of the third elegy: "If ye should rend your garments over him, I will rend my heart and my vitals!"

The Naghid exclaims in the bitterness of his grief, and overcome by his sorrow: "Is there any counsel in death? Is there any escape from the grave? O! do find some balm for my pain and wound, my friends! Do hasten to strengthen my heart with plaster and bandages!" We learn from the elegy that the news of Hai's death called for fasting and mourning in all

[1] See Abraham ibn Daud in *Neubauer's M.J.C.*, I, p. 66.

[2] Bialik-Rabnitzki, *Shire Shelomo ben Yehuda ibn Gabirol*, I, Berlin, 5684, pp. 88-90.

Jewish settlements in Baghdad as well as outside that city. It appeared to the eyewitnesses of that event as if with the death of Hai Gaon the Torah was carried to the grave and buried. It was deeply felt that he left no son who could fill his position as a leader and teacher in Israel.[1] Instead of him the Exilarch Hezekiah b. David became the leader of the school and Jewry. The information given by R. Abraham ibn Daud that the former did not remain long in office, can now be safely discarded since we know from the Diwan of the Naghid that in 1055 he was still in office and exchanged friendly letters with Samuel ha-Naghid in Spain.[2] Through unfortunate intrigues and political machinations he was imprisoned by the Caliph, chained and tortured. He died probably in dungeon, while his two sons escaped to Spain. We learn from the Naghid that his friend Samuel b. Joseph el-Bagdadi would have been the most suitable candidate for the vacant seat of the Gaon.[3] Why he did not return to his native country, but remained in Spain, we cannot say. This is the more surprising since a native of Spain was put at the head of affairs in Baghdad, namely Isaac b, Moses, known as Ibn Sakni, who hailed from Denia. He was one of the five Isaacs, who lived and taught in this period. Of his activities and character, however, we are unable to give any report.[4]

We now come to Abraham, who is mentioned in the Diwan of Isaac, the son of Abraham ibn Ezra. It is impossible to see in him a Baghdadian Gaon, as Poznański suggested.[5] This Abraham, who is styled Rosh Yeshibath Geon Ya'akob, was. moreover, a member of the priestly Geonim from Palestine, who officiated in Ḥadrakh near Damascus, as proved by S. Assaf.[6] There is a gap between Isaac b. Moses, who may have

[1] Sassoon, *Diwan*, pp. XVIII, 11-13.
[2] For a fuller treatment of this date, see Sassoon, ibid., pp. XX, 101.
[3] See above, p. 42.
[4] See MS. Sassoon 1046, p. 66 (*Ohel Dawid*, pp. 1065-1068), where he is called "bar Ḥofni"; Poznański, *R.E.J.*, LXV (1913), pp. 312-316.
[5] Posnański, *Babylonische Geonim*, p. 11
[6] See *Tarbiz*, I, No. 1 (5690), p. 104.

died about 1100 or somewhat later, and the next Gaon about whom we have some more information, namely Solomon b. Samuel Gaon. Thanks to the great discovery of S. Assaf, a good deal of information about the Baghdad Gaonate and the Jews in the East in our period, which was not known to the previous historian of the post-Geonic Babylonian Geonim, the late Dr Poznanski, is now available. We know that Ibn Ezra's son Isaac stayed in Baghdad in 1143, when he composed a poem in honour of Abu el-Barakat Hibbat Allah, a very learned Jew, who became a Moslem.[1] In this period the Gaon Solomon b. Samuel may have been in office. There is a letter written by him and addressed to the community of Mazidiyyah and its surroundings, i.e. Hillah. In an elegy he mourns the death of his son Samuel, who died at the age of twenty, and by his death frustrated the father's fervent hope of seeing him as his successor. Samuel is praised as a wonderful scholar, well versed in Bible, Mishnah, Talmud, Tosefta, Sifra, Sifre, and Aggadic Midrashim. The poor father calls on the sons of Shin'ar and 'Elam, Canaan (Central Europe), Ṣo'an (Egypt) and Sefarad, to lament with him the loss which Judaism suffered.[2] For us the point of interest is that the Gaonate of Baghdad in the middle of the twelfth century was in close connection with the Jewries in Mesopotamia and Persia, Central Europe, North Africa and Spain.

A contemporary of this Gaon was Daniel, who bore the title of Alluf ha-Yeshibah and resided in some Jewish centre in the East. There some cases of disobedience against the Gaon arose, which necessitated energetic interference. The trouble was caused by two men, one of them Aaron b. Meraioth and the other Shealtiel Khalaf b. David ha-Melammed. The latter soon regretted his opposition to the Gaon and at his own re-

[1] See about this man and about Isaac ibn Ezra, below, pp. 85-88.

[2] According to Mann, *Texts and Studies*, pp. 213-214 the Gaon Solomon was not the son of Samuel, and the elegy mentioned here mourns the death of 'Azariah, not of Solomon; see, however, Assaf, *Kobeṣ shel Iggeroth R. Shemuel b. 'Ali wu-Bene Doro*, reprinted from *Tarbiz*, I (5690), pp. 5, 59.

quest as well as through the intervention of influential circles in Baghdad, he received pardon and was entrusted with official duties as well as with the collection of contributions to the Academy. The removal of the previous ban and the proclamation of the reinstallation of Khalaf in his office and dignity was performed by Daniel the Alluf, whose supremacy was imposed by the Gaon on Khalaf and duly acknowledged by him.[1]

The predecessor of the Gaon Solomon was the Gaon 'Ali, the father of Samuel Gaon, the greatest and most important of the Geonim of the post-Geonic period in Baghdad. If we understand rightly the report of Benjamin of Tudela about David Alroy, the Gaon 'Ali must have been officiating before Solomon Gaon. We are told that David Alroy studied under Ḥisdai the Head of the Captivity and under 'Ali the Head of the Academy.[2] Since Benjamin travelled about the year 1173 in the East, and he dates the Alroy events ten years earlier, it follows that Alroy must have studied under 'Ali at least two decades before Benjamin's visit to Baghdad. If so, 'Ali's time on the seat of the Geonim must be put about 1140. This would mean that he was the predecessor of Solomon Gaon.[3] While nothing is known about the activities and character of 'Ali Gaon, the personality and life of his son Samuel are of such importance that we have to devote to him a whole chapter.

[1] *Tarbiz*, I, No.3 (5690), pp. 21-25; see, however, Mann, *Texts and Studies*, I, pp. 212-213.

[2] See M. N. Adler, *The Itinerary of Benjamin of Tudela*, Oxford, 1907, Hebrew part, p. 51, and English part, p. 54.

[3] *Tarbiz*, I, No. 1 (5690), p. 105.

CHAPTER IX

SAMUEL B. 'ALI GAON

SAMUEL B. 'ALI GAON, called Ibn el-Dastur, must have been very young, perhaps in his childhood, when his father died. Therefore a stranger, the aforementioned Solomon b. Samuel, of whom we spoke in the previous chapter, occupied the Geonic seat in Baghdad. This Gaon, as we know from his mournful letter about the sad and early death of his learned son, had hoped that his own son would step into his place. Death decided differently, and apparently the dignity returned to 'Ali's son, namely Samuel. This Gaon was already known before the discovery of the Genizah. He became famous through his dispute with Maimonides and also by descriptions of the travellers in the East, as well as through his correspondence with scholars and by eulogies of a poet of his time. His was a very critical time in the history of the Jews, as evidenced by the Messianic movement initiated by David Alroy. Benjamin of Tudela who visited Baghdad about the year 1170 reports that in the time of this Gaon there were ten Academies in Baghdad. The first and the most important was under the guidance of Samuel b. 'Ali Gaon, the second under his brother, Ḥanaiah b. 'Ali ha-Levy. The leaders of the other schools are also mentioned by their names in the Itinerary of Benjamin of Tudela.[1] Rabbi Pethaḥiah of Ratisbon, who visited Baghdad only a couple of years later, offers a few details about the character of this Gaon, and by the way, some new information about the conditions in Baghdad. It is worth while mentioning here a few details preserved by R. Pethaḥiah which will become clearer in the light of the newly-discovered collection of Genizah letters. R. Pethaḥiah's report on the Geonic office

[1] See Adler, *Itinerary*, Hebrew part, p. 38.

deserves closer attention. He says: "R. Samuel the Gaon wrote and sealed a letter of recommendation on behalf of R. Pethaḥiah advising all to give him safe conduct whithersoever he should go, and that they should show him the graves of scholars and the pious.[1] Such an introduction known as "Iggereth Araḥith", or by the older Aramaic term "Iggereth Diḳar", can be traced throughout the ages from the early Talmudic period up to this very day. We learn further that the Gaon traced his genealogy back to the Prophet Samuel. The Gaon had no sons, but had a very learned daughter well-versed in Bible and Talmud. She gave Scripture lessons to the students. It is instructive to hear that the lady-lecturer imparted her instruction through a window. She herself was within the building while the disciples were outside, below, and could not see her.[2] Samuel's jurisdiction and authority extended over the whole of Babylonia, the districts of Moṣul and Damascus, the cities of Persia and Media. The troubles of which his predecessor suffered apparently disappeared to a great extent. No judge and no teacher was appointed in any of the cities and countries without the Gaon's seal and consent.[3] One must, however, see in Pethaḥiah's information some exaggeration when he writes that Samuel was the owner of about sixty slaves and that he occupied a large residence, "which is covered with tapestry; he himself is clothed in garments adorned with gold".[4] According to the new information derived from the Genizah letters, R. Pethaḥiah must have misunderstood the financial position of the Gaon, for such a rich man of that position would not write such pitiful letters begging for money, unless we assume that the money asked for was mainly for scholars and teachers around him.

[1] Benisch, *Travels of Rabbi Petachia of Ratisbon*, London, 1856, p. 22. For such letters of recommendation, see Sassoon, *Iggeroth Paras we-Teman*, Hazofeh, 5685; pp. 209-223.
[2] Benisch, *Travels*, p. 18.
[3] Ibid.
[4] Ibid., p. 16.

His authority extended even to Europe. R. Moses of Kief turned to him with Halakhic questions, and the Gaon's Responsum is still preserved.[1] It is difficult to decide after so many centuries, in the dispute which raged between the Gaon Samuel b. 'Ali and Moses Maimonides. It is certain that these two leaders could not see eye to eye in many important theological and ritual questions. Maimonides' view about the bodily resurrection after death gave rise to many attacks against the great teacher of Cordova. The critics of Maimonides stirred up unrest and ill feeling among the Jews of Yemen. One of them approached the Gaon of Baghdad, in the year 1189, on this affair. His reply has not been preserved, but is characterized by Maimonides in the following way: "This year, in the year 1502 Sel. (1191), some correspondence written by our colleagues and friends of Baghdad reached us. They mention that a Yemenite enquirer asked about these problems of the Gaon who officiates at present in Baghdad, R. Samuel ha-Levy, and he compiled for them a dissertation on the resurrection of the dead. And he put my opinions concerning this problem partly in a mistaken way, and partly in a form which can be justified. He defended me, but very little help can be derived from his penmanship. After this exchange of letters, the Gaon's dissertation in its original form was sent to me. I saw in it all the homilies and Aggadoth which he compiled. Yet it is well known that scholars cannot be required to relate such homilies and wonderful deeds *verbatim* as women are accustomed to tell them in the house of mourners, but the aim is to explain their subjects till they are clear to the intelligent, or at least nearly so. And more wonderful still are some strange ideas mentioned by him pretending that they are philosophical views on psychology."[2] R. Samuel was not a one-sided Talmudist, but also well read in philosophical works.

[1] See *Sha'are Teshuboth, Responsa of R. Meir b. Barukh of Rothenburgh*, Berlin, 1891, p. 64; A. Epstein, *Das Talmudische Lexikon*, Breslau, 1895, p. 26 (reprinted from *M.G.W.J.*); Poznański, *Bab. Geon.*, p. 54.
[2] See *Kobeṣ Teshuboth ha-Rambam we-Iggerothaw*, Leipzig, pt. 2, pp. 8-9.

It does not amount to much that Maimonides rather deprecates the Gaon's philosophical authorities, for example, the Mutakallimun, or Avicenna's treatise on reward. Yet the Gaon must have been well versed in contemporary philosophy. The Gaon's treatise against Maimonides made such an impression among the Jews of Baghdad that one of them, probably Daniel by name, found it necessary to compile a refutation of the Gaon's attack on Maimonides, a considerable fragment of which was discovered and published by A. Harkavy.[1]

This was not the only controversy between the two great leaders of Jewry. Another Baghdadian, the aforementioned Joseph b. Taber, turned to Maimonides with a question about Hilkhoth Niddah, and from one of these letters we see that Maimonides took part in a local quarrel between the Gaon and the Exilarch. Apparently Maimonides sided with a candidate for this post, who was not favoured by the local Gaon. Now the letters discovered, furnish some more details about this affair. It seems that a vacancy occured for the Exilarchate. This happened in the year 1191. There is preserved a letter written to the communities of el-Raḥbah, to the Jews of el-Raḳah, to el-Ḳal'ah, Serugh, Manbagh, el-Birah, Buza'ah, el-Bab, Palmyra, Ḥamath, Ḥomṣ, Baalbek, Edessa, Ḥaran, the whole land of Syria, and other communities. This circular letter shows that the Gaon had to put before them an account of what was going on in Baghdad. According to his report the Exilarch who pretended to fill that high position was an ignorant man, possessing no knowledge of either Bible or Mishnah.

His only qualifications were his wealth and influence with the Government.[2] Maimonides was in favour of one of the candidates, we do not know which. He was rebuked for taking part in this strife, and people were criticizing him for writing to a man whom he did not know and from whom all scholars

[1] *ZfHB*, II, pp. 125-128, and pp. 181-188.
[2] *Tarbitz*, I, No. 1 (5690), p. 126 f., and No. 2, pp. 62-63.

should keep away.[1] Who was this Exilarch? We know from Benjamin of Tudela that in the time when he passed through Baghdad a man called Daniel was very influential in the circles of the Caliph and the government. This man, with great authority over all the Jewish communities under the rule of the Caliph, may have aspired to become Exilarch. He gave permission to the communities appointing spiritual leaders and Hazzanim. Without his permission no one dared to officiate in any community. After the death of Daniel in the year 1174, there was a serious crisis in the history of the Exilarchate. The deceased Exilarch left no son, and consequently the Jews of Baghdad looked elsewhere for a member of the Davidic Dynasty. Such a family of royal blood existed in Mosul. Here lived two descendants of this family, namely David and Samuel. The Jews of Baghdad were divided in their opinions; some were in favour of the former, others of the latter. Most likely the Gaon supported one and Maimonides the other.

A third cause for ill-feeling between these two lights of Jewry was due to the fact that a member of the Baghdadian Academy, who became later the highest dignitary of that place, Zechariah b. Berakhel, published a very unfriendly criticism of Maimonides' commentary to the Mishnah. Maimonides was informed of this and expressed his opinion about the writer and his master, in a long letter addressed to his own favourite pupil, R. Joseph b. Judah ibn 'Aknin. We see that the fame of Maimonides reached Baghdad and his work was studied diligently by members of the Academy. We have no material to decide whether the action of the critic originated in the desire to exalt himself at the expense of Maimonides and to captivate the applause of the crowd by minimising the great value of the Mishna commentary. Maimonides ridicules and rebukes the indecent habit of some scholars who make believe that they can dispense with the literary production of others and excel them. Maimonides further felt that his faithfulness to God and

[1] Poznański, p. 32.

his religious observance were not quite safe against defamation on the part of his enemies in Baghdad. All these small annoyances disturbed possible relations between Maimonides and the Gaon because the critic was no other than the son-in-law of Samuel Gaon. Mar Zechariah must have been a very conceited and overbearing scholar if the report given by Maimonides is to be taken literally. His criticisms are rejected as foolish and childish, yet Maimonides proposes to deal with the questions asked and objections raised to the Mishnah commentary, in their proper places. It is noteworthy that Maimonides acknowledges some of the mistakes and attributes them to the misleading guidance of some earlier authors and their works such as the Meghillath Setharim by R. Nissim b. Jacob of Kairuwan,[1] the Book of Precepts by Ḥefeṣ b. Yaṣliaḥ,[2] and others which the writer is reluctant to mention.

The same letter of Maimonides makes mention of a second correspondence which took place between Baghdad and Fustat. The Gaon's letter has not been preserved, but from the answer we can gather that a great deal of friendliness and mutual recognition was lacking between the writer and the addressee. Maimonides in his answer cannot suppress his feelings of annoyance and grief at the apparent lack of good manners. Nevertheless he advises his pupil, who made up his mind to leave Aleppo for Baghdad, to pay due respect to the Gaon. Joseph ibn 'Aknin acquired permission from his great master to open a Midrash and Talmud Torah in Baghdad. Ibn 'Aknin is advised to compare the Halakhic Code of Alfasi with the *Ḥibbur*. It seems from all this that personal and religious motives as well as intellectual and scientific reasons caused this deplorable estrangement between Maimonides and Samuel b. 'Ali Gaon.[3]

[1] The fragments of this work were collected by S. Poznański and published in *Hazofeh*, V (1921), p. 177 ff., p. 294 ff., VI (1922), p. 329 ff.

[2] See B. Halper, *A Volume of the Book of Precepts* by Ḥefeṣ b. Yaṣliaḥ, Philadelphia, 1913.

[3] *Ḳobeṣ Teshuboth ha-Rambam*, pt. 2, p. 31.

Finally, there is an exchange of correspondence between the Gaon and Maimonides about a Halakhic question. The correspondence originated through permission granted by Maimonides to cross great rivers such as the Tigris and Euphrates on the Sabbath. This permission was given in writing and was shown by R. Abraham ha-Cohen to the Gaon in Baghdad. The Gaon speaks of Maimonides in glowing terms and gives him his proper titles and mentions that in a letter addressed to Yemen, where some ill-feeling arose against the Halakhic Code of Maimonides, he defended him and praised his work. Yet, in the present case he cannot remain silent, and tries to upset Maimonides' decision, which is regarded as mistaken and misleading. Maimonides examined the arguments brought forward by the Gaon and defended his point of view in a dignified manner.[1]

We may rightly assume that the quarrel arising out of the election of the Exilarch was the chief cause of these regrettable affairs, as admitted by Maimonides himself. After the death of the Exilarch Samuel in the year 1190 the Gaon Samuel went a step further and endeavoured to put an end to the dignity of the Exilarchate. According to him there was no need for such an institution. Not worldly but spiritual leadership was the need of the Jews in the Diaspora. It was waste of money to keep up an expensive Exilarchate instead of combining all forces for the material and spiritual well-being of the Academy which is really the Throne of the Torah, the place of our great teacher Moses, the centre of Judaism.[2] Samuel in his zeal went so far as to consider anyone who dared to raise his voice or contradict the teaching or decision of the Academy as disputing the very authority of our Teacher Moses. It is doubtful whether he succeeded in carrying out his project of abolishing the Exilarchate.

The letters issued by the Gaon are on the whole pleadings

[1] Ibid., pt. 1, pp. 32-33.
[2] *Tarbiz*, I, No. 1 (5690), p. 126.

for support on behalf of the Yeshibah. These letters were sent by special messengers, whose names have to be mentioned here. First of all, Jacob b. 'Ali, who was styled Rosh Be Rabbanan. He was a native of Baghdad, an *alumnus* of the Geonic school, who spent the latter part of his life in Fusṭaṭ. Secondly, Zechariah b. Berakhiah, a native of Aleppo, who succeeded his father-in-law, the Geon Samuel b. 'Ali as Gaon. These representatives went backwards and forwards to all the communities of Syria, Mesopotamia and Persia, where they collected funds for the upkeep of the Geonate and the Yeshibah, settling during their stay all communal and private affairs in abeyance, and looking after the spiritual welfare of the communities. The Jewries of these countries were united and administered by a well regulated organization. The consolidation of the administration was largely due to the energy and the organizing talent of Samuel b. 'Ali Gaon.

No wonder, that a Baghdadian poet, Eleazar b. Jacob ha-Babli, in his admiration of our Gaon extolled in many poems the merits and greatness, the learning and piety of Samuel and of his children. The poet mourns in more than one elegy the death of Samuel's daughter, who, according to Pethaḥiah of Ratisbon and our poet, was a very learned woman whose wisdom is highly praised.[1] The husband of the Gaon's daughter was 'Azariah, who is styled Rosh Yeshibath Geon Ya'aḳob, the son-in-law and pupil of Samuel Gaon. The Genizah letters enrich our knowledge of the Gaon's family by the information that Zechariah b. Berakhiah, also a successor to Samuel, was a son-in-law of Samuel b. 'Ali. There is no need to assume that 'Azariah in the Diwan of Eleazar Habbabli is a mistake for Zechariah in the Genizah letters as suggested by Assaf.[2] It is doubtful whether Pethaḥiah's report that the Gaon had only one daughter, and no sons at all, is

[1] v. Poznański, pp. 64-66. For other learned women in this period see below, p. 83.
[2] *Tarbiz*, I, No. I (5690), p. 108.

quite correct, since the poet also seems to suggest that Samuel Gaon was the father of four children.[1] Samuel b. 'Ali Gaon died on the same day as his daughter, and the Paitan mournfully exclaims: "God has forbidden to slaughter a lamb and its young one on the same day, how could death be so cruel to snatch away simultaneously daughter and father?"

[1] Poznański, p. 63, note 8.

CHAPTER X

THE SUCCESSORS TO SAMUEL B. 'ALI

THE date of Samuel Gaon's death can be approximately established at 1207. His immediate successors were his two sons-in-law 'Azariah, and Zechariah b. Berakhiah, both of whom have been mentioned previously. The former, 'Azariah, is highly praised by the Baghdadian poet as a learned and wise man, as an eloquent preacher and successful teacher, a man of noble birth and heart.[1] How long he held the dignity of Gaon, we cannot ascertain, but it was probably for a very short period. His successor, the more often mentioned Zechariah, was, as stated, a native of Aleppo, where there had been since the cessation of the Palestinian Gaonate an important centre of Jewish learning and religious activities. Zechariah was highly praised by his future father-in-law and was invested already in the lifetime of the latter with rights and privileges of an *Ab Beth Din.* As such he was empowered to appoint secretaries, *Ḥazzanim*, readers, leaders of communities, teachers and judges. He visited all the Syrian communities and a part of the Babylonian congregations in order to look after communal matters.[2] His learning and scholarship must have been very great indeed, in spite of the deprecatory remarks of Maimonides, since his criticism of the Mishnah Commentary induced the master to change his view in so many instances. Nothing, however, is known about his conduct as Gaon, probable because he spent only a very short time on the seat of the Geonim of Baghdad. We are unable to explain why his

[1] Poznański, p. 36.
[2] Tarbiz, I, No. 1 (5690), p. 119 and p. 126.

name is never mentioned in the Diwan of the Babli. Yet that is no reason to strike his name off the list of these Geonim.

A happy discovery from the Genizah throws some new light on the next Gaon in the chain of these dignitaries, who succeeded Samuel b. 'Ali.[1] This Genizah fragment from the Adler collection contains a letter or a circular written by R. Eleazar ha-Levy b. Hillel, who complains about persecutions which he suffered from his godless and deceitful enemies, of the nets of destruction spread out by his adversaries to cause his downfall, and of their treacheries by which his life was endangered. Reading between the lines, we learn that some accusation was brought against him. We gather further that the leaders of the communities, their elders and princes, who were zealous for the Lord, made up their minds to invest him with the dignity of the Gaonate. He, however, in his modesty, was reluctant to accept their offer, and hesitated for a considerable time to heed them, till finally they forced him, against his will, to occupy the honoured seat of the Geonim. When his enemies saw this they sought the aid of the government in order to frustrate this appointment. He was blackmailed before the Caliph. Having heard from an intimate friend that the Caliph ordered his imprisonment and punishment, he sought refuge in hiding. So far the contents of the letter, which is fragmentary. Yet, from another accidental discovery we learn that a Gaon, Eleazar b. Hilal, called ibn Fahd, officiated in Baghdad about this time. It is quite certain that the writer of the letter, Eleazar ha-Levy b. Hillel, is identical with the Eleazar b. Hilal ibn Fahd, as he occurs in an Arabic source. Professor Goldziher found a decree preserved by the Arabic historian, Ibn el-Sa'i,[2] in which the Caliph, el-Naṣir bidin-Allah, appointed, on the ninth of the month Du el-Ka'da 605 H. (= 1209), Daniel b. Eleazar b. Nethanel (Hibbat Allah) as successor to the deceased Eleazar

[1] *R.E.J.*, 70 (1920), p. 107.
[2] Poznański, p. 37.

b. Hilal b. Fahd. This government decree was publicly read and proclaimed in the synagogue of Baghdad. It teaches a few interesting things: first of all that the order was made at the request of the candidate, who apparently had to apply for it, secondly that the right of appointment rested in the hands of the Caliph. This seems like an arbitrary action on the part of the non-Jewish authorities which must have been a departure from previous usage; yet the Genizah fragment mentioned a few lines earlier may supply an explanation. Most probably it was owing to the dissentients and the parties under which Ibn Fahd suffered such a great deal and which brought such a profanation of God's name in the community, that this right of autonomous election was either voluntarily suspended, or forcibly taken away from the Jews and usurped by the government. However that may be and whatever the consequences were, the candidate for the dignity had to prove his worth and character.

His Majesty made enquiries about the qualifications and fitness of the candidate for the office. Having received guarantees, the new Gaon was confirmed in his office and recommended to all communities and acting judges in Mesopotamia as their head and lord. He was distinguished by the attire due to his rank and position, his commands were obeyed and his decisions had to be accepted. All the privileges, judicial and administrative, enjoyed by his predecessors, were vested in him. His fame like that of Samuel b. 'Ali, was not limited to the east, but penetrated also into western Jewry. This was achieved by his literary activities. His name was known to the teachers of Israel on the Rhine and on the Tiber, as confirmed by the authors of the Shibbale ha-Leḳeṭ and Or Zarua' respectively. I am not sure whether the Gaon, or Resh Methibta, R. Daniel, who is mentioned in the Hilkoth Tefillin of Naḥmanides[1] as Daniel 'Aziz Resh Methibta is identical with our present Gaon. The termination of his

[1] MS. Sassoon, 971, p. 167, *Ohel Dawid*, p. 687.

office may be gathered from the fact that when Harizi visited Baghdad about the year 1220, he found Daniel's successor on the seat of the Geonim. Consequently he must have been Gaon from 1209 till c. 1219.

Of his internal activities two letters written by Daniel b. Eleazar, with the surname Ḥasid, addressed to the communities of Wasṭ and Basra, give some information. These communities apparently had the right to appoint a beadle for the synagogue called after the name of Ezra the Scribe. A man called Abu el-Ḥasan and his son Abu Manṣur, who succeeded him, are mentioned in this correspondence.[1]

The next Gaon in Baghdad was Isaac ibn Shweikh, whom el-Ḥarizi describes as Gaon and praises as a liturgical writer. One of his poems is preserved in the Aleppo Maḥazor.[2] The rites of Algiers, Tlemcen and others preserved prayers by a liturgical writer, R. Isaac b. R. Israel, which have been attributed by Poznański to our Gaon. He enumerates five such pieces, containing either confessions for the Day of Atonement or admonitions for the same day. I am enabled to add another Widdui which begins with the words אתודה על עבירות קלות וחמורות which is ascribed in one of my MSS. as a composition of R. Isaac b. R. Israel.[3] The same MS., which is written in a cursive Sefardi hand of the fourteenth century, provides all the Widduyim of this liturgical writer, some of which are different in their wording from the headings given by Poznański and Davidson. The confession for the morning service is copied from a Parma MS. with the heading אתודה ליוצר בראשית פעם שניה while my MS. reads: אתודה ליוצר אור פעם שניה. Similarly, the confession for the Musaf service has a different beginning in the same MS. from that supplied by the Parma MS. The latter furnishes

[1] For fuller particulars, see *J.Q.R.*, *N.S.*, XVII, pp. 409-410.
[2] v. Poznański, l.c., p. 42; Davidson, *Thesaurus*, III, p. 293, No. 998.
[3] MS. Sassoon, 491, v. *Ohel Dawid*, p. 302; Davidson, *Thesaurus*, vol. III, p. 374, No. 459, where, however, the author's name is not given.

the heading אוסיף כהרים קול במוסף while my MS. reads: אוסיף במוסף להתודות. It is remarkable, if these liturgical pieces really emanated from the pen of the Baghdadian Gaon, that they found their place in the ritual of the Spanish Jews, and hence influenced the liturgies of the various provinces in the Maghreb. In favour of the identification of the poet with the Gaon can be advanced the fact that there are rituals and confessions and similar liturgical compositions by another Gaon or Resh Methibta, whose name frequently occurs in MSS. and printed books, designated as a Baghdadian Rosh Yeshibah, e.g. Nissim Rosh Yeshibath Babel.[1] All our witnesses, MSS. as well as editions, designate R. Nissim as Gaon of Babel. Even in MS. Parma, where the Gaon is called R. Assi, instead of R. Nissim, his title and place of origin are unchanged. It is most likely, therefore, that the Jews of the Pyrenees borrowed these pieces from their brethren of Mesopotamia.

This Gaon was in correspondence with Abraham the Naghid. If the eulogies bestowed upon him by Maimonides' son are to be taken at their face value and not as mere compliments, he must have been an extraordinary man, a most distinguished scholar and a worthy leader of his generation. His learning and scholarship are put on a very high plane. Similarly, he was judged by another contemporary, namely the wandering poet, Judah b. Solomon el-Ḥarizi, whose praises and criticisms are, however, not above suspicion. Their value is mostly darkened or enlightened, according to the donor's liberality or meanness. A third witness is the Baghdadian poet Eleazar a-Babli, who was personally acquainted with the Gaon and took part in some more or less lively grammatical or lexicographical skirmishes with him. The Babli, in an elegy dedicated to the memory of a distinguished man of the Baghdad community, used expressions which were criticized by the

[1] His name occurs in several MSS. of various rites in my possession. See *Ohel Dawid* MSS. 338, 972, 651, 657, 686, 687, 659, 634. *The Widdui*, etc.

Gaon. The poet defends them, but at the same time takes the opportunity to eulogize the Gaon. The same poet who survived the Gaon, supplies us in his long elegy composed on the occasion of our Gaon's death with a third testimony of the Gaon's character and importance. After the more or less usual lamentations and personal expressions of grief, the Gaon is described as a man who led the communities with wisdom and counsel, who presided over the academy with his great learning and seriousness, whose authority was duly accepted by those near and far, in Babylon and Persia, by judges and teachers, and whose death was mourned by young and old, by learned and ignorant. He left three sons, Eleazar, Yehosef and Seadyah. The elegy does not supply any material about them besides the usual praises.

The latter witnesses enable us to glance into the inner conditions of the Baghdad community of the time. Besides the distinguished contemporary of our Gaon and of the Baghdadian poet Eleazar, we learn about a vice-president of the Academy, a scholar called Raba.[1] Ḥarizi on his part tells us that besides the Gaon Isaac b. Israel there officiated another Isaac, called by him Ben el-Awani, as president of an Academy. Ḥarizi does not fail to make according to his manner great fun of this unfortunate man. He describes him as a very rich man, but as an equally poor poet. He alleges that he bought his academic dignity for a thousand gold pieces, yet the Academy is ruled by somebody else. Of course it is difficult to say how many of these allegations may be accounted for by the disappointed poet's displeasure. Isaac Gaon is also known as a book-collector. A scribe, Mordecai, copied on his behalf in Elul 1532 Sel. (= 1221) the Arabic commentary to Ḳoheleth written by Abu el-Barakat Hibbat Allah.

Besides these two Isaacs, namely Isaac ibn Shweikh and Isaac el-Awani, there is a third Isaac who is styled Gaon by the Baghdadian poet, but who cannot be identical with either of

[1] Poznański, pp. 45 and 61.

the previous two because he was of priestly origin. It has been suggested that he is the same man who flourished about 1210-1229 and preached in Arabic communities throughout Irak. Perhaps the title Gaon changed in this period into a family name, as for instance, Shem Tob ibn Gaon.

Isaac Gaon was succeeded by Daniel b. Abi el-Rabi' ha-Kohen. Only scanty information about him is available in the poems of the aforementioned poet. We learn that he was a descendant of noble ancestors, learned in the Law and endowed with some poetic talent. A Holy Ark was his heart and his figure like a cherub's. He kept discipline in the communities by being strict with the presumptuous and disobedient elements. Yet he was full of love, mildness and mercy to all those who appealed to him for help and counsel, for sustenance and healing. A real prince of Gold was he in their midst, who provided for all their needs and necessities, who clad the naked in silk, who guided the perplexed in the right way and healed the sick and suffering. So much about his character. As to his family, he had a son, Azariah, who died in the lifetime of his father. A second poem is written in honour of a certain Samuel b. Abi el-Rabi', and a third in honour of a Shams el-Dawlah Abu el-Ḥasan b. Abu el Rabia', on the occasion of the birth of the latter's son, Ṣadid el-Dawlah Abu Manṣur, called in Hebrew Eleazar b. Phinehas. They are all designated as descendants of Geonim, yet their actual relation to the officiating Gaon cannot be established. The suggestion may be advanced here that Ezekiel, called Khawajah Shams el-Din b. Ithamar, to whom a prolific Persian author, Isaiah b. Joseph of Tiflis, who lived in Tabriz[1] dedicated his work Sefer Hakkabod, was a member of the same family.[2] Similarly, it

[1] See *Register of the Jewish Theological Seminary of America*, New York, 1931, p. 176.

[2] See MS. Sassoon, 959, cf. *Ohel Dawid*, p. 552. The dedication in the MS. agrees with MS. Vienna 125, cf. A. Z. Schwarz, *Die Hebraeischen Handschriften der National-Bibliothek in Wien*, Leipzig, 1925. The printed text of *Sefer ha-Kabod* supplies a different name, Elijah ha-Levy b. Hananel

has to be queried whether the famous Sa'd el-Dawlah,[1] whose tragic fate will engage our attention in Chapter XII, is or is not identical with one of the dignitaries mentioned before.

The next leader of the Babylonian school was a scholar called 'Ali, who is known to us from the Diwan of Eleazar ha-Babli. This poet is full of praise of the Gaon's wisdom and learning. He must have attained a high degree of scholarship and well-earned fame for wisdom even before he ascended the high dignity of his later office, for, when he lost a son called Zechariah while he was still a private man in the community, these qualities of his are highly eulogized. In another elegy, written by the same poet on a similar occasion at a time when 'Ali occupied the Geonic seat in Baghdad, he is compared with the Holy Ark. In him, just as in the Holy Ark, dwell law and wisdom. Owing to his wisdom he can bring to life the most hidden secrets of the law. He is designated as "unique among his contemporaries" in the knowledge of the Oral Law. He bore the title "Awḥad el-Zaman", or "Yaḥid ha-Dor", usual in this period. The same poem tells us about the Gaon's family. He had two sons. One of them married the daughter of a leading member of the community, Abu-l-Tayyib b. Faḍlan. The Gaon's son was called Zechariah. This is remarkable since it suggests a peculiar custom among the Jews of Baghdad of naming a new-born child after a dead brother. The bridegroom is styled Vice Gaon. Father and son are equal in scholarship as well as in charity. The second son was Safi el-Dawla Joshua, who was the crown of the Academy. The poet celebrated him in one of his poems at the time when he finished the Torah, which probably means on the occasion of completing the Torah. This 'Ali, like some of his predecessors,

[1] See about him, *Obermayer*, p. 156 f.

ha-Levy, see *Maamar Sod 'Es ha-Da'ath,* Jerusalem, 1891, f. 38 b, as pointed out by A. Marx, *J.Q.R., N.S.,* XVI, p. 341. It is to be added, however, that the *Sod 'Es ha-Da'ath* by the same author is dedicated to Elijah b. Hananel ha-Levy in the edition, f. 1a, as well as in MS. Sassoon, 1060, cf. *Ohel Dawid*, p. 1070. About a MS. New York, v. *Register of the Jewish Theological Seminary of America*, New York, 1931, p. 176.

is also to be found among our liturgical writers and poets. Dr. Poznański discovered an 'Akeda which bears the acrostic 'Ali Gaon, and is ascribed by him to our Gaon.[1]

Considering first the fact shown above, that the title Gaon became in the course of the thirteenth century and further on more of a family name, secondly the extraordinary lack of modesty in calling oneself Gaon in an acrostic, and finally the character of the 'Akedah itself, which is merely a slavish imitation of 'Abbas Judah Samuel's well-known poem, it seems to me unlikely, that this liturgical compilation should be the much-praised Gaon's work. This name shared the same history as that of the names of Ḥaber, Ḥazzan and Dayyan. However that may be, the lack of poetical work or ability does not detract in the least from the Gaon's greatness. More serious is the fact that the Baghdadian poet's wish that one of the Gaon's sons should step into the high office of their father was not fulfilled. Whether this was due to the fact that Zechariah and Joshua died before their father, or to any other reason of which no report is preserved, cannot be said. We know that the last Gaon of Baghdad was Samuel b. Daniel ha-Kohen.

Although there is no evidence, it is most likely that this Gaon who succeeded 'Ali II was the son of Daniel b. Abi el-Rabi' ha-Kohen. We owe our knowledge of his official position to the rather sad events which agitated all Jewries from the Seine to the Euphrates in connection with the anti-Maimuni movement newly initiated by Solomon b. Samuel Petit. He left his native country, France, and came to Acre where he zealously and bitterly fought against the memory of Maimonides. He made such an uproar that Maimonides' descendant, David, had to repair to that city in order to prevent further mischief. His activities aroused such ill feeling that the Exilarchs of Damascus and Mosul together with the Gaon of Baghdad issued two letters, dated October, 1288,

[1] See Poznański, p. 78.

condemning the activities of Solomon Petit.[1] These letters are remarkable documents revealing the change of attitude in Baghdad towards Maimonides. While previously we had to record the antagonism, existing between the Gaon of Baghdad and Maimonides in the lifetime of the latter, now, eight decades after Maimonides' death, all responsible leaders of Jewry joined in the defence of his works. Our sources do not enable us to to tell much more about this last Baghdadian Gaon, unless we add he had two sons, Hananel and Aaron. Here our information ends, and the history of the Baghdadian Gaonate comes to an abrupt conclusion. We cannot tell whether Hananel or Aaron, or neither of them, succeeded Samuel b. Daniel ha-Kohen in the father's dignity. Nor can we tell whether the Gaonate ceased for ever or whether an up till now unknown and undiscovered Baghdadian poet has not preserved in his lost Diwan many more Geonim, whose names may come to light one day.

[1] *Kobak's Yeshurun*, VII, pp. 76-80; Poznański, p. 52.

CHAPTER XI

INTELLECTUAL LIFE IN BAGHDAD IN THE TWELFTH CENTURY

A LATE Baghdadian chronicler, who compiled in Hebrew a history of the Moslem rulers, knows of two prominent Jews in Baghdad who became Moslems. He reports that in the year 555 of the Hijra (1160) died Muḳtafi, Caliph of Baghdad. In his days lived the apostate Abu Barakat Hibbat Allah.[1] In the year 575 of the Hijra (1179) died the Caliph Mustaḍi. In his days another apostate, Samuel b. 'Azariah, was very active in combating his late co-religionists with intellectual and spiritual weapons. The notice taken of these apostates by the late chronicler of the nineteenth century is an undeniable proof of the fact that the memory of these faithless men survived till modern times. Yet this alone would not suffice to record their names and recall their memories in this monograph dedicated to the Jews, and not to the apostates of Baghdad. Their literary activities, however, offer us some material for the description of the inner life of the Baghdad community, the intellectual atmosphere within which it flourished and the relation of its members to some personalities outside their assemblies. The writer who is called Samuel b. 'Azaria, is actually no one else but Samuel b. Judah ibn Abun, or in Arabic Samaual b. Yaḥya el-Maghrebi, the author of the Ifḥam el-Yahud, i.e. the Silencing of the Jews.[2] In spite of the fact that Maghrebi was the pupil of Hibbat Allah, his importance justifies a deviation from the chrono-

[1] See above, p. 61.

[2] The greater part of the material about el-Maghrebi used in this chapter is based on an essay by Martin Schreiner in the 42nd volume of the *Monatsschrift*, 1898, under the title Samau'al b. Jaḥja al-Maghribi und seine Schrift "Ifḥam al-Jahud", which is here gratefully acknowledged.

logical order to treat the pupil before the master. The history as well as some stray remarks in his polemical work may be used for our purpose.

The apostate was the son of a rabbi, a liturgical writer whose poem is recited on the two days of New Year in the liturgy of the Sefardi rite in various countries, the lamentation of a grieved and unfortunate father who mourns the son, who became spiritually and morally dead to him by acknowledging Islam. Judah b. Abun, the father, hailed from North Africa and emigrated to Baghdad, where he was known under his Arabic name Abu el-Baḳa b. 'Abbas el-Maghrebi. Here he married the daughter of Isḥaḳ b. Ibrahim el-Baṣri el-Lawi, who hailed from Basra and lived in Baghdad. He was a learned man and as such became the son-in-law of one of the leading members of the Baghdad Jews, Abu Naṣr el-Dawudi. His three daughters were reputed to have been well versed in Hebrew and religious studies. It may be noted by the way that Samuel b. Ali's daughter,[1] as we have seen above, was also famous on account of her scholarly attainments, which throws light on the intellectual standard of Baghdad women in this century. Samuel was educated in the Torah and commentaries till his Bar Mitzvah. Then his father sent him to teachers of secular knowledge. It is interesting to see the curriculum of a Jewish student in Baghdad and to become acquainted with his teachers. Sheikh Abu el-Hasan el-Daskari taught him Indian arithmetic and the knowledge of astronomical tables. The philosopher Abu el-Barakat Hibbat Allah b. 'Ali, who has been mentioned above (page 61), taught him medicine. An uncle of his, probably the brother of his mother, Abu el-Fatḥ b. el-Baṣri, was his guide in practical medicine and surgery. Besides elementary arithmetic and practical medicine he attended the lectures of Abu el-Muẓaffar el-Shahrzuri, who instructed him in political accountancy and

[1] See above, p. 64, and p. 70.

surveying. He devoted his time to geometry, especially to the books of Euclid. Meanwhile he continued his medical studies and was able to earn his livelihood as a medical practitioner. On his travels in 'Irak, Syria, Adarbizan and Kuhistan he searched after all available medical works, so that he could boast of great proficiency and knowledge in medicine. He was also very fond of historical and poetical writings. The study of the latter, and some of his dreams in which the Prophet Samuel plays a part, induced him to abandon his religion for Islam.

It would be out of place to give a detailed account of this renegade's views and opinions, his accusations and mystifications, but a few illustrations gathered from this polemical work may be mentioned. In speaking of Ezra the scribe, the author records that near his grave in Baṭaiiḥ el-'Iraḳ a light is to be seen up to this very day. Naturally the shrine of Ezra at el-'Ozeir is meant.[1] Some of his remarks about the relation of the Moslems to the Jews may be of interest. The advent of Islam found the Jews under the rule of the Persians, with the exception of the Arabs in Ḥebar who adopted Judaism. According to him, Jewish worship was often prohibited by the Persians, presumably an exaggeration to suit the purposes of this apostate that the Jewish prayers contain curses against the gentiles. The Jews in order to evade the persecution of the Persians introduced the Ḥizana (poems) in the place of their ordinary prayers. Yet, the Moslems never molested the Jews, the Ahl el-Ḍimmah, in their religious services. The views of Jews about Islam and its founder are duly recorded. The designation of Muhammad as "Pasul" or "Meshugga" and of the Ḳoran as "Ḳalon" is corroborated by other sources as well.[2] He gives an account of post Biblical Jewish history, the chief feature of which is the division between the Rabbanites and

[1] For further references to the miracles connected with the shrine of Ezra, see my article "The History of the Jews in Basra", *J.Q.R.*, *N.S.*, XVII, p. 411 ff.

[2] Steinschneider, *Die Polemische und Apologetische Literatur*, Leipzig, 1877, p. 302 ff.

Karaites. In speaking of the Mishnah and Talmud he preserves some noteworthy facts. A Mishnah manuscript filled in his time about eight hundred written leaves, while a copy of the Talmud comprises the load of a mule. Naturally, he points out teachings, either maliciously or for his own justification, which might put Judaism in a bad light. The attitude of Talmudic Judaism towards gentiles is especially scorned. He shows a more friendly attitude towards the Karaites than to the Rabbanites, because many of the former embraced Islam. Finally it has to be mentioned that el-Maghrebi preserved some information about a pseudo-Messianic movement which agitated the Jews of Baghdad a great deal in this time. The centre of this movement was the false Messiah, Menahem b. Suleiman ibn el-Rukhi. According to ibn el-'Atir this took place in the year 487 of the Hijra (1094). At that time, this apostate tells us, the Jews of Baghdad were so excited that they hoped to be able to reach Jerusalem by flying in a night's journey. There are some objections to the historical value of this report; nevertheless even an apostate would not make fun of his late coreligionist's credulity without any reason. Besides, this characteristic feature attached to messianic expectations and hopes may have repeated itself many a time.

The impression which this book made in Baghdad may have been greater than our historical knowledge indicates, for it was not limited to Baghdad. Its influence must have spread to the Jews of Yemen, for otherwise Maimonides would not have taken the trouble to contradict it in his famous letter addressed to them. Maimonides speaks of the apostates in the plural, for Samuel el-Maghrebi was not the only one who left Judaism. Besides him R. Nethanel or Abu el-Barakat, the philosopher and Jewish scholar, who lived in Baghdad, has been mentioned.

Ḥarizi accuses Isaac the son of Abraham ibn Ezra, whom we have already mentioned above,[1] of having followed the

[1] See above, p. 61.

example of these two men and embraced Islam. Ḥarizi writes in laudatory terms of Abraham ibn Ezra and praises also the poetical activities of the son, yet he adds: "When he (Isaac) arrived in eastern countries, the glory of God did not shine upon him, for he divested himself of the precious mantle of religion and put on strange garments."[1] Thanks to the publication of H. Brody, derived from the Diwan of Isaac ibn Ezra, which is still in manuscript, it is known that Isaac vehemently resented such a libel and denied it with the greatest indignation.[2] Maybe, however, that his association with Abu el-Barakat led Ḥarizi to the assumption that Isaac followed the ways of his friend.

A biography of Abu el-Barakat, with his full name Hibbat Allah b. Malka, is given by el-Ḳifti (1172-1248) in his famous lexicon of learned men.[3] According to him Abu el-Barakat spent the greater part of his life as a Jew and only in his old age became a renegade. As a cause for this deplorable change of religion el-Ḳifti says that after having healed a Seljuk Sultan who bestowed upon him honours and enriched him with great wealth, on his return to Baghdad he was greeted with rhymed insults by a certain Ibn Aflaḥ (about whom nothing more is known), which greatly offended his vanity. In his spleen he thought his conversion to Islam would increase his respect among his fellow townsmen. It throws light on his character that his grown-up daughters remained faithful to Judaism and he himself took great care that they should not be deprived of their father's inheritance. Another reason is given by ibn el-Zagani. According to the latter, Hibbat Allah acted as court physician to Sultan Maḥmud. He attended the Sultan's wife, who was also the Sultan's cousin, in her last illness. The Sultan fell into great mourning for her death and

[1] *Taḥkemoni*, ed. Kaminka, Warsaw, 1899, p. 42.

[2] See H. Brody and K. Albrecht, *The New Hebrew School of Poets of the Spanish-Arabian Epoch*, London, 1906, p. 159 f.; H. Brody, *Mibḥar ha Shira ha-'Ibrith*, Leipzig, 1922, pp. 209-210.

[3] See Poznański, *M.G.W.J.*, 48, pp. 50-52.

could find no comfort or consolation. Hibbat Allah thereon, fearing blame or even loss of life, safeguarded himself by embracing Islam. However divided opinion may be about Hibbat Allah's conversion, writers are unanimous in their praise of his great learning and scholarship. He compiled several works on philosophical subjects such as logic, metaphysics and science. A number of his books are listed by Steinschneider.[1] He was distinguished by the title of Awḥad el-Zaman (the Unique of the Generation). It is interesting that the famous physician Sa'id b. Hibbat Allah, a Moslem, in his intolerance did not permit Jews and Christians to attend his lectures. Hibbat Allah, who came either from Basra or from a place called Balad on the Tigris near Mosul, persuaded the porter to allow him to attend in the corridor of the lecture room that he might listen to the master's teaching. Thus he continued for a whole year. Then, in disguise, he participated in a scholarly discussion in which he greatly distinguished himself, whereon the intolerant professor could not help allowing him to attend his lectures. There is also a report about Hibbat Allah in an old Jewish source which is worthy of consideration. An old chronicler of the Baghdad Jews[2] dates this conversion to Islam in the reign of the Caliph Muḳtafi, and gives as reason for this action that the servants and the ministers of the Caliph offended the doctor's vanity and pride by their rudeness in not rising before him. The writer notes also that the convert became blind, impoverished and smitten with leprosy at the end of his days. It is not certain whether he died as a Moslem or returned to Judaism before his demise. The latter may account for the fact that a Gaon expressed the desire of having Abu el-Barakat's work in his library.[3] To the same reason may be attributed the fact that an earlier Gaon, Samuel b. 'Ali,

[1] *Die Arabische Literatur der Juden*, Frankfort/M., 1902, p. 182 f.
[2] See *Ohel Dawid* p. 371.
[3] See above, p. 77, and Poznański, p. 42, about the colophon of the Gaon's manuscript.

possessed the same author's Kitab Mu'taber among his books. Surely the Gaon would not go so far in his tolerance to quote from a work of an apostate.

This leads us to give an account of Abu el-Barakat's literary activities. First of all his Arabic commentary on the book of Ḳoheleth, which he wrote long before his conversion. This work called for an eulogy which is preserved in a poem by Abu Sa'd Isaac b. Abraham Ibn Ezra of Cordova. The latter says: "God made thee Nethanel the Yahid ha-Dor as a standard of nations, the ruler of his people the righteous; with thy wisdom thou makest wise their elders and with thy words thou teachest their youth; thou hast surpassed earlier sages and didst become strong like Khalkol and his friends." These lines were written in Baghdad, Siwan 1454 Sel. (1143).[1] He was, as we have seen, the friend of Isaac ibn Ezra and the teacher of el-Maghrebi. These three personalities are clear proofs of the influence of Moslem culture on educated Jews. They are, further, an additional testimony to the necessity of Maimonides' great work and the need for a Guide to the Perplexed. Hibbat Allah reached the age of eighty, but his last years, when he was deaf and blind, were rather unhappy.

[1] See L. Dukes, *Kokhbe Yiṣḥak*, pt. 24, p. 21; Harkavy, *Ḥadashim Gam Yeshanim*, VI, p. 47; *ZfHB*, XV (1911), p. 159.

CHAPTER XII

THE POLITICAL CONDITIONS IN BAGHDAD DURING THE PERIOD OF THE LAST GEONIM

When Benjamin of Tudela visited Baghdad in the year 1168, Mutanjid billah Yusuf (1160-1170) ruled as Caliph in Baghdad. The number of Jews, which amounted to 40,000, and the considerable number of synagogues, twenty-eight, will convey some idea of the importance of the Jewish community in Baghdad. At the same time it will allow some conclusions as to the political conditions, which must have been favourable to the Jews. They lived in the eastern part of Baghdad, and in Kark, situated on the other side of the river Tigris. Benjamin says that he travelled two days from 'Oḳbara to Baghdad, which he calls the "great city and the royal residence of the Caliph Emir el-Muminin el-Abbasi". He is the head of the Muhammadan religion, and all the kings of Islam obey him. He occupies a position similar to that held by the Pope over the Christians. He has a palace in Baghdad, three miles in extent with a great park full of trees and animals. The whole is surrounded by a wall, and in the park there is a lake whose waters are fed by the Tigris. Whenever the king desires to indulge in recreation and to rejoice and feast, his servants catch all manner of birds, game and fish, and he goes to his palace with his counsellors and princes. The Caliph's palace and life must have greatly impressed the travelling Spanish Jew, so that he speaks of them at greater length. This he does the more willingly and sympathetically because the Caliph is kind unto Israel, and many Jews could be found in his entourage. It is difficult to establish the veracity of Benjamin's report about the Caliph's knowledge of languages and Jewish law. We have no means to verify or gainsay whether he really read and wrote Hebrew. His noble character, his truthfulness, trustworthiness, peaceful endeavours and high esteem for work must have been well known in Baghdad and the provinces when Benjamin travelled in those parts. We shall not endeavour to find the reason for Benjamin's lengthy description of the Caliph's life and habits, but turn to the material contained in the pages of his work.

Very important and which interests us in this chapter is the report about the Exilarch. Previously, in the Geonic period we spoke of many bearers of this title, and pointed out their relation to the Geonim on the one side, and to the government on the other side. In Benjamin's time Daniel b. Ḥisdai was the head of the Captivity of all Israel. By this title he was called among Jews. The Arabs called him Sayyidna bin Daud. His power and rights over all the Jews were confirmed by the Emir of Baghdad. He was granted a seal of office over all the congregations. Jews and Moslems alike were bound to rise before him and salute him. In an interesting account the Exilarch's weekly visit to the palace and the honours shown to the Jewish Prince are described. The appointment of the Exilarch had to be paid for to the Caliph, to the princes and to the ministers. The Exilarch on his part had the right to appoint the heads of the Academies and instal them in their office. His authority extended over all the communities of the Abbasid empire, including Shinar, Persia, Khurasan, Yemen, Diarbekr, Mesopotamia, Armenia, Georgia, up to the Caucusus. In all these countries spiritual guides and judicial officials, teachers and readers had to apply for the consent of the Exilarch for qualification or permission to function within the communities, courts and synagogues, in one capacity or in another. The political and spiritual powers involved in this patronage cannot be underrated. As a matter of fact it was shown in a previous chapter that this right vested in the Exilarch was, later on, transferred from the Exilarch to the Gaon. We have seen further that the appointment of the respective Geonim was later on made by the government and not by the Exilarchs. Altogether the historical function of the Exilarchs gradually ceased and the Geonim concentrated all the religious as well as political privileges in their hands. Owing to lack of material the deeper causes of this by no means unimportant change of power must remain obscure.

When R. Pethaḥiah of Ratisbon arrived at Baghdad the Exilarch, Daniel b. Ḥisdai, was no more among the living. He left no heir, only daughters. The community was divided and could not come to an understanding. One party favoured R. David and the other R. Samuel, both of Mosul, who traced their origin to the Exilarchs of Baghdad (v. above, page 67).

There is no greater contrast than between the reports of these two travellers on one side and that of the poet Juda el-Ḥarizi on the other. He visited Baghdad during the reign of the Caliph el-Naṣir bidin-Allah (1180-1225), and unrolls before our eyes a most vivid picture of decline and degradation. In the age of the former travellers Baghdad was a seat of wealth and learning, the Jewish community populous and full of religious vigour, free and happy, industrious and charitable; now it was pleasure-seeking and forsaken, bereft of the pious and full of sinners. Even the places of the great synagogues and the buildings destined for and devoted to the study of the Torah, divine worship and charity, were either in ruin or alienated to some profane purpose. In the middle of the thirteenth century came the great tragedy which overcame Baghdad and put an end even to this poor remnant.

The year 1258 saw the downfall of the Moslem dominion and the entrance of the Mongols into Mesopotamia. This event is connected with the name of Hulago Khan, a grandson of the more famous ruler of the Tartars, Genghis Khan. We do not know whether or not Jews suffered at the siege of Baghdad when the last Abbasid, el-Musta'ṣim-billah, was captured and executed. One thing we know for sure is that the Mongol Khans employed members of a Jewish family as their physicians and viziers. Sa'd el-Dawlah, whose father, grandfather and great-grandfather were attached to the Mongol rulers, was sent to Baghdad in the year 1284 by Argun Khan, the grandson of the conqueror of the Abbasids, as governor of Mesopotamia. This Jewish governor, sitting on the throne of the Caliphs, raised Baghdad to a great height of wealth and importance. The integrity and great financial skill of the governor was fully and duly recognized by his master and he was elevated to the dignity of Chancellor of the Empire. A Persian historiographer gives the genealogy of Sa'd el-Dawlah. Unfortunately all the names and titles like Safi el-Dawlah and Muhaddib el-Dawlah are not very helpful in finding the key for identifying them with other bearers of such and similar titles. The fact alone is worth recalling that a Jewish family held such high offices in the surrounding of the Mongol Khans for four generations. The family hailed from Abhar in the north of Persia. The great minister was so successful in fostering the interests of his royal master that he did not fail to make bitter enemies for himself. This was the common lot of all loyal and faithful Jewish Viziers. Sa'ad's loyalty and integrity led to an awful tragedy, to the Vizier as well as to his fellow Jews. The jealousy and enmity between Mongols and Arabs finds a clear and lively expression in the rhymes of contemporary poets. In the days of the Vizier's strength and power many feared him and flattered him. They changed their attitude, however, as soon as his political star began to decline, Argun Khan became dangerously ill and the Vizier, who was by profession a medical man, could not help his master. Then his enemies and rivals took the opportunity of overthrowing the Jew and bringing about his death. One of the poets describes the Vizier's struggles, offering by the way some very interesting details which throw light on Sa'd el-Dawlah's humane character and religious attitude. We hear that in his distress and peril he spent lavishly in distributing money among the poor and needy, scholars and Rabbis, asking them to intercede in prayer for the health of his royal master. The death of the master brought the end of the Vizier's life. The mob of Baghdad, however, not satisfied with the cruel death which Sa'd el-Dawlah suffered at the hands of his enemies, turned the whole Jewish quarter of the city into a pool of blood, such as was witnessed by Jews in German cities in the darkest Middle Ages or in the dark Russia in the time of pogroms.

Additional information about this episode in the history of the Baghdad Jews, and about the extraordinary personality of the minister, Sa'd el-Dawlah, is provided from Arabic and Persian sources by Professor Edward G. Browne.[1] We learn that the Vizier acquired his master's confidence by his knowledge of languages, e.g. Turkish and Mongolian. The significance of the minister's influence and position is eloquently reflected in the following lines of a contemporary poet:

"The Jews of this our time a rank attain,
To which the Heavens might aspire in vain,
Theirs is dominion, riches to them cling,
To them belong both Councillor and King."

Yet this poet envied the Jew's greatness and does not believe in or at least does not wish for the stability of the Jew's dominion and influence. He expresses the innermost hope of his heart that he will soon sing of the Jew's downfall and misfortune. Unfortunately his sinister prophecy soon became true. And another poem reports the general pogrom among the Jews in Baghdad, saying:

"Grim captains made them drink Death's cup of ill,
Until their skulls the blood-bathed streets did fill,
And from dwellings seized the wealth they'd gained,
And their well-guarded women's rooms profaned."

[1] *A Literary History of Persia,* Vol. III, Cambridge, 1928, pp. 31-6, cf. *The Jewish Guardian* (London), No. 515, 9th August, 1929.

The whole scene reminds us of George Eliot's famous words, "Where first Mongols thanked God for the blood of the Moslems, and then Moslems thanked God for the blood of the Mongols". Unfortunately the Jews had to suffer from both.

In spite of these terrible happenings and awful events, some of the succeeding Khans appointed Jews to high offices and responsible places of trust. It is true that some of these dignitaries could not resist the temptation, and abandoned Judaism in order to become Moslems. Some of these converted Jews are mentioned by travellers and historians. Under one of the succeeding Khans the old distinguishing signs for Jews and Christians and a special tax for both of them was again introduced. It is remarkable that in contrast with the sad plight of the Baghdadian Jews there were many distinguished Jewish families in various Persian cities and in other parts of Mesopotamia. It seems that the first half of the fourteenth century witnessed a final collapse of the Jewish Community in Baghdad.

CHAPTER XIII

JEWS IN THE SURROUNDINGS OF BAGHDAD

THE correspondence of Samuel Gaon opens up a long list of places populated by Jews, some of which are of interest to us here. Such are Arbil near Mosul, Basra, Daḳuḳa, Hamadan, Wasiṭ, Kufaḥ, Kirkuk, Hillah, Manbagh, Mardin, Seruj, el-Ḳal'ah, and Raḳḳah.

The Jews inhabited Arbil from the earliest date up to the present time. The Babylonian Amora delivered lectures on many occasions in this city, as suggested by Obermayer.[1] The Small Chronicle (Seder'Olam Zuta) preserves the information that the Exilarch Hezekiah died in Arbil on the Tigris.[2] In the same century, we are told by a Syriac writer that the monks of a Catholic convent were captured by the leader of the Nestorians, Barsauma, and put under the guard of a Jew in Arbil.[3] Benjamin of Tudela visited Arbil. Similarly, Judah el-Ḥarizi' speaks of pious and learned men whom he met in this city.[4] Ḥarizi's information about the learning and character of the Jews in Arbil is borne out by the praises heaped upon them in the letter of the Gaon Samuel b. 'Ali. A testimony for the interest in learning can be adduced from the fact that a copyist, Joseph b. 'Ali ha-Kohen, wrote in Arbil a copy of Maimonides' Guide to the Perplexed in Arabic, which is now in the Bodleian Library in Oxford.[5] For centuries our sources are silent about the Jews in Arbil. In or about the second half of the sixteenth century a Yemenite Jew, Zechariah b. Se'adyah b. Jacob el-Ḍahri, visited Baghdad and its

[1] See Obermayer, p. 139, based on Yerushalmi Sota, 4, 4.
[2] See Rappaport, *'Erekh Millin*, p. 191; Obermayer, p. 140.
[3] Labourt, *Le Christianisme*, p. 136; Obermayer, p. 140.
[4] *Taḥkemoni*, ch. 18.
[5] Neubauer's Catalogue, No. 1237.

surroundings, and described his experiences in those cities in his essays. He went from Baghdad to Arbil. On the way, he says, there are many cities, big and small, situated on the Tigris, in one of them a most wonderful synagogue, where the graves of Daniel, Hananiah, Mishael and Azariah are shown;[1] but the Jews there are full of sins, iniquities and guilt. About the Jews in Arbil our traveller and poet tells us that the women are God-fearing and hospitable. The men are also praised as wise and scholarly men, fond of poetry at this time just as in the age of Ḥarizi. Here he was induced to compose, among others a poem on the Zohar and in glorification of R. Simeon b. Yoḥai.[2] It seems that an author, R. Abraham b. Ḥalafton mentioned by el-Ḍahri in the same chapter, was a native of Arbil. Of more recent date is a legacy of 150 Krans made by a Jew in Arbil in favour of the Jews in Tiberias in the middle of the nineteenth century[3].

The next place which calls for some comment is Daḳuḳa which is mentioned in a letter of Samuel Gaon, and may be identical with Raḳuḳ occuring in the list of geographical places, e.g. Waṣṭ, Ḥillah, Baṣra, Maḥmudiyyah, Baṣliyyah, where an otherwise unknown preacher, R. Isaac Sar Shalom, delivered sermons in the years 1210-1232.[4] Steinschneider gives a short account of some material contained in the homilies of Isaac Gaon (meaning Isaac Sar Shalom). We gather from them that the preacher was accustomed to deliver occasional addresses at births, weddings and funerals. It seems incomprehensible that the preacher should have "confirmed" girls according to the usage of reform rabbis of our times, as Steinschneider suggests.[5] Of greater interest promises to be Steinschneider's information from the manuscript that the

[1] See below under Kirkuk, p. 98.
[2] MS. Sassoon, 995, *Ohel Dawid*, p. 1022; cf. also H. Brody, *Maṭmone Mistarim*, Cracow, 1894, pp. 9-15 and pp. 20-26.
[3] MS. Sassoon, 791 (C), cf. *Ohel Dawid*, p. 393.
[4] See Assaf, *Tarbiz*, I, No. 1 (5690), p. 121; MS. Bodleian, 1001, cf. Neubauer's Catalogue, col. 214.
[5] See *Hebraeische Bibliographie*, 1862, p. 37.

preacher delivered a sermon at the dedication of a Holy Scroll given by Sheikh Ṣadaḳah to some synagogue.[1] In spite of the fact that the name Ṣadaḳah was quite frequent in the beginning of the thirteenth century and in eastern provinces, nevertheless it may be mentioned here that there is a tombstone preserved of a Sheikh Ṣadaḳah who lived near Hillah and died in 1232. His full name was R. Ezra el-Sheikh Ṣadaḳah, b. R. Israel known as Ben 'Athira.[2]

Hamadan is famous for the mausoleum of Mordecai and Esther, erected in this place. The inscription to be found on the graves bears the names of Jamal Satem and the brothers, the doctors and the leading members of the community, Jamal el-Dawlat Yeḥizḳiah (Hezekiah) and his brothers Jeshu'ah and Jemuel. The identity of these names is a matter of conjecture. It was suggested that we have here the Hebrew name of the Khan's Vizier, Sa'd el-Dawlah, mentioned in the previous chapter. Benjamin of Tudela, who visited the place, says that there were about 50,000 Jews in that city, which is probably exaggerated.

Waṣṭ is mentioned in the report of Nathan ha-Babli, together with Basra, as contributing a sum of 150 golden dinars for the upkeep of the Academy of Sura.[3] The Gaon Daniel ben Eleazar Ḥasid addressed two letters to the congregations of Waṣṭ and Basra in which reference is made to a man called Abu el-Ḥasan, the beadle of the synagogue of Ezra the scribe in el-'Ozeir, and to his successor Abu Manṣur, who held certificates from the Gaon Samuel b. 'Ali and the Exilarch David, respectively.[4] The place was visited by Benjamin of Tudela, who found there about 2,000 Jews, and el-Ḥarizi, who met a R. Samuel who, according to him,

[1] *Homiletisches und literarisches Beiblatt als Anhang zur Bibliothek juedischer Kanzelredner*, ed. by M. Kayserling, II, Berlin, 1872, pp. 17-19.

[2] See *Ohel Dawid*, p. 567.

[3] See further my *The History of the Jews in Basra*, *J.Q.R.*, *N.S.*, XVII, p. 408.

[4] See *J.Q.R.*, *N.S.*, XVI, pp. 395-397; and ibid, XVII, pp. 409-410.

was "a tower of strength to all the Jews, and quite unique in his liberality among Babylonian Jews".

Inscriptions of the tenth to the thirteenth century show that Hillah had in this period a large Jewish community. Two inscriptions, those of Ḥasan b. Faḍlan and Bisher b. 'Ali el-Salubi, are without dates; a third one, dedicated to the memory of R. Ezra el-Sheikh Ṣadaḳah b. R. Israel, called ben 'Athira, is dated 1543 Sel. (=1232 C.E.).

Near Hillah, at el-Kifil, is to be found the famous shrine of the prophet Ezekiel. This shrine is still visited by the Jews of Baghdad during Pentecost. On this occasion they use a Scroll called the Scroll of Ezekiel of which several copies, with dedications, are preserved. The inscriptions in the synagogue of Hillah and in the shrine are of recent dates, mostly of the beginning of the nineteenth century, yet the place was already well known as a place of pilgrimage in the time of Benjamin of Tudela. Here may be mentioned that the Jews of Baghdad and of Kerkuk hold a tradition that Daniel and his three companions are buried at Kerkuk near Baghdad. A Scroll called Meghillath ha-Nabi Daniel wa-Haberaw, containing special prayers for pilgrims to the graves of these men of renown, appeared in print in Baghdad in 1912. The aforementioned Yemenite traveller knew both shrines, that of Kifil as well as that of Kerkuk.[1] Several Jews of the eighteenth century are known to us by their correspondence with Baghdadians, e.g. Moses ben Abraham b. Ṣaleḥ and David b. Joseph b. Elijah Baba.

There must have been an important community in Mardin. From this place hailed Obadia Kamal el-Dawlah 'Abd el Khalik, the son of Jonah of Mardin, for whom Azariah the Prince, the son of Yahalalel the Prince of Baghdad, copied in that city (Baghdad), in the year 1341, Ibn Kemmune's Tanḳiḥ el-Beḥath.[2] A manuscript of Maimonides' Halakhic

[1] For full details of the facts in the text see *Ohel Dawid*, pp. 558-564, 567-569 and 1022.

[2] See Steinschneider, *Polemische und Apologetische Literatur*, p. 37.

Code, with the glosses of Meir ha-Kohen, written in Germany by Jacob b. Joseph ha-Levy the martyr, in the year 1355-6 on behalf of Mordecai b. Moses, was dedicated in the year 1566 by R. Nissim of the family Hazzan Joseph to the synagogue of Mardin.[1] Most probably the synagogue of Mardin was named, like so many other synagogues of the East, after Elijah the Prophet.[2] From the entries attached to this manuscript and dated 1590, we make the acquaintance of many Jews resident in Mardin.[3] Among them we find members of the following families: Sa'arti, Hazzan, Imdi, Jelal and others. From entries we learn further that the community and the synagogue existed at the end of the last century, and were visited by Jews from Palestine.

[1] MS. Sassoon, No. 1043, *Ohel Dawid*, p. 1084.

[2] See S. Krauss, *Bate Kenesiyyoth 'Attiḳim be-Ereṣ Yisrael wube-Arṣoth ha-Ḳedem*, p. 2, and p. 16.

[3] For particulars, see *Ohel Dawid*, p. 1085.

CHAPTER XIV

THE FOURTEENTH AND FIFTEENTH CENTURIES

OUR sources are suspiciously silent about the Jews in Baghdad in the fourteenth and fifteenth centuries. What we learn about them is by mere accident. The terrible persecution of the Jews in Baghdad at the downfall of Sa'd el-Dawlah must have had a very baneful influence on the fate of the Jews in that city. A good many perished and many more must have emigrated to other parts of the East. Yet there is some evidence that the continuity of the Jewish settlement was not interrupted. In the year 1341 we meet a member of a noble family, who copied an Arabic book for Obadiah Kemal el-Dawlah 'Abd el-Khalik, son of Jonah of Mardin. His name was Azariah b. Yahalalel b. Azariah b. David, who was a descendant of the Exilarchs, and, like his father, bore the title of Prince. The descendants of this Nasi continued his dignity in Baghdad. Genealogical lists and poems furnish names of his descendants. The list to be found in the Shem Tob Bible supplies the name of Sar Shalom the Nasi b. Phinehas the Nasi.[1] A Genizah fragment informs us that father and son were descendants of Solomon and David; consequently they must have been the descendants of the Exilarchs. Moreover, the poem dedicated to Sar Shalom Nasi was composed by no one but Azariah the Prince. The colophon informs us that Sar Shalom had many sons; all of them were, to judge from their titles, high dignitaries and officers of the Crown, like Malkiṣedeḳ, called Khawaja Khalifah, Phinehas styled Khawaja Badi'el-Zaman, Hezekiah with the title Khawaja Bazur Jamhar, and the fourth, Joshiah, whose

[1] MS. Sassoon 82, *Ohel Dawid*, p. 3.

pedigree is also found in a Genizah fragment. This family gave leaders and poets to the Jewish community of Baghdad. At the end of the fourteenth century, in the year 1376, a Nasi, David b. Hodayah of Baghdad, probably a descendant of the old Baghdadian Exilarchs, signed a document in favour of Samuel of Schlettstadt.[1] From this time onward till the middle of the sixteenth century all our sources keep silent about the existence and the fate of the Jews in Baghdad. This silence cannot be interpreted as evidence for the non-existence of the Jewish community in Baghdad. The traveller Zechariah el-Ḍahri, who visited Baghdad during the second part of the sixteenth century, describes his experiences and Jewish conditions in Babylon. A few details of his description may be quoted here. He says: "I travelled from Hormuz (Persia) to Babylon, which is situated on the Tigris. I carried 500 musical instruments for sale in order to make joyful the weary and the exiled. After forty days' journey on the sea I landed in Basra, whence I boarded a boat for twenty shekels on the Tigris. Passing on the river I saw the grave of Ezra the Scribe and that of Ezekiel b. Buzi. After another forty days' journey I arrived in Baghdad, where all my trouble and sorrow ceased. I hired temporary lodgings with board. This happened on a Friday. I went to the bath to refresh myself. Then I went to the Great Synagogue, where I offered my prayers and read out of the Book of the Lord. I vowed twenty gerah for oil for the perpetual lamp; then I went with the community to fulfil the duty of visiting the sick."[2] We learn from this report that there must have been a considerable Jewish community, since the poet speaks of the Great Synagogue in Baghdad. As to the religious conditions prevailing at that time among the Jews of Baghdad, the custom of visiting the sick after divine worship on Sabbath may be especially pointed out.

[1] Poznański, p. 119.
[2] MS. Sassoon, 995, p. 33 ff, *Ohel Dawid*, p. 1022; Brody, *Maṭmone Mistarim*, pp. 9-15 and pp. 20-26.

CHAPTER XV

THE ADMINISTRATION OF THE BAGHDAD COMMUNITY

In this chapter I will endeavour to give an account of the size, the financial upkeep, the internal administration and organization of the Baghdad community during the course of its history. One must admit at the outset that the historian is handicapped by two drawbacks. First of all by the very fact that Baghdad was a centre of world Jewry for many centuries, the local significance and importance was overshadowed and forgotten. Secondly, owing to the interruption in the continuity of our knowledge of the history of the Baghdad Jews, a good deal of information is lacking.

What was the size of the Baghdad community during the fourteen centuries of its existence? The answer cannot be exact. It is known that ancient writers are not always reliable when giving figures. Thus, medieval chroniclers speak of huge crowds attending or witnessing some of the events which took place in Baghdad, as described in the previous chapters. Apart from reasonable doubt as to the exactness of the figures, the question arises whether all of them were members of the Baghdad community, or a part of them were visitors from abroad and from the neighbourhood. In the days of Benjamin of Tudela or Pethaḥiah of Ratisbon, the community was still of a considerable size. The exact number again is missing, but the number of synagogues and scholars in Baghdad permits a conjecture. When Arab writers speak of hundred thousands of Jews in Baghdad who dwelt there in the days of Sa'd el-Dawlah, the historian cannot use such information without criticism and precaution. These writers are hostile to the Jews, and experience teaches that in the past as in our own days in western countries, these agitators have the tendency to exaggerate the number of Jews who are naturally looked upon as aliens and even intruders, and so these anti-Semites forge their weapons with which to incite the mob against the Jewish community. Reliable figures about the exact number of Jews in Baghdad cannot be furnished from these reports; nevertheless, they indicate that a large Jewish population did inhabit Baghdad.

It is interesting to know that in the year 1308 Hijrah (1890-1891) the number of contributors to the military tax, as given in Daftar Tawzi' Badalat el-'Askariyyah (Register of Military Tax Assessment), came to 2,483. There are various statistics which speak of about seventy or eighty thousand Jews in Baghdad. Furthermore, there are no means of estimating the fluctuation which must have occurred in the Jewish population during the generations owing to political and economic causes on the one side, and pestilence and flood on the other.

The income of the community was not derived by direct taxation. As in all primitive countries and conditions, people prefer indirect taxes to those of direct payments. The chief source of income is the "gabelle", or meat tax. Another source of income was from the sale of intestines of sheep at the abattoir. A fee of 2½ per cent. is charged by the community on marriage contracts, and ½ per cent. on the purchase of property and on mortgages. The community as such possessed landed properties, houses and shops, which were known as "Waḳf" property, acquired by legacies or gifts. Finally, free-will offerings (Mi she-Berakh) by individual members of the community, the sale of Miṣwoth, called Ḍamayin, and charitable gifts in the various boxes of the synagogues, augmented the budget of the community. The income was used for communal purposes.

This was the credit side of the yearly budget. The debit side consisted of payments made to the Ḥakham Bashi and the other communal officials. Charitable and educational institutions were kept up by the community. Some hospitals and some schools, synagogues and other religious institutions received grants from the communal funds. In the year 1893 the total amount paid to the officials, the Ḥakham Bashi included, was 2,225 Kirsh (Piastres) per month. The expenses for the upkeep of the shrines of the Prophet Ezekiel and Ezra the Scribe, namely, 1,250 Piastres and 1,500 Piastres, respectively, were also defrayed from this income. The monthly expenditure reached the total of 25,375 Piastres equal to 3,625 Rupees at that time. The correspondent to whom we are indebted for these figures, complains of a deficit in the budget of 250 Turkish pounds.[1] Such information about the finances for the Geonic age and post Geonic period is lacking. The very fact that the Geonic institutions were supported by world Jewry, makes it doubtful whether Baghdad Jewry shared the expenses of the upkeep of the Geonate. Nevertheless, the merchant princes and other prominent members of the community may have contributed their share to the upkeep of the Geonate as well as to that of the local institutions. Up to the beginning of this century, under the Turkish regime, government taxes were collected by the community. These taxes consisted of contributions known under the name of 'Askariyyah (military tax). The Turkish government fixed annually a certain sum to be paid by the community as a whole. A committee was appointed which assessed the individual payments to this sum. This may have been the case in earlier centuries as well, when the leaders of the community were responsible for the payment of taxes to the government. This method of payment opened the door to injustice and quarrels such as we shall see later on (Chapter XXVI).

Just as the management of the military tax necessitated an organizing body to discharge its duties, in the same way the

[1] *Maggid Mesharim* (Calcutta), No. 15, Calcutta, 18th January, 1894.

collection of the communal income required some authority for handling the different funds and the allocation of expenditure. At the head of the community stood—and here again one notices a continuity from olden times up to the most recent days—a political and religious body. In early times the former was represented by the Exilarch or by the members of the most prominent families, the latter by the Gaon and his successors; in more recent days the spiritual side was in the hands of the Ḥakham Bashi, and the communal management in those of the Nasi. The beginnings and origins of neither of these offices can be traced historically. The Ḥakham Bashi was not merely a spiritual leader but in the first place was a man of affairs representing the community before the government and conveying its orders to the community. Much skill was needed to satisfy both parties. The Nasi was also carrying out similar duties, but more unofficially. He, like his predecessors in the Geonic age, owed his dignity to his wealth and to favouritism in government circles. This favour was not always without danger. Some of the Nesiim enhanced their position within the community by their learning and piety, charity and wisdom. Next to these two leaders, there was a council of ten men who were known as 'Asarah Nibḥarim. It speaks eloquently for the conservative mind of the Baghdadian that this body should occur in early Geonic documents as well as in more recent reports. The clerical work of administration was combined with that of the Beth Din, whose Sofer discharged both duties. Fuller information about the two dignitaries will be given in some of the following chapters.

CHAPTER XVI

THE MIZRAḤI FAMILY

The first authors who claim our attention, after a considerable gap in our narrative, are members of the Mizraḥi family. Two brothers, Jacob b. Jonah b. Benjamin b. Abraham Mizraḥi and Simeon b. Jona Mizraḥi, shall be the subject of this chapter. The former added marginal notes and glosses to the Calendar of Abraham b. Samuel Zacut. Jacob Mizraḥi mentions one of his books on the Calendar called Luaḥ ha-Teḳufoth, which he compiled in the year 1685 in Aleppo. The same author compiled further dissertations on the Calendar which are preserved under the title Kehillath Ya'akob. In this work the author reports his visits to places such as Safed, Aleppo and Damascus. The author's interest in astrology is evidenced by his ownership of such treatises and compilations on this subject ascribed to Hamai Gaon and Abraham ibn Ezra respectively. He signs his name in three different scripts in Hebrew, Arabic and Syriac, a sign that he knew these three languages. His brother Simeon was also engaged in the study of the calendar, and a work of this type is recorded in a manuscript which bears the title Kanfe Yonah.[1] We further possess from his pen a foreword to Phinehas b. Isaac Ḥariri's Kabbalistic commentaries Darkhe No'am and Em ha-Melekh, with a number of poems bearing the acrostic Simeon b. Jonah Mizraḥi. The preface was written in the year 1714 in Baghdad. It may be that the vocabulary to the Zohar by Jonah Mizraḥi, which is preserved in the same manuscript, was compiled by Jacob and Simeon Mizraḥi's father. Simeon was also a lover of books and collector of

[1] MS. Coronel, see *Steinschneider, Monatsschrift,* 49 (1905), pp. 506-509; *Ohel Dawid,* p. 512.

manuscripts. A miscellaneous manuscript containing some Kabbalistic works and Maimonides' Ethical Will to his son, written by a Spanish scribe, Abraham b. Ḥayyim, in the fifteenth century, was in the year 1680 in Simeon Mizraḥi's possession. From the entry preserved one can gather that the owner was simultaneously a diligent student of the manuscript. According to a declaration made by Aaron b. David Barzani, Chief Rabbi and Hakham Bashi of Mosul (1901), the Rabbis of Mosul were for about 200 years members of the Barzani family, who on their part claimed to be the descendants of Simeon Mizraḥi, the Baghdadian Rabbi in about 1700. The aforementioned author of the Ḳabbalistic work, Phinehas b. Isaac Ḥariri, was of Persian origin. Besides his Ḳabbalistic work there is preserved a collection of poems by him, his son Ḥayyim, Se'adyah Sirbani (Sheherbani), Shabbethai, Samuel b. Nethanel Barzani, Ebiathar, and others. Most probably the Mizraḥi family also hailed from Persia and may have been related to Ḥariri. We see that Baghdad in the latter part of the seventeenth century was the seat of Kabbalistic and astronomical studies.

Simeon Mizraḥi, as mentioned by Aaron b. David Barzani, was the ancestor of the Barzani family, which supplied many spiritual leaders to the Jewish communities in the East and many writers, poets and book collectors. Thus an old MS. of the Sheiltoth, a full description of which will be found in *Ohel Dawid*, was in the possession of Sason b. Mordecai Barzani, who lived about 1846 in Mosul, where he signed some marriage contracts. David b. Mordecai Barzani, whose name occurs in marriage documents dated 1833 and 1837, and who exchanged letters with Ṣaleḥ b. Joseph Maṣliaḥ about 1780 to 1790, was a brother of the former. Aaron and Moses, the sons of David Barzani, may be considered as the sons of the latter. Aaron officiated as Chief Rabbi and Ḥakham Bashi in Mosul, and was anxious for the appointment of his son David Barzani as preacher in the synagogue built by Sason 'Abdallah. This appointment was contested by Raḥamim 'Abdallah, who preferred to see his own son in that office. An earlier member of this family, Aaron b. Raḥamin Barzani, who lived about 1786 in Surat, corresponded with a Jew of Cochin, by name Sliman Ḳaṣar. A Joseph Barzani, whose date cannot be ascertained but who probably belongs to the eighteenth or early nineteenth century, compiled a geomancy containing additions to the Shoshannath Ya'aḳob of Jacob b. Mordecai of Fulda. Of a very recent date is Yaḥya b. Reuben Barzani of Mosul, who wrote a poem to be said at the tomb of the Prophet Nahum and in the Cave of Elijah the Prophet. He was ambitious enough to request the printer, Ezra Dangoor in Baghdad, to insert the same at the end of the Maḥazor for the Festivals, used by the Baghdadian Jews. The ancestor of the Barzani family is, according to the genealogy preserved by the Chief Rabbi of Mosul, identical with R. Samuel Barzani, who is mentioned in the Visions of Hayyim Viṭal.[1] Of special interest for us is the information that Isaac Barzani officiated as Rabbi of Baghdad. His date can be ascertained from the fact that he is mentioned as a contemporary in the works of Rephael Solomon Laniyado and Judah Diwan.[2] Since both flourished in the early seventeenth century we may assume that Isaac Barzani occupied the Rabbinate in Baghdad before Simeon Mizraḥi, that is about 1600. The exact family relationship between Isaac Barzani and Simeon Mizraḥi cannot be established. Yet it is not impossible to assume that Simeon Mizraḥi himself may have been a descendant of Isaac Barzani, and that the latter may have been the son of the Kabbalist and poet Samuel Barzani, who was held in high esteem by the Kabbalists of the Safed school. Members of a family named Barzani are to be found in lists of Jews compiled for fiscal purposes as late as the end of

[1] *Hezyonoth*, Baghdad, 1866, f. 5a.

[2] v. *Beth Dino Shel Shelomo* by Laniyado, Constantinople, 1777; and *Hut ha-Meshullash* by Diwan, Constantinople, 1739.

the last century. It may be added here in conclusion that a member of the Ḥariri family, Moses b. Abraham Ḥariri, who was an elementary school teacher in a village near Baghdad, only recently published a work under the title wa-Yibḥar Mosheh.[1] It is most likely that these Ḥariris are descended from the Kabbalist and poet Phinehas.

[1] Baghdad, 1930.

CHAPTER XVII

MOSES B. BENJAMIN AND HIS CONTEMPORARIES

THE next Rabbi of the Baghdad community was Moses b. Benjamin. He was a prolific writer. His works are partly printed and partly in manuscript. He wrote a commentary on the Biblical Masora under the title Maṭṭeh Mosheh; a book of sermons and homilies based on the weekly portions of the Torah under the title Hoil Mosheh; sermons for festivals; and finally a book containing Halakhic decisions. None of these books has appeared in print, in spite of the fact that the author speaks of his Pesaḳim as printed. Our knowledge of their existence is derived from the author's catalogue of his works in the prefaces of his works Ma'aseh Rab and Sha'are Yerushalyim. The former, comprising a commentary on various Rabbinic Aggadoth, especially of the stories of Rabbah bar bar Ḥannah, appeared in Constantinople in 1736. The author was enabled to publish this book by the support received from a member of the Baghdad community, Joseph b. Nissim Gabbai. This patron of literature participated with another Baghdadian worthy Moses b. Mordecai Shindookh, in erecting a wooden catafalque and a marble slab over the grave of Ezra the Scribe at el-'Ozeir. The second work is preserved in manuscript and bears evidence of the continuation of Ḳabbalistic studies in Baghdad. The preface to the Sha'are Yerushalyim offers some scanty material for the biography of the writer. We learn that before the year 1731, that is the year of writing the Sha'are Yerushalayim, the author lost all the members of his family in the plague which raged in Baghdad. He made up his mind to emigrate to Palestine and settle in Jerusalem, but owing to many causes, hinted at as well known to the readers of his introduction, but unknown to us, he gave up his project and devoted himself to these mystical studies in memory of Jerusalem, whence the name the "Gates of Jerusalem" was derived. The work itself is divided in three parts under three different titles, Mishpaṭ Ṣedeḳ, Sha'are Ṣedeḳ, and Hin Ṣedeḳ, and comprises fifty-two chapters. The name of the author is nowhere mentioned in the manuscript, but is, with certainty, established by a reference to the printed Ma'aseh Rab in the body of the book and by the comparison of the catalogue of treatises by our author in the introduction of the printed and the written works.

In the same year that the "Gates of Jerusalem" was written, a contemporary of the Kabbalistic writer, Ezra b. Ezekiel ha-Babli of Baghdad, compiled moralistic poems under the title "Tokhahoth Musar" which were printed in Constantinople in the year 1735. The poems are partly in Aramaic and partly in Hebrew. Like all moralistic writers, our poet depicts the spiritual and moral conditions in a gloomy light. Thus he rebukes the rich who boast of their wealth, neglecting spiritual treasures for material gain. Generally he complains about those who neglect prayers, who indulge in spreading evil reports about their fellow men, and condemns jealousy and envy, indecent speech and pride, drunkenness and meanness, pleasure-seeking and frivolity, and calls on man to repent and walk in the paths of righteousness, humility and goodness. Without more literary evidence and historical documents it is impossible to establish how far this moralist's rhymes reflect the actual conditions of the Baghdad community in the first decade of the eighteenth century, and how much of his poems mirror conditions borrowed from other, earlier and contemporary moralists.

Another contemporary of these two authors, and perhaps of greater importance than both of them, was a scholar, a poet and a collector of Hebrew manuscripts, Sliman b. David Ma'tuḳ. He hailed from 'Ana, which is situated on the site of the ancient Neharde'a, where his ancestors lived for centuries. He was the owner of many manuscripts, some old and others of more recent date. Among them was an Arabic translation of the Pentateuch, five Scrolls, (Ecclesiastes being omitted), Proverbs, Job and Daniel, and the poem Mi Khamokhah; the Kabbalistic work ha-Ḳanah; a geometrical manuscript with a commentary and a treatise on the Astrolabe, to which are added tables and mathematical notes by the owner; and a commentary on geometry copied from a manuscript written by Solomon b. Simeon Mizraḥi; a miscellany written by Abraham b. Ḥayyeem ha-Sefaradi in the fifteenth century which had previously belonged to Simeon Mizraḥi; and the Talmudic Methodology of Jeshu'ah b. Joseph of Tlemcen, which was written by the owner's paternal uncle, Joseph b. Sliman Ma'tuḳ, in the year 1680. Consequently Joseph Ma'tuḳ was a contemporary of the Mizraḥis in Baghdad. His son's date can be inferred from the inscription which is found over the doorway of the shrine of Ezra the Scribe at el-'Ozeir, dated 1739. From the entries attached to these manuscripts one is enabled to compile a pedigree of the Ma'tuḳ family from the seventeenth century almost to the present day. Sliman Ma'tuḳ is reputed to have been the possessor of a large library of about seven thousand volumes—manuscripts and printed books. Of this collection some books came into my library, for instance, Jonah Gerondi's Sha'are Teshubah, Fano 1505, Judah ha-Levy's Kuzari, Fano 1506, and David ibn Yaḥya's Leshon Limmudim, Constantinople, 1542. They all bear Sliman Ma'tuḳ's signature and traces of his interest in and study of literature. The poetical and liturgical collections written and compiled from the year 1800 and onward contain a number of poems composed by Sliman Ma'tuḳ.

CHAPTER XVIII

ṢADḲAH B. SE'ADYAH ḤUṢEIN

Ṣadḳah Ḥuṣein officiated first as Rabbi in Aleppo, whence he came to Baghdad. His election to the Rabbinate of Baghdad must have taken place about the year 1742 or 1743, when his predecessor Solomon Mizraḥi died in the Great Plague. During this catastrophe the community lost most of its leading members and scholars, so that the Nasi, Moses b. Mordecai Shindookh, had to turn to Aleppo for a candidate to fill this important post in Baghdad. At the recommendation of Samuel Laniyado, the leading Rabbi of Aleppo, Ṣadḳah b. Se'adyah Ḥuṣein, was elected for the Chief Rabbinate in Baghdad. Ḥuṣein's name was well known and recognized before he entered Baghdad. The Laniyados, father and son, Samuel and Solomon, consulted him on ritual and scholarly questions, as can be seen from the numerous references in the printed works of these worthies. Most of his works are still in manuscript. To these belong his Responsa and sermons. A part of his works containing Responsa to the four parts of the Shulhan'Arukh appeared in print under the title Seḍaḳah wu-Mishpaṭ, edited by Isaac Nissim b. Rahamim, of Baghdad.[1] The printed Responsa furnish many details for the history of Baghdad Jewry in the second half of the eighteenth century. We learn that a new synagogue was built and a special honorary officer appointed for this function, endowed with full powers. A document issued for this purpose was signed by Moses b. Mordecai the Nasi and a number of communal worthies. The Nasi, who is styled "the great prince, the ruler over this city", died before the building of the synagogue was

[1] Jerusalem, 1926.

completed. Now the honorary officer entrusted with the building of the synagogue lodges two claims against the members of the community who signed the above-mentioned agreement. First of all he claims sums which he advanced in the lifetime of the Nasi, who for some unknown reason ceased to supply money for the building, so that the honorary officer had to advance his own money for that purpose. Secondly, he asserts that the Nasi, having no money for building purposes, referred him to a gentile who lent a certain sum which was applied to the work carried on in connection with the building. The money received from the gentile was derived on account of some sale of oxen belonging to the government, so that the loan was contracted from the public treasury. Some time after the death of the Nasi the relations between the Moslems and Jews in Baghdad became strained, and the Jews were accused of having received money from public funds. The honorary officer was summoned before the authorities and forced to return the money which he had borrowed. Now the honorary officer claims that the original money was spent for the building and the money paid to the government was his own; consequently the community owed him that sum. The reply of Ṣadḳah Ḥuṣein is entirely in favour of the claimant. We learn further from the Responsum that the Nasi acted as the banker of the government, which throws light on the action involved in the second part of the claim. The Nasi accordingly deputed the honorary officer to receive the money from the gentile who sold cattle belonging to the government as their agent, and was liable to deliver the amount realized on the sale of the oxen to the Nasi. Further we gather that a man called Aṣlan b. Ezekiel acted as deputy to the honorary officer. The date of this Responsum[1] can be established by the fact that the case was raised after the death of the Nasi, Moses b. Mordecai. He is known to us as the ancestor of a famous Baghdad family, the Shindookh. He was the owner of a manuscript of the Urim

[1] v. *Ṣedaḳah wu-Mishpat*, f. 96a ff.

we-Thummin, written on his behalf at Mosul in the year 1728, by Nissim Ḥazzan. The Nasi was still alive in the year 1740, as is seen from the inscriptions in the shrine of Ezra the Scribe at el-'Ozeir. Consequently, the Responsum was written shortly before the election of Ṣadḳah Ḥuṣein as Rabbi of Baghdad.

Another Responsum[1], the date of which is uncertain, throws light on the power exercised by the Nasi, and offers some glimpses into the economic conditions prevailing among the Jews of Baghdad. A certain man lived in strife and quarrel with the Nasi, who with the help of the local government, banished him from the city. The exiled person was a well-to-do man, and the father-in-law of the Nasi's brother.

We learn further of the commercial relations between the Jews of Baghdad and of other places like Aleppo and Ḥasba.[2] Of greater importance is a fourth Responsum, which offers some important biographical details about Baghdadian worthies and communal information in the fifties of the eighteenth century. A deplorable quarrel broke out between Ṣadḳah Ḥuṣein and the Nasi, whose identity is not stated, and will be discussed later on. Ten years after Ṣadḳah had officiated as Rabbi and judge in Baghdad, the Nasi protested against the Rabbi's decision as illegal, since he acted singly. Moreover he (the Nasi) appointed three scholars who were to act as members of the local court (Beth Din). Ṣadḳah saw the cause of this agitation in underhand dealings of evil-minded people who tried to oust him from his position and spread rumours about his alleged erroneous decisions. The Nasi's attempt to deprive Ṣadḳah of his sole authority as judge by insisting on having two more judges added to Ṣadḳah's court, caused him great annoyance. Thereupon his previous rights were withdrawn and a new court constituted. Two congregations sided with Ṣadḳah and could not acquiesce in the decision of the Nasi, especially since the newly appointed

[1] Ibid., f. 99 d.
[2] Ibid., f. 95a.

judges were not considered qualified either by their learning or by their age. In his Responsa he devotes a special enquiry to this incident, and naturally concludes in his own favour.[1] He disqualifies the authority of the newly constituted Beth Din, first of all on the ground of the members' rivalry to the local Rabbis; secondly owing to their youth; further, because they were foisted upon the congregation by an arbitrary act of the Nasi which was based on an error; and finally, because the majority of the community did not consent to the new arrangement. Of further interest is the fact that Ṣadḳah was blamed for not collecting the sums due in cases of divorce or death, the sums guaranteed in the marriage document according to the status of the woman. At that time Ṣadḳah Ḥuṣein had reached the age of fifty-four years; therefore he must have come to Baghdad at the age of forty-four, that is in the year 1743. He officiated in Baghdad for forty-three years, and died there in the year 1778, at the age of seventy-nine.

Besides his printed work we possess two manuscripts—one entitled 'Abodath ha-Ṣedaḳah, containing his sermons delivered on various occasions,[2] and the other his Responsa. The sermons were delivered in the year 1770-1773. The oldest is a sermon for Sabbath of Repentance, dated 1770. In one of the sermons there is a prayer for the leaders of the communities in Baghdad. In this prayer are mentioned the contemporary Nesiim, Ezekiel b. Mordecai, David b. Mordecai Kohen, Isaac the Nasi, and his brother Michael. A funeral oration in memory of the victims of that calamity preserves their names and those of other dignitaries and worthies of the community. In the year 1765 the above mentioned Michael b. David b. Jeshu'ah Gabbai married the daughter of Ṣaleḥ b. Aaron Gabbai, who was also a victim of that plague.

From the codicil, in Arabic, which is added to the marriage

[1] Ibid., f. 92c ff.

[2] Copious extracts from Ṣadḳah Ḥuṣein's sermons are to be found n *Kesef Ṣaruf* by Joseph b. Joseph Hebroni, Jerusalem, 1928.

contract, we learn some details about the wealth of the bride. These are: גורדלוג משאט (i.e a long gold chain which goes round the neck reaching to the waist, at the end of which a large almond-shaped locket is suspended with comb-like ornaments hanging from it) valued at 273 Asads; שנוף מע לולו (i.e. pearl ear-rings) valued 300 Asads; גורדלוג סמך (i.e. another chain such as described above, with small fishes suspended from it) valued 300 Asads; סוואר מפתול (i.e. plaited bracelets) worth 700 Asads; היכל גנב (i.e. an amulet with magic inscriptions and figures, worn on the side) valued at 68 Asads; כצר קבצת כנגר (i.e. dagger-shaped pieces of amber worn as a bracelet) worth 182 Asads; קראמיל מע דגם דהב (i.e. gold buttons) value 282 Asads; טלצם מע משווכאת (i.e. talisman with golden ornaments) valued at 160 Asads; סת טנאטיף (i.e. six necklaces consisting of small differently shaped pieces of gold) value 520 Asads; תלת מחבם וטצטין וזגירין (i.e. three rings, two golden plates worn by women over their caps, with a tassel in the middle of the plate) worth 140 Asads; ספיפי לולו (i.e. some material ornamented with pearls to cover the cheeks and chin, which is joined on to the cap by means of some golden hooks) value 500 Asads; אידין ספיפי מע ארבתעש דהב (i.e. a similar ornament with fourteen gold pieces, worn on the arms) value 370 Asads; דנבוס ודע וארבע דנאבים דהב (i.e. pin with shell head and four gold pins) value 60 Asads; חנאדה וצדפה וקנתין פצה (i.e. mother-of-pearl and two small silver toilet boxes) value 60 Asads; הגל דהב וטוק (i.e. gold foot-ring and chain) worth 1,000 Asads; סת קביין וגבה (i.e. six upper garments and one cloak) value 926 Asads; סבע זבונאת (i.e. seven gabardines) value 580 Asads; סבע קמצאן (i.e. seven under vests) value 560 Asads; סבע פווט (i.e. seven silk kerchiefs) value 460 Asads; סבע צראקיג (i.e. seven trouser girdles) value 160 Asads; ארבע כפיפי (i.e. four handkerchiefs) value 160 Asads; תלת ישמאגת (i.e. three pieces of fancy cloth used for head wear in the house) value 265 Asads; תלת גיתאייאת זר וארבע גיתאייאת (i.e. three kerchiefs embroid-dered in gold and four ordinary ones) value 190 Asads; איזארין (i.e. two wrappers) value 150 Asads; הזארי ומעצב (i.e. woven stuff from Hazaribagh, and ornaments to be worn on the plaits) value 160 Asads; גכגור וכיליי ופוטה חמאם (i.e. trousers, veil made of horsehair and bath towel) value 380 Asads; מנאשף (i.e. bath-sheets) value 100 Asads; ארבע בקג (i.e. four silk squares for wrapping up garments) value 150 Asads; בית מנאמה (i.e. night gowns) value 570 Asads; צנדוק ומרפע (i.e. chest) value 60 Asads; סת וצל נחאס (i.e., six pieces of copper for household use) value 100 Asads; מרי (i.e. looking-glass) value 25 Asads; זולי (i.e. carpet) value 27 Asads; in addition, 1,010 Asads in cash, so that the whole dowry reached the sum of 10,651 Asads.

Interesting material can be derived from the Responsa about the life in the Jewish community in Baghdad. We learn that people left the city during the plague and further that Jews and non Jews had frequent business connections. Some details are given about the various occupations of the Jews in the city, their customs and their origin. Thus we find German Jews settling in the city. Another Responsum contains material about business connections between Jews in Baghdad and Hebron. For example, Ṣaleḥ Aaron was trustee for the Four Provinces of Palestine. Difficult questions arose about the persecutions suffered by the Jews in Persia. For instance, the oppressions had forced many to become Crypto-Jews. These, in order to prevent gentiles from marrying their girls, pretended that these were their wives. Now a certain man fearing lest an orphan girl should be taken away by a gentile, in order to confirm what he had said about her being his wife, gave her betrothal money, and this without witnesses. Moreover, he then married her, but without a Kethubbah. Later, owing to persecutions, he was forced to leave the country. The question then arose whether this marriage was valid or not. Ṣadḳah in his reply compares the Eastern Marranos with those of the West, the problems of the secret Jews of the eighteenth century with those of their unfortunate brethren of the sixteenth century, and refers to the earlier decisions. It is most likely that descendants of these Marranos in Persia secretly kept their ancient religion up to the latter part of the nineteenth century, for a marriage contract in Arabic and Persian dated August, 1867, is witnessed by two Jews who sign in Hebrew, which would be very extraordinary if the bridal couple had been genuine Moslems. These Marranos are known under the name of Jedid el-Islam, or New Muhammedans.

Many Responsa furnish us with material about inflation of money in the author's time, when the gold coin Zar el-Maḥbub, which was originally worth six silver Rupees less two-and-a-half Shahis, became dearer by royal decree, and went up to six Rupees. This change of value led to many complications in religious law and commercial life. The Baghdad Jews, as well as their Persian brethren, still kept the ancient law that a betrothed bride requires from her bridegroom a letter of divorce if the betrothal be annulled. In a case mentioned, a man who betrothed a girl in Barwagard in Persia sent the letter of divorce through a certain man in Hamadan to Baghdad. Other Responsa throw light on Jewish customs in Baghdad (about which more will be said in a special chapter dealing with them), on the piety and devotion of the Baghdadians, especially their love for Palestine, their liberality in furnishing sacred appurtenances for synagogues, and the prevalence of the vow of a Nazarite in these days among them. A certain Baghdadian Jew who changed his domicile from Baghdad to 'Ana took upon himself the vow of a Nazarite owing to some trouble with his brother; later on regretting this, he asked for annulment of his vow. Among the Rabbis who corresponded with Ṣadḳah Ḥuṣein, only Isaac Laniyado is mentioned by name. The others are all anonymous. These details convey a clear idea of Ṣadḳah's activities and Jewish life in his days in Baghdad.

CHAPTER XIX

ISAAC PASHA

A VALUABLE source for the history of the Jews in Baghdad about the middle of the eighteenth century is opened by the Diwan of the Baghdadian poet, Ṣaleḥ b. Joseph Maṣliaḥ. Ṣaleḥ eulogizes Sliman b. David Ma'tuḳ, Jacob Ṣurganah, a "messenger" from Jerusalem, who visited Baghdad in the year 1750, Moses Shapira, who, as we know from other sources, wrote in the year 1748 the geometrical manuscript referred to in the previous chapter, Ṣaleḥ b. David b. Jacob in the year 1755, Jacob Elyashar, a "messenger" of the Jewish communtity in Hebron to the Jews of the East in the year 1763, and especially Isaac b. David b. Jeshu'ah Gabbai, who held the dignity of Nasi about the year 1763. This Nasi was known under the name of Isaac Pasha. He earned this name by exercising stern discipline among the Baghdad Jews which is illustrated by an episode described in an article under the title Ma'aseh Rab in a Calcutta periodical,[1] a brief resumé of which may be of some interest to the readers of this chapter. This Nasi deserved to be called Isaac Pasha by the manner of his government, ruling his flock like a Turkish Pasha. He inflicted corporal punishment when communal statutes were transgressed. Such a case was one submitted to the local Rabbi, Ḥakham Ṣadḳah Ḥuṣein, who found the transgressor guilty. Thereupon the man was flogged in public by the order of the Nasi and fined. Naturally the man gave vent to his feelings of anger and humiliation by cursing the Nasi. Apparently the mansion of the Nasi was open to all the members of the community, and evil minded tale-bearers reported the words of

[1] *Maggid Mesharim*, I, No. 39, Calcutta, Ab. 28 5650 (14th August, 1890).

abuse which they heard from the mouth of the scourged man. Thereupon the Nasi summoned him to his presence, where he was offered a glass of wine and invited to repeat all the abuses and curses. The Nasi, according to Oriental custom, held a rosary in his hand, and counted the curses on the beads. When all the beads were counted, he asked if he had any more abuses. The man replied yes, and went on. When the Pasha had counted again half the rosary, the man stopped. Invited to continue, the poor man had to admit his inability of doing so. Thereupon he was dismissed and the tale-bearers handed over to the communal beadle for flagellation. He was a great benefactor of Baghdad Jewry and was praised for his charitable and kind deeds. Among his benefactions was a gift to the Midrash[1] of the first full printed edition of the Talmud, which was used by the students and scholars for their regular studies. A fly-leaf preserved contains entries giving an account of the completion of the Tractates Meghillah and Mo'ed Ḳaṭan. Isaac had three brothers, Abraham, Moses and Michael. From a funeral sermon preached by Ṣadḳah Huṣein we learn that this Nasi and his brothers were the victims of the Great Plague which raged in the year 1773. As previously mentioned in a prayer for the leaders of the communities in Baghdad, by the same author, Isaac Pasha is mentioned, together with two other leaders of the community, Ezekiel b. Mordecai and David b. Mordecai Kohen.

[1] In eastern countries the term Midrash signifies the house of study, that is Beth ha-Midrash.

CHAPTER XX

THE NESIIM OF BAGHDAD

At the head of the Jewish notables and lay leaders of the community stood the Nasi. The beginnings of this dignity are shrouded in darkness. We find traces and names of its bearers in the Baghdad of the Geonic period. In the new period the Nesiim were selected from among the wealthy members of the community, and acted as chief bankers or as a kind of minister of finance to the Pashas or Walis of Baghdad. This was only natural, since their business made them responsible for the financial activities of the government and their dignity among their brethren responsible for the contributions of the Jews in the city or in the district. The first Nasi of this type was Moses b. Mordecai Shindookh, who was mentioned in a previous chapter in connection with the rebuilding of the synagogue in Baghdad.[1] Another bearer of this office was Isaac Pasha, whose romantic and tragic career was the subject of the previous chapter. In this one the unique and tragic history of these Nesiim will be fully described, based on a report written in Arabic by a Baghdad Jew who emigrated to Sidney in Australia.[2] By the way we learn the interesting fact that the Diaspora of the Baghdad Jews extended as far as Sidney, where numbers of Jews hailing from Baghdad settled and formed an Arabic speaking Jewish colony in New South Wales.

According to our anonymous reporter, Sheikh Sason officiated for thirty-eight years as Nasi and at the same time

[1] See above, p. 113 ff.
[2] *Maggid Mesharim*, VIII, Nos. 46-48, Calcutta, 26th August-9th September, 1897, respectively.

acted as Sarraf Bashi (chief banker) to the government. Owing to old age he retired from communal life, and Ezra b. Joseph b. Nissim b. Menahem Gabbai was appointed in his place. He and his brother Ezekiel were called after their mother Rachel (Ezra b. Raḥel and Ezekiel b. Raḥel), who was a native of Constantinople and married into a Baghdadian family. The Nasi and his brother had a very tragic history. On one side biographies remind us of the sad fate which befell such worthies in Jewish history as Joseph ha-Nagid in Spain, Sa'd el-Dawlah in Baghdad, and many others who paid with their life for their political activities. On the other side, they are aptly set in an environment and circumstances full of memories and scenes of the Thousand and One Nights. The two brothers, Ezra and Ezekiel, the former in Baghdad and the latter in Constantinople, became very influential in government circles. Ezekiel was a favourite of Ḥalat Effendi, the Keeper of the Seal to Sultan Mahmud II. He exercised his influence not only through the Effendi, but also directly at the Sublime Porte. A lucrative business was carried on in selling good posts of Pashas and Walis all over the Turkish Empire to the highest bidders. Sometimes as many as fifty or sixty Pashas crowded the antechamber of this high standing Jew. Naturally such life and activity could not be carried on in secret and in darkness. As a consequence enmity and jealousy raised their heads and brought about the downfall of Ezekiel. His end is so like that of the famous Aḥiḳar, only with the exception that the Sultan's regret was too late and his pardon did not reach the victim in time. The earlier position and ultimate death of Ezekiel alternatively influenced a great part of the history of the Jews in Baghdad. When Sheikh Sason gave up his office, an important change took place in the government of Baghdad. The Wali, Suleiman Pasha, retired, or rather fled from the city. His place was taken by Daud Pasha, who was a native of Georgia and originally a slave in the household of a wealthy Beg, Muṣṭafa

Beg ibn Muhammad Beg Arbi'i. Until this time no one had been allowed to enter upon the rank and status of a Pasha unless he was a native of the city. Daud Pasha, however, in spite of his lowly origin, by his cleverness and his mastery of the Arabic and Turkish languages aspired to this high office. He was chosen for it, but could not achieve the necessary confirmation by Firman from the government of Constantinople. Daud's friendly relations with the Nasi of the Jews, Ezra ibn Rahel, induced the latter to plead before his brother in Constantinople for the confirmation of Daud as Pasha. At his request, the Nasi dispatched to Constantinople his own son Joseph Rahamim, who returned with the Firman in favour of Daud Pasha in his pocket. It was a unique event in the history of Baghdad, that a Jew should have been commissioned to deliver an imperial Firman to the chief officer of such an important province, which extended from Diarbekir in the north to Basra in the south, and included such important commercial and industrial centres as Aleppo, Damascus, Mosul, etc. But this honour was a double-edged sword, for from this time jealousy and greed darkened the relations between gentiles and Jews. Next to Daud Pasha, two wicked people brought misfortune and unhappiness into the life of the community as well as into that of individual Jews. The first was a man intimately connected with the Pasha, namely his instructor and teacher Mulla Muḥammad, called by the Jews "el-Moser", i.e. the informer. The other, a helper of the informer, was the apostate Jew, Ibn Yayi, originally Abraham b. Shalom. He was a married man with children. He became infatuated with a common Moslem woman, a dancing girl, and, ignoring the advice and counsel of his brethren, sank deeper and deeper in the mire until he gave up Judaism and became a Moslem. Being well acquainted with the personal conditions and the material circumstances of his late co-religionists, he served as an informer to his new master, the Moser, who on his part extorted sums of money, and persecuted the Jews. In the former case he divided his ill-gotten gains with the Pasha.

This wicked triumvirate thus brought great misfortune and many hardships on the Baghdad Jews. In consequence of their extortions and intrigues many members of the community emigrated to distant parts where the hand of Daud Pasha could not reach them. They left Baghdad, some for Bombay, Calcutta and Sidney, others for Aleppo, Damascus and Alexandria. These are the farthest geographical points where the refugees from wickedness established new homes. After the tragic end of Ezekiel b. Raḥel, Daud Pasha forgot all the kindness and material benefits he had received through Ezra b. Rahel. At the instigation of the apostate Jew and the greedy Moslem, Ezra and also David, son of Sheikh Sason and Joseph b. Moses (the latter being brothers-in-law, having married sisters) were imprisoned. The unhappiest of the prisoners was Ezra b. Rahel, who paid with his life for all the goodness he had shown to the Pasha. The second prisoner, David Sassoon, who was also in great danger of his life, escaped in a miraculous way. His father pleaded on his behalf before the Pasha, who was very reluctant to free his prisoner. Somehow or other Sheikh Sason succeeded and his son David was liberated on the condition that he left his native city immediately. So it happened that a special boat was hired which carried David Sassoon straight to Basra. He was told by his father not to tarry in Basra, but to leave at once for Bushire. After leaving the custom house in Basra he was lucky to find a boat leaving for his destination otherwise the messenger of the Pasha who had cancelled his previous decree of release, and now ordered the return of the prisoner, would have caught him in Basra, which was under the jurisdiction and power of the Wali of Baghdad. Meanwhile David Sassoon continued his journey and settled first in Bushire, where he was followed by his father, who ended his days there in the year 1830. Soon afterwards David Sassoon left for Bombay, where he established a firm under his own name, which has been famous for generations. His religious and communal activities in his new home in India will be described later in Chapter XXXII.

The third prisoner was also released ultimately and afterwards played the rôle of a leader in the community. He may have been Nasi for a short time. The next Nasi was Isaac Gareh. The years of leadership of this Nasi were likewise beset with misfortunes and trouble. Plague, flood, famine, and siege combined to decimate the population of the city and drive almost the whole Jewish community into exile and despair. It is difficult to say which of these experiences was the most cruel. The city was besieged by 'Ali Pasha, who was sent from Constantinople to depose Daud Pasha, who was considered a rebel against the Sultan. For many months the city was surrounded by 'Ali Pasha and his soldiers. During the siege famine raged in the city. Finally 'Ali Pasha entered the city and Daud Pasha was sent to Constantinople. The apostate Jew, Abraham b. Shalom ibn Yayi and his friend Mulla Muḥammad el-Moser, continued their wicked work, this time against Isaac Gareḥ the Nasi. Ibn Yayi had an old standing grudge against the Nasi, for which he cried for vengeance. The work of ibn Yayi finally led to the tragic death of the Nasi. Thus we see that the life of the Nesiim of Baghdad was not enviable. The only consolation that can be found is the fact that the authors of all these misfortunes, the Moslem Mulla and the Jewish renegade, did not leave this world without their due punishment; and further that the victims of Turkish misrule and Moslem persecution found new homes where under British fairness and tolerance happier conditions prevailed, and they were enabled to contribute to the welfare of the community at large.

After the tragic death of Isaac Gareḥ, Saul Laniyado acted temporarily as his successor. He was in office on April the 8th 1824, when the missionary Joseph Wolff entered the city. He was introduced to Saul, whom he designates "the Prince of the Captivity".[1] At that time there were 1,500 Jewish families in Baghdad, in whose hands the whole commerce of the city was concentrated. They are described as rich and prosperous. Wolff also made the acquaintance of Rabbi Moses, i.e. Rabbi Moses Ḥayyim, whom he calls "the High Priest of the Jews". The missionary was shown four beautiful synagogues which he admired. Later on Abraham Turki took over the dignity of the Nasi. He was joined by Mordecai Shasha, who was looking after the monetary affairs, while Turki devoted himself to the internal management of the community. Unfortunately they soon had to declare insolvency; and thus with the financial failure of the leaders ends the rather tragic chapter of the Baghdad Nesiim. The traveller R. David D'Beth Hillel informs us that during his stay in Baghdad, in the twenties of the last century, two of the Nesiim were put to death. His words are: "In the course of my stay there (which was about a year) two Israelites' chiefs were killed in this manner and their adversaries succeeded them."[2]

[1] The details about Laniyado are derived from W. T. Gidne's *Sites and Scenes*, pt. II, 2nd ed., London, p. 131.
[2] *The Travels of Rabbi David D'beth Hillel from Jerusalem, through Arabia, Koordistan, part of Persia and India, to Madras*, Madras, 1832, p. 64.

CHAPTER XXI

ṢALEḤ B. JOSEPH MAṢLIAḤ

THE successor to Ṣadḳah Huṣein in the Rabbinate was Ṣaleḥ Maṣliaḥ. He is referred to in the homilies of his predecessor as Ṣaleḥ Ḥazzan. Perhaps he earned this title, which was, and is, an honourable one in the East, by his liturgical and poetical compositions, which are still preserved, partly in manuscript and partly in print. Also before he was elevated to the dignity of the Rabbinate he acted as Ḥazzan. Some of his poetical compositions, to which reference has been made in a previous chapter, were written about the middle of the eighteenth century. A collection of his letters, which are preserved in MS. Sassoon, 229, show that this elevation must have taken place in the year 1778, for in the letters addressed to him before that date he is styled as the "Head Precentor of the great Synagogue of the Nasi, the sweet singer in Israel", but in the subsequent correspondence he is addressed as Hakham Ṣaleḥ. This collection further shows him in correspondence with individuals in various cities of the East, e.g. Aleppo, Damascus, Shiraz, Basra, Wardiawa, Bushire, Hillah, Mosul, 'Ana and Awran. Closer connection between Baghdad and Damascus existed in the eighteenth century. In a letter dated 1778, addressed to the poet Ṣaleḥ Maṣliaḥ in Baghdad, Rephael de Lisbona, a worthy of Damascus, is mentioned.[1] The son of Maṣliaḥ, Nissim, dedicated a poem in honour of Hayyim b. Amram, another worthy of Damascus, who desired a treatise on the eclipse from the poet in the year 1797[2]. Incidentally, these details, which can be supplemented

[1] MS. Sassoon 229(B), *Ohel Dawid*, p. 399.
[2] MS. Sassoon 57, *Ohel Dawid*, p. 243.

from other sources, show the continuity of the Jews in Damascus. Among other correspondents are, Maṭloob b. Rahamim b. Mordecai of Aleppo, Joseph b. Saul Ḳolmar also of Aleppo, Zechariah b. Rahamim of Shiraz, Jacob b. Joseph Elyashar of Jerusalem, Aaron b. Saleh b. Joseph Gabbai of Basra, Hayyim b. Moses Gabbai of Bushire, Moses b. Abraham b. Ṣaleḥ of Hillah, David b. Mordecai Barzani of Mosul, Moses Sidon of Damascus and others of unknown places. Some of the letters are expressions of friendship, others are of a business character. Many are of communal interest. We learn that about 1780 a certain Michael Nasi was the lay leader of the community. There were a number of Baghdadian Jews in Shiraz, in Persia. One of them, Israel b. Joseph ibn Sa'id, acted as banker to 'Abdallah Pasha, the Kurd, before whom the Jews lived in great fear. This banker died in dire poverty, leaving nothing except the clothes he wore.

The Jews of Basra at that time were in many ways dependent on the Jews in Baghdad. In religious matters as well as in their political troubles they turned to their brethren in the sister city, Baghdad, for intervention and counsel. R. Jacob Elyashar placed an order with a professional scribe in Baghdad to write a Scroll of the Law for a certain Hakham Abraham Turgeman in Palestine; further he begs for intervention on behalf of the Jews in Basra, who were in great distress owing to the persecutions whose memory is preserved in the Meghillath Paras. The unhappy event which took place in Basra had a harmful influence on the religious life of the community. On the one side, the men had to leave the city; on the other side, women were not allowed to leave the gates of Basra. Thus the levirate marriage, or the release from the same, obligatory according to Jewish law, could not be performed. We learn further that Baghdadian Jews dedicated Holy Scrolls in memory of their deceased relatives to synagogues in Hebron. Owing to the prevailing troubles Jacob Elyashar was forced to leave Basra, and asks in a letter written in Gurna, that his family be received and protected in Baghdad. These letters show that at this time, 1780, Ṣaleḥ was well recognized as the spiritual leader of Baghdad Jewry. The political position of the Jews in Basra is described in a letter written in Hebrew-Arabic by Aaron b. Ṣaleḥ b. Joseph Gabbai to this Hakham. In consequence of the intervention of a high Moslem official styled Zara Elji at the Sublime Porte at Constantinople, the Pasha, who was the cause of all the trouble and distress in Basra, was removed from his post, and Selim Pasha was appointed in his place. The arrival of the Firman in Basra on Sabbath Hanukha 5540, was greeted with great joy and caused immense happiness among the inhabitants of that city, Jews, Moslems and Christians alike. Persian Jews turned with their affairs and cases to the court of Hakham Ṣaleḥ, seeking his decision. As a true spiritual guide to his community he was asked to administer justice and keep his watch over the young, that they should remain in the fold and be brought up in the spirit of the Torah. The correspondence reveals the importance of the Baghdad Rabbinate in religious matters, as well as that of Baghdad as the commercial centre for the Jewish communities far and near. Thus we hear of Baghdad Jews travelling to Damascus who were held back on the journey for forty days, hungry and thirsty, in the desert of Palmyra.

One letter supplies material for the history of Jewish immigration. The members of a family which for generations lived in Urfa left for 'Ana where they were in possession of an orchard and garden. One member of this family left 'Ana for Deir el-Gharbi, and before leaving leased that property to non-Jews. This was taken amiss by the other Jews of the place, especially by the members of a family called Khalaf. Similarly in Baghdad, the Jews were permitted to acquire houses, by purchase or otherwise. The Hakham acted also as trustee for sums deposited with him by various people. A certain Yahya b. Elijah sent an orphan boy to the Hakham in order to arrange for his studies in Talmud which he could not pursue in his native place. The expenses for the upkeep of the orphan were defrayed by the writer of the letter, who was very anxious that the capital left to the orphan should not diminish. They were sent to Hakham Ṣaleḥ in half-yearly instalments.

In most of these letters the writers refer to the Hakham's son Nissim, who in an official capacity assisted his father in carrying out the duties of his office. The gratitude of the Baghdad Jews to their late Hakham was so great that even his late descendants enjoyed a legacy named after Hakham Ṣaleḥ. From the dates and the persons mentioned in the numerous poems of Hakham Ṣaleh and of his son, Nissim, we may infer that Ṣaleh died about 1785. Nissim composed a poem on the occasion of the rebuilding of the New Synagogue in Baghdad in the year 1797. The following members of the community distinguished themselves on this occasion by their munificence as special benefactors: Sason the Nasi b. Ṣaleḥ, 'Abdallah b. Joseph and Joseph, a descendant of Sliman b. David Ma'tuk. It is noteworthy and characteristic that Suleiman Pasha el-Kebir, who governed Baghdad in the name of the Sultan of Turkey in the years 1779-1800, is included among those who helped in the restoration of the building of this synagogue. This is the more remarkable since the Turkish Pashas generally were not conspicuous in their pro-Jewish attitude. For Nissim's date and his part played in communal life after his father's death a few documents are available. In the year 1812 he signed a communal ordinance (Haskamah) made under the leadership of Sason the Nasi. His signature stood among those of many others and not in a prominent position, which shows that he did not succeed his father in his dignity. In a letter which is addressed to the Rabbis in Baghdad from India, dated in the year 1797 or thereabouts, his name occurs in the third place of the addresses.

CHAPTER XXII

SASON B. MORDECAI SHINDOOKH

A CONTEMPORARY of the last named Rabbis, father and son, was Sason b. Mordecai b. Moses Shindookh. He belonged to one of the most prominent families of Baghdad. Among his ancestors we find Moses b. Mordecai Shindookh, who was the Nasi officiating before the arrival of Ṣadḳah Ḥuṣein in Baghdad, as pointed out previously. Although he never officiated actually as Hakham, he may be placed here on account of the ordinance mentioned above, in which he was entrusted with the performance of weddings for the whole city of Baghdad. Besides, he was the author of numerous works and scribe of many manuscripts. Some of his works are printed. His Ḳol Sason is a moralistic work with interspersed poems. The love of God, fear of God, honour of God, service of God, are put in antithesis to love of pleasure. Faith and trust, modesty and patience, the ready acceptance of chastisement and devotion of the heart, the intensity of prayers and observances, good manners and study, decency and ethics, love and hatred, jealousy, envy and honour, mockery and flattery, falsehood and slander, peace, strife, and perjury, obscenity and robbery, liberality and meanness, laziness and zeal, shyness and arrogance, pride and anger, frivolity and immorality, repentance and instruction are the serious subjects of the author's meditation. He gleaned his material from many sources which were open to him in printed books and manuscripts, yet wealthier than all these were his experiences derived from life. Most attractive are the parables and anecdotes quoted in his work. The work reached two editions; one was printed in Livorno in 1859, the other in Baghdad in 1891. His second work appeared under the title Mizmor le-Asaf, comprising the usual rules connected with the prayer book, arranged accordingly. In this work the reader finds again many poetical pieces scattered all over the work and occasionally some moralistic homilies. The latter are divided according to the days of the week and festivals. It appeared only once in Livorno, 1864. According to the autograph manuscript in my possession, the work was completed in 1798. His third work appeared under the title Dabar be-'Itto, in two parts, printed in Livorno in 1862-1864. The work is somewhat similar and almost a continuation of the previous one, treating in the same style the laws of Sabbath, New Moon and Festivals. This is followed by Imre Sason, also a moralistic compendium with some poems, printed by Solomon Bekhor Ḥuṣein with a preface by Isaac b. Mordecai, a grandson of the author, and which appeared in Baghdad in 1891. Further I have to mention Tehillah le-David, a commentary on Psalm 145 with homilies and poems, edited by Solomon Bekhor Ḥuṣein (Baghdad 1892), and Sedeh Laban, a Kabbalistic exposition of the same Psalm with a poetical introduction edited by Ben Ṣion Mordecai Ḥazzan (Jerusalem 1904). Besides these printed books there are others which are mentioned in manuscripts. Thus the Sha'are Ṣedeḳ was extracted by his great grandson Moses b. Simeon b. Moses b. Sason, and Shir Yediduth, mentioned by the author himself. Shindookh was a very prolific poet. In another place I have enumerated 113 headings of his poems.[1] In the year 1770 he wrote a prayer book according to the rite of the Baghdad Jews. There is further a manuscript of the counting of the 'Omer with Kabbalistic annotations in my collection, which was written by him. Sason officiated as Ḥazzan of the Great Synagogue. According to the Haskamah referred to above, the right of performing wedding ceremonies was, in the year 1810, officially entrusted to him and to his representatives. In some of the letters

[1] *Iggeroth Paras we-Teman*, Budapest, 5686, p. 15 ff., reprinted from *Hazofeh*, vol. IX (5685), pp. 209-233.

addressed to Hakham Ṣaleḥ he is mentioned as the Hakham's equal in office and in dignity. As Hazzan he was interested in the calendar, and two works of this branch of knowledge were copied by him. From the trend of his mind one can easily gather that he was interested in Kabbalistic writings. It is not surprising to find him among the owners of Kabbalistic manuscripts, such as a Kabbalistic compendium by Joseph Gikitilia and the Kawwanoth of Ḥayyim Viṭal. We find him as witness in marriage documents in the years 1765 and 1793. His descendants enjoyed equally with those of Ṣaleḥ Maṣliaḥ and others certain shares due to them according to the local custom of Baghdad from every participant at a wedding invited by the bridegroom during the seven days of festivities. This rite is called Minhagh Ḳirsh Rumi. In the year 1841 his grandson, Aaron b. Samuel, sold this right to his cousin, Simeon b. Moses, for 2,500 Kirsh Rayich. He lives in the memory of the Baghdad Jews and Moslems alike as the destroyer of the superstitious influence of the Moslem Marabut, Abu Sifain. In Baghdad there was a tomb of a man called 'Abd el-Kader, who was celebrated as Abu Sifain, i.e. man of two swords. His mausoleum bordered on the Jewish quarter. It was a magnificent building to which Moslems made pilgrimages in order to find relief in their physical troubles. Jewish women imitated their neighbours and repaired to this place. When Hakham Sason saw this abuse and dangerous superstition he counteracted it by hiring a courtyard opposite that place, where he spent a time in solitude nullifying by his Kabbalistic performances the magic power of Abu Sifain. In consequence of this the spell of Abu Sifain was broken and both Jews and Moslems neglected his shrine and were healed from their superstitions. This ruin is mentioned in a document dated in the year 1853 as Ḥanuth Abu Sifain.[1] Sason died on the 6th

[1] See *Ben Yehoyada'* by Hakham Joseph Hayyim, vol. 2, Jerusalem, 1899, f. 24d; *Sedeh Laban*, introduction; J. J. Benjamin, II, *Eight Years in Asia and Africa*, Hanover, 1863, p. 148, where the Hakham's name has to be added.

of Tebeth, 5590, at the age of eighty-three. His descendants played a considerable part in the life of the community during the nineteenth century, and up to the present day the privilege of their ancestor to act as official registrar of marriages is still in their hands.

Finally, it may be recorded here that Hakham Sason was reputed as an artist who modelled a miniature Tabernacle exactly according to the description given in the Bible, and I was told that after the reading of section Terumah (Exodus XXV-XXVII, 19) he used to show it to the congregants present. Solomon b. 'Abed Twena, a later prolific author, who hailed from Baghdad but spent his days in India, refers to this masterpiece, in recording at the same time a similar construction by another member of a Baghdadian family, Faraj Hayyim b. Solomon b. Ezekiel Judah, who was the author of wa-Tithpallel Hannah, Jerusalem 1889-90.[1]

[1] See the *Jewish Gazette* (Pacrah), VI, No. 35. Calcutta, 15th February, 1884.

CHAPTER XXIII

MOSES b. ḤAYYIM B. MOSES B. 'ABDALLAH

This Ḥakham was eulogized by the son of his predecessor, Nissim Maṣliaḥ, in the year 1780. He was already at that time a well recognized spiritual leader in the Baghdad community. In the year 1812 he signed immediately after the Nasi the statute regulating the performance of marriages. From a Hebrew-Arabic account book of the years 1820-1821 we learn that the writer of those accounts gave 100 Rumis to the Hakham in order to provide books for the students of the Midrash, which surely was under his supervision. In these years the authority of the Hakham of Baghdad was extended to the new settlements of Baghdad Jews in India, especially in Bombay and Calcutta. We learn that the leading Jews in these places turned to the Rabbinate of Baghdad for guidance and instruction, especially in cases of ritual and law, as in the case of 'Aghunoth, or as to their relation to the Bene Israel in marriage law (MS. No. 897, page 67). One of the first Jewish settlers in Bombay who hailed from Baghdad, Sliman b. Jacob b. Sliman, allotted a part of the income derived from his house to the Hakham and his two sons, 'Abdallah and Elijah. Not long before the Hakham's death he approbated the Peath ha-Shulhan by Israel b. Samuel of Sklow, a pupil of the Gaon of Wilna, which appeared in Safed, 1836. It may be mentioned here that this work was printed with the support of a Baghdadian, Ezekiel b. Reuben b. Manasseh, the founder of the Midrash Abu Mnashshi in Baghdad. A contemporary of this Hakham who shared with him the Rabbinate was Reuben b. David Nawi. His name occurs in the Haskamah in 1812, and in various Responsa, e.g. in those of Ḥakham

Joseph Ḥayyim and in the works of his pupil, Jacob b. Joseph b. Jacob ha-Rofe, who was the author of a commentary on Tractate Beṡah, Constantinople, 1849, Shir Ḥadash and Nawah Tehillah, commentaries on the Song of Songs and the Psalms, respectively, printed in Calcutta in 1843, and in Jerusalem in 1845. In 1847 he signed a letter written by the Rabbinate of Baghdad to the community of Bombay in the affair of the property of Sliman b. Jacob b. Sliman, and a judgment (Pesak Din) in 1835, with Moses b. Ḥayyim. Other members of the Court at this time were Jacob b. Fathi b. 'Abayyid and Elijah b. Solomon Kohen.

After the death of Ḥakham Moses Ḥayyim, in the year 1837, we find Elijah b. Joshua b. Obadiah as spiritual leader of the community. We have his signature on a document dated 1841. In that year he was removed from his office, yet he survived this and reached an age of 107. He died on the 14th of Tebeth, 1895.[1] Even after his removal from his office he was still active and took great interest in a lawsuit which made a stir among the Baghdad Jews in the sixties and seventies of the last century.

The case was this. A Baghdad Jew, by name Jacob Ṣemaḥ, who left his native town for Bombay, where he became wealthy, bequeathed all his considerable property in Bombay to a Beth ha-Midrash in Baghdad, called after his name, Midrash Jacob Ṣemaḥ. His will gave rise to a lawsuit by his daughters. This case came before the Rabbinate of many cities, such as Aleppo, Jerusalem and Smyrna, and resulted in the success of the daughters against the community. Before this decision was given, Elijah b. Joshua b. Obadiah approached the brothers Sir Albert David Sassoon and Elias David Sassoon on the one side, and Sir Moses Montefiore on the other, to intervene in favour of a settlement. It may be noticed here that there existed a synagogue called Midrash

[1] v. *Maggid Mesharim*, vi, Nos. 15 and 16, Calcutta, 7th and 14th February, 1895, respectively.

Jacob Ṣemaḥ, founded by Jacob b. Ṣemaḥ, the account book of which is preserved in MS. Sassoon 230.

After the removal of Ḥakham Elijah the congregation was divided into two parties. One was called Ḳa-ṣini and the other 'Abeidi. These designations were derived from the names of the two rival Hakhamim. The one was Raphael b. Elijah Ḳaṣin, the other Obadiah b. Abraham ha-Levy. Little information is preserved about the latter. All we know is that he was a native of Damascus. He came to Baghdad as a messenger of the Safed community. His coming to Baghdad was the beginning of an unfortunate communal strife. He was instrumental in the removal of the then acting Ab Beth Din, Elijah b. Joshua b. Obadiah from his dignity, and became active with a view to stepping into the place of the removed Dayyan, which aim he ultimately achieved. Yet his victory was short lived, for Raphael Ḳaṣin was elected Ḥakham Bashi, and reinstated the rival Dayyan Elijah b. Joshua b. Obadiah in his former office, naturally removing the acting Dayyan Obadiah b. Abraham ha-Levy. The latter signed and verified documents dated in the years 1847-1852. So much about the head of the 'Abeidi party. More is known about his rival.

He was a descendant of a Spanish family that after the expulsion from Spain settled in Aleppo. He was the only son of Elijah Ḳaṣin, born in 1790. To judge from the number of his books published and in manuscript, he must have been a remarkable man and worthy of his appointment as Ḥakham Bashi by the Turkish government and the support which he received by a considerable section of the community. A work under the title Derek ha-Ḥayyim, printed in Constantinople in 1848, is a noteworthy refutation of the Nethiboth 'Olam (1840), a mischievous work written in Hebrew by Christian missionaries to spread Christianity among Oriental Jews, and to catch their souls in the nets of the Church. This defence of the Jewish religion was reprinted and furnished with a Judeo-Spanish translation, under the title Liḳḳuṭe Amarim, Smyrna. This Baghdadian Ḥakham fought with great courage, wide knowledge and high intelligence against the destroyer who threatened evil to the House of Jacob. His name must also be mentioned among those who defended their faith against the assaults of Moslem scholars. In a pamphlet of his, under the title Iggereth Maggid Meṣarim, he gives an account of his travels among the Jews in many Persian cities, such as Shiraz and Ispahan. He also appeals to the Jews of Europe, mentioning among others Sir Moses Montefiore, to come to the rescue of the Jews suffering from cruel persecutions at the hands of the Persians in Khorasan, Ispahan, Urmia, Hamadan, etc. According to his biographer he also compiled a compendium on the fourth part of the ritual Code of R. Joseph Ḳaro, glosses on Shabbethai Kohen's Toḳfo Kohen and Yayin Harekaḥ, containing homilies on the Pentateuch. The latter three are still in manuscript.[1] Owing to the strife in the community, the details of which are not recorded, Ḳaṣin was forced ultimately to yield to external force and retire to his native place, where he spent the evening of his life, and died in 1871.

As colleagues of Elijah b. Joshua b. Obadiah we find several scholars who shall be mentioned here. First of all 'Abdallah Khḍeir b. Sliman who was a member of Elijah's court in 1844. We learn further that 'Abdallah Khḍeir officiated as Dayyan, together with Abraham b. Isaac Aṣlan and 'Abdallah b. Ezra b. Jacob, and earlier, in 1829, with Simeon b. Raḥamin Shoḥeṭ and Nissim b. Shalom Ḥuṣein. He was the scribe of MS. Sassoon 960, containing a special liturgy for the 15th of Shebat according to the Baghdad rite, written on behalf of the unfortunate Nasi, Ezra b. Joseph in the year 1819. Several poems and liturgical pieces were composed by 'Abdallah Khḍeir, some of them printed in

[1] v. the genealogy of the Kasin family in J. S. Kassin's *Peri Es ha-Gan*, vol. I, Jerusalem, 1931, pp. 128-131.

various compilations, others on inscriptions and in manuscripts. Thus in an inscription which is to be found in the mausoleum of the Prophet Ezekiel, restored by David Sassoon in the year 1859, there is 'Abdallah Khḍeir's poem which begins ענו לאל במהלל ושירים. Another contemporary of the rival Hakhamim was the son of their predecessor, Elijah b. Moses Ḥayyim, the author of Midrash Eliyyahoo, a Kabbalistic commentary on the Bible and Talmud (Livorno, 1862). He died at the age of forty-eight, 7 Elul, 1859. Further, Gabriel b. Jacob b. Elisha, whose work Shem Ya'akob is frequently mentioned by Solomon b. 'Abed Twena in his Nofeth Ṣufim, (Baghdad, 1879), was, we learn, the nephew of the well-known Baghdadian poet, Ezra b. Sason b. Ezra.

CHAPTER XXIV

'ABDALLAH B. ABRAHAM SOMEKH

THIS Hakham, who was a pupil of Moses Ḥayyim, claimed to be a descendant of R. Nissim, who generations before him held the dignity of a Rosh Yeshibah in Baghdad. We have no means of establishing the date and activity of this Gaon. He may or may not have been identical with a Gaon of the same name who very frequently occurs in various liturgies as an author of a Confession used in many rites for the Day of Atonement. It is true that in earlier manuscripts the name of the author is either entirely omitted, or spelt as R. Assi or Issi Gaon. Since both are unknown, it is difficult to establish the actual relation of these Geonim to the Somekh family on one side, and to verify or ignore the tradition of the latter on the other.

In 1828 'Abdallah wrote a commentary on the Passover Haggadah, collected from various sources, among them one by an earlier Baghdadian writer, the Haggadah commentary of Solomon b. Isaac b. Hayyim, and another by an anonymous writer designated as מע״ל after the numerical value 150, meaning the year of its compilation, 5550, i.e. 1790. Besides this he wrote glosses and notes on the second part of the Shulhan 'Arukh, which were printed under the title Zibḥe Ṣedeḳ (Baghdad, 1904), with the support of Abraham b. Ezekiel Gabbai, the son of Joshua, who was the scribe of Somekh's Haggadah commentary (MS. Sassoon 193). This work contains also a number of Responsa bearing on all the four parts of Joseph Karo's Halakhic Code. These Responsa offer some material for the knowledge of the religious conditions, communal affairs and political status of the Baghdad Jews in his time.

From near and far the Rabbinate of Baghdad was consulted in matters of religion and law. Indian and Chinese, Persian and Mesopotamian Jews and Jewish communities turned with their difficulties and troubles to Hakham 'Abdallah, who in agreement with his colleagues and pupils, summarized under the title Bene Yeshibah, discussed and decided these matters. Some are very interesting as manifesting the influence of modern achievements on the mind of the Jews in the East. Thus the question crops up whether travelling on railways on the Sabbath and festivals is permitted or not. The Jews in Bombay were faced by this special problem for local reasons, and sought such a permission from the Rabbinical authorities not for general travelling, but only for the area within the Sabbath limit. A booklet under the title Imre Shabbath by Ḥayyim Jacob ha-Kohen of Safed (Calcutta, 1873) and Jerusalem, no date, has a bearing on the same subject and owes its origin to the same movement. Even before the spread of the railways in India the Jews used the palanquin, which gave rise to the question as to whether it is allowed for use on Sabbath and festivals. Another sign of the times is to be found in an inquiry whether the services of a Jewish medical practitioner who has officially or unofficially severed his connection with Jewish law and custom are allowable for Jews on the Sabbath.

There are plenty of traces of the relationship existing between the Jews of Baghdad on the one side and those of Damascus on the other. We learn of Baghdad Jews travelling from Baghdad *via* Kerkuk, Kantarah, Arbil, Mosul, Zaku, Jezirah, Nisibis, Mardin, Diarbekir, Aleppo to Damascus. The commercial activities of the Baghdadians were not limited to Baghdad but extended over the whole province of Mesopotamia. Thus we find a Baghdadian Jew who travelled near Kut, selling his corals among the Arabs. Another acts as goldsmith or silversmith to Moslems. These travels were not without great danger, for the numerous

'Aghunah cases were the result of these occupations. Interesting are the indications of special local customs among the Jews of Baghdad. An old Turkish law exempted professional scribes of Holy Scrolls, etc., their sons and the sons of the Ḥakhamim, from paying the military tax, called 'Askariyyi. For some reason or other the leaders of the Baghdad community in the days of this Ḥakham decided to remove this privilege. There exist lists of 'Askariyyi payers, one dated Baghdad, 1892, containing the names of 1,905 contributors, and the other dated 1899, containing 2,483 of these taxpayers. The taxpayers were divided into different classes according to the amount of their assessment. The highest assessment was thirty Ḳirsh and the lowest ten Ḳirsh. Of special local customs it may be mentioned first of all, that the circumcision rite was performed in the precincts of the synagogue, and secondly that the order of the Blessing of the Moon (Birkath ha-Lebanah) was preceded by the recital of Psalm 19. An interesting inquiry is made by some Jews in China whether the Ethroghim (festival citrons) grown in Hong Kong may be used for the ritual or not. It seems that those fruits imported from Egypt did not satisfy them, either because they did not arrive in time, or if they did, not in a state fit for the observance of the law. A Bombay Jew was engaged in the pepper trade, importing that article through his non-Jewish agent from Malabar. In the time of this Ḥakham there spread a superstition among the Jewesses of Baghdad—which they must have adopted from their Arab surroundings, and which was called in Arabic "Kabsah"—that the first part of the ritual benedictions prescribed for the wedding ceremony, called Birkath Erusin should not be uttered on the cup of wine but should be accompanied merely by handing over the money of the ceremony (Kesef Ḳiddushin). For the commercial relations of the Jews in the east to the west may be noticed that our Hakham was interrogated as to whether pickled olives from London might be used or not. Finally, we learn that a kind of honey, called in

Arabic Mann el-Sama, was brought from Persian cities and sold in the market of Baghdad.

Ḥakham 'Abdallah died on the 18th of Elul, 1889, and was buried on the Saturday night following, 19th Elul, in the building where the shrine of Joshua the High Priest is situated. A few days after, however, at the instigation of the government, the body had to be removed; yet the grave of another Baghdadian Hakham, namely Jacob b. Joseph Harofe, who found earlier his eternal rest in the same place, was not disturbed.[1]

[1] *Maggid Mesharim*, I, No. 1, Calcutta, 13, Ḥeshwan, 1889 (7th November, 1889), and ibid. Nos. 2, 4, 9, especially 10; also *Zichronoth Eliyahu* (*Jerusalem* 5696), p. 6 ff, where the extraordinary circumstances surrounding this episode may be found. [Since the above was written a biography of R. A. Somekh has appeared entitled *Toledoth Harab 'Abdallah Somekh* by Abraham Ben-Jacob, Jerusalem, 5709.]

CHAPTER XXV

ELIJAH B. SLIMAN MANI

THE great influence exercised by Ḥakham 'Abdallah made itself felt by the great number of scholars studying in his college, who planted and spread the wisdom of the Torah either in Baghdad itself or in distant communities. A pupil of Ḥakham 'Abdallah was Ezekiel b. Ezra b. Joshua ha-Levy,, who published several works: (1) Pizmonim, containing six poems, all with the acrostic of his name, (Baghdad); (2) Pithe Teshubah, prayers of repentance, Jerusalem 1926; (3) The Book of Psalms with a commentary called Tehillah we-Tifereth, Jerusalem 1914; (4) Haggadah Shel Pesaḥ with the Arabic translation and a commentary entitled Simhath Yom Tob; and finally addresses which were delivered on festivities occasioned by the completion of the Tractates of the Talmud, and sermons for Sabbaths, under the title 'Arughath ha-Bosem (Jerusalem, 1903), with some poetical supplements in Hebrew and Arabic. In the preface 'Abdallah's educational and communal activities, piety and charity are eulogized. The author also sat at the feet of Isaac b. Mordecai b. Sason, a contemporary Bagdadian Ḥakham. A more prominent place is due to Hakham Elijah b. Sliman Mani, a native of Baghdad, born 5578 (= 1818), who became later the brother-in-law of his teacher by marrying his master's sister. He excelled as scholar and Hasid. Of his scholarship his Siyyaḥ Yiṣḥaḳ, a moralistic and ritualistic compendium gives evidence; it was published by his son Sliman Menaḥem Mani, Jerusalem, 1902.[1] A number of other works are mentioned by the editor, comprising many branches of Jewish literature, for

[1] The date given in the biography, p. 2a, as 5588, has to be corrected to 5578, as in the text.

example, Responsa, decisions, homilies and Kabbalistic essays which remain in manuscript. A characteristic feature of this scholar was his asceticism. He spent most of his life in solitude, shunning society and luxuries, keeping a vegetarian diet and being satisfied with the bare necessities of life. Real friendship existed between him and R. Elijah b. Moses Ḥayyim, with whom he studied the wisdom of the Kabbalah. In the year 1856, a new movement impelled by real love for Zion and Palestine, arose among the Jews in Baghdad, which resulted in many of them leaving their native city and immigrating into Palestine. Among them was our Rabbi who, after a strenuous journey full of miracles and adventures, arrived in Jerusalem. After a short stay there, in 1858, the Jews of Hebron invited him to occupy the seat of learning and teaching in that ancient community. Here he found ample room for his scholarly and religious activities. His colleague was Moses Pereira, formerly Rabbi in Sarajevo, with whom he shared the Rabbinate. He established a school and a synagogue with a number of pupils and fully qualified teachers. Further, he travelled in order to find means for erecting a house of worship in the neighbourhood of the Sepulchre in Hebron held by the Arabs. His efforts were futile, owing to the obstinacy manifested by the Arabs. He went to Damascus in order to approach the Pasha. In spite of the financial support accorded to him by a wealthy member of the Damascus community, he had to return to Hebron without result. With the support of the Jews in Egypt, India and Beirut, he was enabled to establish the synagogue Beth Ya'aḳob with special liturgical and ritualistic usages, as described in the author's Siyyaḥ Yiṣḥaḳ. With the help of Ezekiel b. Joshua Gabbai of Bömbay and of the sons of Ḥakham Eliyyahoo b. Moses Ḥayyim of Baghdad, he renewed an old Midrash, where among others, Ḥayyim Joseph David Azulai, the famous bibliographer, studied, and he called it Midrash Eliyyahoo. This college was provided with a large library, augmented with new acquisitions under the special care of the Ḥakham. Another synagogue, erected with the help of the members of the Mosciri family of Cairo, was known as Yeshibath Ma'aseh Nissim, so called after Nissim Moseiri. This family supported the Rabbi's activities throughout for many decades. The Jews of Bokhara, headed by Barukh Jihan, were also among the supporters of this Rabbi.

In spite of all his piety and charity, there arose strife and quarrel embittering the life of this saint. It is established that Mani officiated first in an honorary capacity for fourteen years; later he consented to receive a small salary which would keep him and his family alive. Owing to his real humility in order to avoid greetings and honour he was attired like an Arab, searching for opportunities to help the hungry and needy, to assist widow and orphan. Yet for personal reasons there arose against him three men, namely Mercado Romano of Constantinople, Raphael ha-Levy and Nissim Lahbah, the latter being styled as Ḥakhamim, dependent materially and morally on the former. Mercado, who was an influential man in his native city and acquainted with the Pashas at the Porte, spread slanderous rumours about Mani's arbitrary handling of the sums sent to the Holy City without giving account of the income and expenditure. Mani offered to show them his accounts, yet the other party was not satisfied. The opposition against Mani grew daily with the greatest intensity. The enemies would not be satisfied unless the Ḥakham was carried as prisoner to Constantinople, where he would be called to account. Yet the supporters of Mani prevented such a disgraceful step. Then Mercado Romano turned to R. Shalom Moses Ḥai Gagin, threatening with strong measures to bring Mani before his court. Mani was called upon to deliver the keys of the hostel which was under his control, which he did, and repaired to Jerusalem in order to show his accounts, which were found correct. The court published a declaration exonerating him and approving his conduct. The enemies, however, did not acquiesce in this step and were untiring in their efforts to deprive the saintly man of his Rabbinate. They achieved so much that two-thirds of the city turned against Mani. In a pathetic letter Mani describes his troubles and his anxieties. The affair assumed greater and greater dimensions. There developed a large correspondence in which several Rabbis in Jerusalem, Sefaradi and Ashkenazi, the *Consistoire* of the Jews in Constantine, the Rabbis of the same place, Tunis, Bombay and Calcutta took part.[1] At the end the accusers had to give in and acknowledge the wrong done to a real saint. Thus this sad and unworthy episode ended without diminishing the general love and great reverence for Ḥakham Elijah Mani. He died on the 7th of Tammuz, 1899, at the age of eighty-one.

Besides his printed book, his biographer mentions his Ma'aseh Eliyyahoo containing Responsa; further, Zikhronoth Eliyyahoo,[2] an alphabetic compendium on the four parts of the Turim, and Derushim (homilies), all of them still in manuscript. At the end of the book Siaḥ Yiṣḥaḳ there are some funeral orations by Simeon Ben Sion ibn Nayim, the Hazzan of the Bokharian Jews in Nahalath Shib'ah.

[1] The literature of this unfortunate affair is to be found in Abraham Ḥayyim Finso's *Minḥath Kenaoth Mazkereth 'Awon* by the secretary of the Sefaradic communities in Jerusalem, Jerusalem. Further *Dim'ath 'Ashukim* by the Ḥakhamim and representatives of the Jews in Hebron, Jerusalem, 1879; Habazeleth, Jerusalem, vol. IX (1879); and the *Jewish Gazette*, Paerah, II, No. 1, 20th June, 1879, containing the announcement of the leaders of Calcutta Jewry, in Hebrew.

[2] Since the above was written, Part I of Zikhronoth Eliyyahoo on the first two parts of the Shulḥan 'Arukh, was published by Rabbi Yiṣḥaḳ Nissim Raḥamim in Jerusalem, 5696, with an Introduction giving details of the author's family and with a work at the end entitled *Barukh Mibanim* being responsa by Abraham Baruch Mani a son of our author. Also there was published since this chapter was written, a biography of our author entitled *Rabbi Eliyyahoo Mani* by Menasseh Mani, Jerusalem 5696.

החכם המקובל מו״ר ח׳ יוסף חיים זיע״א

ḤAKHAM YOSEPH ḤAYIM

[*Facing page* 149

CHAPTER XXVI

ḤAKHAM JOSEPH ḤAYYIM

HAKHAM JOSEPH ḤAYYIM was a pupil of Ḥakham 'Abdallah and a grandson of Ḥakham Moses Ḥayyim, and he was the last of the great Rabbis of modern times in Baghdad. He was elected at the age of twenty-six (Elul, 1859), soon after the death of his father, Ḥakham Elijah, spiritual leader of the most important and populous community in the East. He officiated for fifty years, until his death (Elul, 1909), and he was also an authority recognized by the Jewish communities in India and China. His modesty and piety, his love for learning and students, his more than ordinary zeal for Palestine and feelings for the community of Israel in general are especially praised, and they endeared his memory long after his death. From the first a wealthy man, he could afford to devote all his time to study, religious exercise, solitude, and service to his fellow men. Nearly every Sabbath he would address crowds of people in the Great Synagogue, men and women, who eagerly listened to his eloquence. For hours he would expound Halakhah and Aggadah to the delight of his hearers. On certain Sabbaths of the year his was the privilege to preach in the Ṣlat el-Kebirah, or the Great Synagogue, when all the other Rabbis of the numerous synagogues came to listen. The fruits of his studies are laid down in his numerous printed works, which will, as far as possible, be detailed here. Some of them are anonymous, but on good authority they can be included in this list. (1) *Adereth Eliyahoo*, homilies on the Pentateuch and the Readings from the Prophets, Livorno, 1864. (2) *Birkath Aboth*, commentary on the Pirḳe Aboth, Livorno, 1865. (3) *Rab Berakhoth*, Responsa, novellae and the order of service for the 7th of Adar, Baghdad, 1868. (4) *Tiḳḳun Tefillah*, corrections of and additions to prayers and poems, with usages and customs introduced by the author, based on material gathered from the writings of Isaac Luria and Shalom Sher'abi, Baghdad, 1870. (5) *Seder ha-Yom*, Kabbalistic prayers and additions to the liturgy, Baghdad, 1870, second edition 1894. (6) *Refuath ha-Nefesh*, a special liturgy for the Shobabim Fasts with many messianic poems at the end, Baghdad, 1870. (7) *Eben Shelema*, *Em ha-Melekh*, *Ḳeren Yeshu'ah*, homilies on the Canticles, Ruth and Esther, Livorno, 1870. (8) *Mamlekheth Kohanim*, a special ritual compiled for the pilgrims to the graves of the three priests situated around Baghdad, namely, Ezekiel the Prophet, Joshua the High Priest, and Ezra the Scribe, Baghdad, 1873. (9) *Or Zarua'*, a collection of R. 'Akiba's sayings mentioned in the Talmud and Midrash as a special ritual for the Day of Atonement, the day when the Tanna suffered martyrdom at the hands of the Romans, Baghdad, 1874. (10) *Meir Bath 'Ayin*, a similar compilation of R. Meir's sayings for the 14th of Iyyar, the anniversary of his death, Baghdad, 1874, second edition, 1905. (11) *Shib'ah be-Adar*, a collection from the Bible, Talmud and Zohar about Moses for the 7th of Adar, and a similar compilation for the 5th of Ab in memory of Isaac Luria, Livorno, 1874. (12) *Haḳḳafoth le-Simḥath ha-Torah*, poems and prayers for the Day of Rejoicing of the Law, Livorno, 1875. This booklet includes a section entitled *Shira Ḥadashah*, which contains further poems by the Ḥakham, for the same occasion. (13) *Hillula Rabba*, readings from the Talmud and Zohar, prayers and poems in honour of R. Shimon b. Yoḥai to be said on the 33rd day of 'Omer, Livorno, 1877, second edition, Baghdad, 1908. (14) *Mishmereth ha-Ḥodesh*, a liturgy for the New Moon, Baghdad, 1879, second edition, no date, probably 1898 or 1900, third edition, 1908. (15) *Kether Malkuth*, a special liturgy for New Year's days, the Day of Atonement and Hosha'na Rabbah, Baghdad, 1897, second edition, with the name of the author, Jerusalem, 1906. (16) *Ben Ish Ḥai*,

Aggadic and Halakhic homilies and expositions on the weekly portions, Jerusalem, 1898, second edition, Baghdad, 1902, third edition, Jerusalem, 1932. (17) *Ben Yehoyada:* Part I, comprising expositions of and commentaries on Aggadic portions in the Tractates Berakhoth and Shabbath, Jerusalem, 1898; Part II on Tractates 'Erubin, Pesaḥim, Yoma, Rosh ha-Shanah, Sukkah, and Beṣah, Jerusalem, 1899; Part III on Meghillah, Ta'anith Ḥaghighah, Moed Ḳatan, Yebamoth, Kethubboth, Giṭṭin, Jerusalem, 1900; Part IV on Nedarim, Nazir, Soṭah, Ḳiddushin and the three Baboth, Jerusalem, 1902, and Part V, on Tractates Sanhedrin, Makkoth, Shebu'oth, 'Eduyoth, 'Abodah Zarah, Horayoth, Zebaḥim, Menaḥoth, Ḥullin, Bekhoroth, 'Arakhin and Niddah, Jerusalem, 1904. (18) *Rab Pe'alim,* Responsa on the four parts of the Shulḥan 'Arukh, 4 volumes, Jerusalem, 1901-1912. (19) *Ben Ish Hayil,* homilies for the Sabbaths of Repentance, of Remembrance, the Great Sabbath and Shabbath Kallah (the Sabbath before Pentecost). There are added sermons delivered on the Jahrzeit days of the preacher's father (7th of Elul), under the titles Shene Eliyyahoo and Neweh Ṣaddiḳim. The latter include funeral sermons for the preacher's uncle, R. 'Abdallah, who died in 1865, R. Raphael Meir Panigel, and others, Jerusalem, 1901, Part II, 1910. (20) *Benayahu,* comprising the *Tiḳḳune ha-Zohar,* with a commentary, 2 volumes, Jerusalem, 1903. (21) *Benayahu,* commentaries and novellae on Aggadic passages in 'Ein Ya'aḳob, Jerusalem, 1905. (22) *Leshon Ḥakhamim,* Kabbalistic prayers and annotations to the prayer book, in two parts, Jerusalem, 1905 and 1910, a second enlarged edition edited by David b. Solomon Laniyado, Jerusalem, 1925. (23) *Ḳanun el-Nisa,* (Rules for Women), a ritualistic and moralistic compendium in Arabic for women, Baghdad, 1906, second edition edited by Ben Ṣion Mordecai Ḥazzan, Jerusalem, 1926. The latter edition embodies a booklet by the same author called *Hazoorayat wa-Tafsirhum,* that is, the Solutions of the Riddles contained in the 58th chapter of the Ḳanun, which was printed in Baghdad in 1910, in a separate booklet (see further, No. 28). (24) *Pirḳe Aboth*, with a comprehensive commentary *Ḥasde Aboth*, with notes by the author's son Jacob, under the title Zekhuth Aboth, Baghdad, 1907, second edition, 1911. (25) *'Alim le-Terufah*, charms by the author. This little booklet contains also the well-known moralistic letter of Nahmanides addressed to his son, a similar letter by the Gaon of Wilna, Elijah b. Solomon Zalman, and the famous ethical will, known under the name of Orḥoth Ḥayyim, ascribed to Asher b. Yehiel, Jerusalem, 1907. (26) *Imre Binah*, questions to test the knowledge of students in all parts of Biblical and Talmudic as well as secular studies. At the end there are two sermons delivered in honour of the dedication of two religious educational institutions, one called Midrash Nuriel and the other Midrash Aaron Ṣaleḥ, both in Baghdad; Jerusalem, 1908. (27) *'Od Yosef Ḥai*, homilies on the weekly portions with special sermons under the title Kunṭris Maroth Yeḥezḳel, comprising sermons delivered at Kifil in the synagogue attached to the shrine of the Prophet Ezekiel, and Halakhic notes on the weekly portions, Jerusalem, 1910. (28) *Ḥazoorayat wa-Tafsirhum*, Baghdad, 1910 (see above, No. 23). (29) *Da'ath wu-Thebunah*, expositions on Isaac Luria's Ḳabbalah, Jerusalem, 1911. (30) *Moda'ah we-Gillui Da'ath*, a special prayer, Baghdad, 1912, second edition, Jerusalem, 1914, third edition, Jerba, 1916. (31) *Niflaim Ma'asekhah.* This is a collection of 164 stories and anecdotes gleaned from the numerous works of the Ḥakham, and although compiled by Ben Ṣion Mordecai Ḥazzan, Jerusalem, 1912, should be recorded here. The collection is a valuable source for folkloristic studies and the history of comparative literature and religion. This work comprises also the well-known Ḳa'arath Kesef, by Joseph Ezobi. (32) *Mashal we-Nimshal*, collectanea from the works of the Ḥakham, compiled and edited by Ben Ṣion Mordecai Ḥazzan, Jerusalem, 1913. To this list may be added some works of R. Joseph Ḥayyim which are in manuscript—a memorial oration delivered on the 28th of Adar II, 1894, at the death of Solomon David Sassoon, some Responsa sent to Ispahan in Persia, and Rangoon in Burmah and finally, some of his liturgical compositions for the 15th of Shebaṭ and for the Passover service.[1]

These works indicate on the one side his industry and learning, his activities as scholar and orator, and on the other, his great influence on the religious life and practice of the Jews in Baghdad. Many of these works manifest a practical tendency in introducing Kabbalistic innovations and alterations in the synagogue and its liturgy. Some of these innovations gave rise to newspaper polemics initiated by the historian and geographer of Babylonian Jewry, Dr. Jacob Obermayer. As a correspondent of the Hebrew journal ha-Maggid, from Baghdad, he drew attention to these practices and innovations, which he disliked. He condemns the asceticism of the Rabbi as well as his alterations in the text of the prayers and changes in well established ancient usages. His literary activity, especially his collection of sermons called Addereth Eliyyahu, is the subject of severe criticism owing to the use of methods like Remazim, Gemaṭriyoth, etc. Obermayer finds fault with the author for not seeking approbation as usual since the invention of printing. Obermayer is not altogether free from personal invectives, in which the great material wealth of the author is unduly emphasized. A number of textual alterations in the litanies and poems made by the Ḥakham are rejected as useless. A few words may be added to show Obermayer's wrath aroused by Ḥakham Joseph Ḥayyim's reforms. First of all he said that the Kapparoth for the eve of the Day of Atonement should be white fowls, and further that people should not walk barefooted but in cloth shoes on the

[1] For the Memorial Oration, see MS. Sassoon, 484, *Ohel Dawid*, p. 89. About the Responsa, see MS. Sassoon, 588(D), *Ohel Dawid*, p. 204; MS. Sassoon, 961, *Ohel Dawid*, p. 977; MS. Sassoon, 581 (B), *Ohel Dawid*, p. 205, (the Responsum sent to Calcutta is to be found in print in the author's *Rab Berakhoth*, ff. 178b-191a). About the author's liturgical compositions, see MS. Sassoon, 483, *Ohel Dawid*, p. 231, and Ibid., p. 236.

Ninth of Ab. Then he ordered the Jews of Baghdad to fast on the 7th of Adar, the anniversary day of the death of Moses, and to spend the night before in study and reading. To the public fast days he added the 5th of Ab, the day when he celebrated the *Jahrzeit* of R. Isaac Luria Ashkenazi. Among other new rules of the Ḥakham there is first of all his prohibition that the slaughterer may not kill a fowl or an animal in the sight of another animal. Then he remarks about the Ḥakham sitting all day in his library removed from the world, and his four wealthy brothers carrying on business for him. Obermayer deprecates the religious conditions prevailing in Baghdad and surroundings, and the Ḥakham's inactivity.

So far we have heard only the accuser without having any recourse to the plea which the accused may have put forward. Obermayer's account may furnish us with some details about the religious and social conditions of Baghdad in the middle of the seventies of the last century. He tells us that fifteen synagogues were open and frequented for divine worship. Three of them he regards as very ancient; three others were built in the last twenty years by Manasseh b. Ezekiel Reuben, two more from the estate of Jacob b. Semah, and another by Saul b. Joseph Moses. A good many more synagogues were founded in the last forty years by wealthy members of the community, after whom they are mostly named. None of the synagogues have any outward beauty. The Scrolls of the Law are kept in cases covered with silver and rich silks. The prayers are delivered according to the Sefaradi rite. Most of their precentors are members of the Beth ha-Midrash; they have a good delivery and read correctly; besides, they have the advantage of a fine pronunciation, owing to their knowledge of the Arabic tongue. Obermayer complains of the paucity of singing in the service. Most of the synagogues have their permanent preachers who gather their material from the works of well-known moralists. Here again Obermayer finds fault with Ḥakham Joseph Ḥayyim, whose sermons are unduly deprecated. The preachers receive no salary and act in an honorary capacity. As one of the peculiarities of Baghdadian Jewish life the pilgrimages to the graves of Ezekiel the Prophet and Ezra the Scribe by Baghdadians, men and women, young and old, are pointed out. In these places, in Kifil and in el-'Ozeir, synagogues and caravanserais were erected, the former for study and prayer, the latter for the accommodation of the pilgrims. On every eve of New Moon it is customary to visit the shrine of Joshua the High Priest, which is on the right side of the Tigris, about half-an-hour's walk from Baghdad. Obermayer mentions further a small synagogue in the Jewish quarter of Baghdad, with a grave, called by the people the Shrine of Sheikh Yisḥak, which is considered a place of worship by them. The writer as a German Jew is not very favourable to these practices, just as he cannot appreciate the predilections of Eastern Jews for the study of the Zohar. Altogether Obermayer's account about the apostacy and superstitions, bad manners and habits of the Baghdad Jews must be accepted only with the greatest reserve. Surely he, as a stranger imbued with Western culture and brought up in an entirely different Jewish environment, could not judge impartially the Jews of Baghdad, just as they may have looked askance at the manners and ways of the Bavarian Jew. Obermayer's letters, therefore, cannot be considered as a reliable source for the inner history of the Jews in Baghdad.[1] They are the outburst of a superficial observer out of sympathy with the people and customs he wrote about.

This criticism of the stranger within their gates, in spite of his high position as teacher of French in the palace of the Persian prince, 'Abbas Mirza, did not detract from Ḥakham Joseph Ḥayyim's saintly conduct and the general reverence paid him by his fellow Jews. It is true that the Ḥakham's first journey to Palestine and his acquaintance with Kabbalistic

[1] Obermayer's letters are printed in *ha-Magid*, vol. XX, Lyck, 1876, pp. 58 f., 65 f., 76 f., 84 f., 103 f., 113, 120 f., 130 f., 138 f., 146 f., and 155.

BURIAL GROUND, BAGHDAD

In the centre is the grave of Ḥakham Yoseph Ḥayim

[*Facing page* 156

lore made such an impression upon him, that for the good of his flock he introduced some changes and alterations. Yet the reader of his sermons and of his other books will never acquiesce in Obermayer's verdict of condemnation. Nor did his contemporaries consent to it. He was acknowledged near and far as a holy Rabbi to whom they journeyed for help and advice, for instruction and enlightenment. His last days were crowned by a call received from Jerusalem to become the spiritual leader, the chief Rabbi of the Jews in the Holy City. He refused to accept this dignity. He set out, as usual, in the month of Elul, to go to the grave of Ezekiel the Prophet, but on his way there he died on the 13th of Elul, 1909.

CHAPTER XXVII

THE OFFICE OF THE ḤAKHAM BASHI

Exact information about the origin of the Office of the Ḥakham Bashi in general, and in Baghdad in particular, is not available. In a previous chapter two bearers of this title, Raphael Ḳaṣin and Obadiah b. Abraham ha-Levy, were mentioned. Their tenure of office was not a happy one, as our description some pages earlier has shown. It seems that their successors were no happier in their high office. The cause of all the strife, before and afterwards, was their dependence on the lay authorities. The real leaders of the community in spiritual as well as in legal matters were the Ḥakhamim, whose life and work were the subject of the preceding chapters, which show the weight attached to their personality and teaching on the one side, and the influence exercised by their saintliness and benevolence on the other.

The next Ḥakham Bashi, Sason b. Elijah Smooḥa, a native of Baghdad, who for thirty-five years officiated as Rabbi and later as Ḥakham Bashi, had to face many troubles and was the centre of deplorable quarrels. After Obadiah ha-Levy's death, Sason Smooḥa was appointed his successor. In the year 1879, the whole Jewish population turned to the leading Rabbis, 'Abdallah Somekh and Joseph Ḥayyim, to sign with the members of the community a petition addressed to the Pasha of Baghdad to the effect that the Ḥakham Bashi be removed from his office. The charges voiced aloud against him were of an extraordinary nature. Bribery and embezzlement of the military tax, called 'Askariyyah, were the most serious. The Pasha himself, who at first naturally favoured the Ḥakham Bashi, owing to the great services which he had rendered to the Turkish government, ultimately yielded to the claims of the Jewish community and consented to the removal of Sason Smooḥa from his post. In the interval the affairs of the Rabbinate were entrusted to a court of three, and public affairs to a board of representatives consisting of ten members. For twenty months the matter remained in abeyance. Smooḥa did not rest, and, with the influential intervention of the Ḥakham Bashi in Constantinople and other wire-pulling, he was so far successful, that in the spring of 1881 the provincial Mejlis in Baghdad reinstated him in his former dignity. The reason given for this rehabilitation was that by the removal from his office his Firman, which was issued to him by the Sublime Porte in Constantinople, and the various orders bestowed upon him by the Sultan for his services, had not been invalidated. Thereupon Smooḥa dismissed the court appointed at the time of his removal and took over the determination of legal and religious causes. This high-handed action aroused general dissatisfaction. The leaders, spiritual and lay alike, gathered together in order to protest, yet they tried peaceful means in offering Smooḥa 2,500 Kirsh Rayich per month for his retirement from office. This was not accepted. Smooḥa rejected the peaceful offer made to him by his brethren, and relied on the influence and protection of his non-Jewish friends. Feelings became more and more embittered, telegrams were sent to all quarters, Rabbis and representatives were determined, the whole community restless and at strife till finally Smooḥa left his post. The inner peace of the community was broken, and the general condition affected by strife, illness and unemployment, so that the local Mejlis had to interfere, and the authorities in Constantinople finally agreed to the removal of Smooḥa from his office and the appointment of Elisha b. Nissim Dangoor as Ḥakham Bashi of Baghdad.

Among the documents concerning this affair there is a remarkable letter addressed to the leaders of the Baghdad community, Joseph b. Ezra b. Abraham Gabbai and Ḥakham

Joseph Ḥayyim, by the Ḥakham Bashi of Constantinople, Moses ha-Levy, in which he pleads on behalf of the deposed Ḥakham and his family. The community is not entitled, he asserts, in spite of all the accusations lodged against their Ḥakham, to deprive him and his family of the bare necessities of life. He threatens and enjoins them to provide for the livelihood of their Ḥakham Bashi. The writer of an unsigned letter to the "Paerah" in Calcutta intends to vindicate the case of the former Ḥakham Bashi at the expense of the newly elected one. The former is praised as a man of wisdom and of the world, capable of representing Jewish affairs before the government; he is industrious and zealous in settling all pending cases, while the latter lacks personality and worldly wisdom. This letter truly reflects the change of opinion which took place in Baghdad in favour of Smooḥa against the new Ḥakham Bashi Elisha Dangoor. Joseph Goorji, who was instrumental in the early stage of this deplorable strife, now turned into a partisan of Smooḥa, and, together with another leader of the community, Ṣaleḥ b. Daniel, and his son Menahem, endeavoured to reinvest Smooḥa with the rights and the title of the Ḥakham Bashi. This movement could not have been very popular, since handbills and leaflets in Hebrew and Arabic, and other languages spoken and used by the inhabitants of Baghdad, were stuck in all the streets and squares denouncing Smooḥa and cursing and reviling his new protectors. Many people, among them the Wakil (Acting) Ḥakham Bashi, Israel b. Sason Israel, were imprisoned and tortured. On the other hand the Smooḥa party also suffered imprisonment from the Wali and excommunication from the Ḥakham Bashi and his followers. The affair assumed such dimensions that Ḥakham Elisha Dangoor was publicly abused and wounded on his way to divine worship. Prominent among the people who caused this new trouble were the sons of the former Ḥakham Bashi and his helper, the tax collector, Abraham Baṣooṣ. These cases engaged the attention of the courts for a long time.

The only actual change recorded in our sources is that the duty of tax collecting was taken away from the Ḥakham Bashi and transferred to Joseph Goorji, who became responsible for the execution of this task. A new development occurred when Joseph Goorji collected signatures for a declaration that the present Ḥakham Bashi should also be removed and an intermediary or an agent between the Jews and the government should be appointed instead; and further that the number of representatives should be reduced from ten to seven. Goorji induced some Ḥakhamim, among them the leading Ḥakham 'Abdallah Somekh, to sign such a document under duress. When, however, this Ḥakham and his entourage became aware of the wrong done to the Ḥakham Bashi Elisha Dangoor, they regretted their complicity and signed another document favouring the retention of the present spiritual head of the community. Both documents were sent to Constantinople, where the confusion they caused puzzled the officials in the high places. The matter was sent back to Baghdad for explanation, which was offered by 'Abdallah Somekh and his colleagues. As a result of these contradictory requests addressed to Constantinople, the lay heads and the spiritual leaders suggested that in the meantime one of the members of the court, Abraham b. Moses Hillel, should officiate as Wakil Ḥakham Bashi. From the documents we further learn that the Ḥakham Bashi of Constantinople addressed a letter to Elisha Dangoor advising him to send in his resignation at once to the authorities, otherwise it might be too late. As a matter of fact when the case was dealt with before the Wali Pasha of Baghdad it was decided against him, and his removal from office was officially announced. The troubles and quarrels increased owing to several irregularities and blunders on the part of the leaders. Thus the sums fixed in the tax books were tampered with, figures increased and doubled, against the statute laid down at the time when this affair was regulated. There was another irregularity which added to the trouble.

Certain members of the community were ex-officio exempted from paying taxes. This privilege extended to the sons of Ḥakhamim, the scribes and their sons, etc. In spite of it their names were put on the register and, against the decision of the Ḥakhamim, were threatened with gaol in case of refusal. Some people whose taxes had been doubled were actually imprisoned. Then the old trouble of finding the writer of the handbills was still agitating the minds and occupying the attention of the court. Reuben, the son of Ḥakham Israel Sason, was suspected and imprisoned. Finally through the incompetence of the communal leaders, some acres of land which had served originally as burial ground, and now (1884) had been discontinued for more than eight decades, was sold by public auction and fell, for the small sum of about seventy Rupees, into the hands of a Moslem, while the Jews had the same option to acquire it. The party of Goorji discovered that a society of 372 members had been formed, under the leadership of Moses b. Ṣadḳah Sofer, whose aim was to punish the leaders of the Goorji party and abuse them. In order to prevent the escape of the ringleaders of this society, Joseph Goorji petitioned the Wali Pasha to imprison these people. This was done by the order of the Pasha with the help of the local municipality and police. Moses Ṣadḳah Sofer was also suspected of writing and sticking the handbills. Now a new trouble arose in searching for the writer or reporter of the discriminating reports and letters about this regrettable affair in the Calcutta newspaper *Paerah*. A man Ezekiel b. Ḥakham 'Abdallah Ḥanein, was suspected of being the author of these much disliked newspaper articles. He would have fared badly, in spite of his claim that he had been suffering for more than six months from illness, had he not been a British subject, which fact entitled him to escape the jurisdiction of the Turkish court. His case was put before the British Consul, who naturally tried to look impartially on this case. The opposition against the Ḥakham Bashi grew from day to day. Unfavourable rumours were spread about his manipulations of money sent to him from various sources in India and Europe for charitable purposes. It is difficult to say whether these rumours were correct or false. Anyhow they must have changed the minds of even the most eager of his friends and supporters, such as Ḥakham 'Abdallah Sokmeh, and assured the victory for Joseph Goorji's plans. In short, now almost the majority of the community agreed to the removal of the Ḥakham Bashi. This news made a very bad impression, so that a man who signs himself "Lover of Truth" (Oheb Emeth), in Calcutta, protested against such awful calumnies spread against such a saintly man as Elisha Dangoor. Another correspondent in Calcutta, Rephael Moses Toledano, reveals the fact that the opposition of the Goorjis against Dangoor was due to the Ḥakham's reluctance to further the selfish and private interests of Goorji and his party. Goorji left nothing unturned, pursuing his one aim to remove the Ḥakham Bashi from his office. This narrative cannot give all the details of the protracted transactions and meetings which took place at this stage of the affair, owing to their ambiguous character, yet it has to be pointed out that Goorji and his party did their utmost to make the position of the Ḥakham Bashi intolerable. Many considerate writers deplore the humiliation brought about by these events upon the venerable and generally revered spiritual leader Ḥakham 'Abdallah Somekh, owing to the conduct and ways of Joseph Goorji. Finally the better nature of the latter prevailed, and on the Day of Atonement of the year 1884, he asked Ḥakham 'Abdallah Somekh's pardon. This was granted under the condition that Goorji would make his peace with the Ḥakham Bashi.

As soon as peace was concluded another unfortunate incident disturbed the harmony. Apparently many of Goorji's partisans were not pleased with their leader's peaceful move. They eagerly waited for the least opportunity to kindle the strife of fire anew. The occasion was offered by the charitable activities of some members of the community who endeavoured to establish a society to provide medicine free of charge to the poor in Baghdad. This medicine had to be procured and brought from European countries. By collections, and thanks to a large contribution from the heads of the community, such a society was finally founded. A house serving as a dispensary was built next to the school for this purpose. The leaders of the community claimed that the whole building should be registered as communal property; otherwise the charitable work of this committee would be discontinued.

Further reports furnish us with some new details about the development arising out of the Ḥakham Bashi affair. Goorji still kept his faith in the future of Ḥakham Smooḥa and agitated accordingly in Constantinople. But when he saw that his protégé had no hope of being reinstated in his office, he induced an acquaintance of his, a certain Rabbi Israel b. Shalom, to come to Baghdad and occupy the post of Ḥakham Bashi. This man actually accepted this invitation and travelled to Baghdad, but death overtook him when he reached 'Ana. Afterwards a famous and worthy scholar of Aleppo, Abraham b. Raphael Ḥamwi, an author of several treatises, proficient in four languages spoken in the East, visited Baghdad, and was entreated to occupy the vacant seat of the Ḥakham Bashi. He preached several times, was well connected in Jewish as well as in non-Jewish circles, and was generally revered and highly esteemed, so that he appeared to be the right man for the post. For some reason he refused to accept the dignity conferred on him. Then on the advice of Ḥakham 'Abdallah a list of five candidates was put forward out of whom the Ḥakham Bashi should be chosen.

Ḥakham Elisha Dangoor still remained in office, and in this capacity he expressed the feeling of great mourning caused among the Jews of Baghdad by the death of Sir Moses Montefiore.[1] He died on Saturday, 27th Adar, 1895.[2] His rival,

[1] *Ḥabazeleth*, Jerusalem, 1885, Elul.
[2] *Maggid Mesharim*, VI, No. 24, Calcutta, 24th April, 1895.

Smooḥa, lived another fifteen years, and died in 1911. Ḥakham Elisha's successor as Ḥakham Bashi was R. Isaac Shoḥeṭ, who occupied the post for seven and-a-half years, till 1905, when he was removed. Then David Papu was brought to Baghdad in 1906, and officiated till 1912, when his predecessor's fate overtook him. He was succeeded by R. Yeruham Elyashar, who left Baghdad for Jerusalem when the British entered the city. Then followed R. Moses Shammash for six years, till he died at the age of ninety. With the Dayyanim, Ḥakhamim and notables of Baghdad, he signed the regulations of marriage customs, dated 12th of Iyyar, 1921, as "Wakil Ḥakham Bashi Baghdad wa-Rayyis el-Ruḥani". The last bearer of this title was Ezra Reuben Dangoor (died 13th January, 1930).[1]

[1] *The Jewish Chronicle*, 14th February, 1930; the *Jewish World*, 13th February, 1930.

NEW SYNAGOGUE, BAGHDAD

It is to be noted that the space between the sides and the centre of the Synagogue is not covered.

[*Facing page* 165

CHAPTER XXVIII

SYNAGOGUES, SCHOOLS AND CHARITIES

THE number of synagogues in Baghdad impress all visitors. Benjamin of Tudela, Petachia of Ratisbon and other travellers do not omit to mention this. At the present day the Baghdad Jews have altogether about twenty-six synagogues for divine worship. Some of them are large and go back many centuries, others are smaller and of a more recent date. In order to do justice to this feature of the history of the Jews in Baghdad, a description of the present synagogues must be the starting point.

The most important among these places of worship is the Great Synagogue, called Ṣlat li-Kbiri.[1] This is in size and in origin the most important of the Baghdadian synagogues. According to tradition it is situated on the very spot where the last king of Judah who was exiled to Babylon, King Jehoiachin, erected a small sanctuary with materials brought by the exiles from the Holy Land.[2] In the course of this history we hear of rebuildings of this synagogue during the seventeenth and eighteenth centuries. The last renovation took place in the year 1854-55. The expenses were defrayed by the well-known benefactor of Baghdadian institutions, Manasseh b. Ezekiel. A word or two may be added here about the structure of this synagogue, which may serve as a commentary to the illustration. The synagogue is square. It looks like the courtyard of a Baghdadian mansion.

[1] Where the letter "r" does not stand next to the letter "g" the Jews of Baghdad pronounce it as if it were "gh", for instance, li-Kbiri is pronounced li-Kbighi, but Grab is pronounced by them Ghrab, and not Gghghab.
[2] cf. the letter of Solomon Bekhor Ḥuṣein in ha-Lebanon, Paris, V (1868), No. 49, pp. 782-4.

It is divided into Hekhaloth, i.e. twenty-seven divisions, with sitting accommodation consisting of masonry divans covered with carpets. These are situated on three sides of each Ḥakhal, leaving the fourth side open. The Hekaloth are divided as follows: fourteen of them are under vaulted archways along the walls; the remaining twelve are around the Tebah on three sides. The Tebah stands in the centre of the synagogue and is covered by a roof which extends only over the adjoining twelve Hekhaloth. Consequently the space between the Hekhaloth along the walls and those around the Tebah is open. The chief Hekhal, which is the centre one on the western wall, has accommodation for the Holy Scrolls. Here was the seat of honour reserved for the Nasi, Sheikh Sason and his descendants. Probably other Nesiim and their families shared the same privilege. The Ḥakhamim sit on the Tebah. One of the pillars of the Tebah shows on the photograph a small box, which serves as a receptacle for the 'Erub of the city. Seating accommodation for women is provided over the Hekhaloth in galleries behind lattice-work of wood. In case the women's gallery is too crowded, some of them repair to the roof, where they listen to the service. For the use of the roof for such purpose there is a Talmudic reminiscence, when Samuel and his disciple Rab Judah were taking part in a service on the roof of the ancient synagogue of Shaf we-Yathib in Neharde'a.[1] The Great Synagogue is richly endowed with Holy Scrolls. In 1910, there were more than seventy. Some of them are enclosed in beautiful cases of gold and silver; others in cases covered with velvet. These cases retain their old Mishnaic names Tiḳ. These Tiḳs are provided with inscriptions commemorating the names of the donors and their parents in whose memory they were dedicated. There is a special regulation as to the seasons and preferences to be given to individual Scrolls. In the middle of the last century, in the time of Ḥakham Elisha Ṇissim, the use of the Holy Scrolls

[1] Niddah, 13a.

on special days caused some trouble and led to new regulations. There is no Ner Tamid (Perpetual Lamp) in any of the Baghdad synagogues, but in this synagogue there are suspended glass vessels, called Ṭiriyyat, hanging on chains which contain lamps kindled in memory of the deceased by their relatives.

Near the chief entrance to the synagogue there is a small stone in the wall with the inscription Eben me-Eres Yisrael (a stone from the Land of Israel), which is touched with the fingers and kissed at entering and leaving the synagogue. This stone was brought by Ḥakham Joseph Ḥayyim when he returned from Palestine, in the year 1868. On the same occasion he brought several sacks of Palestinian earth, which were spread on the floor of the synagogue. I found in this synagogue a Parokheth (curtain) of quite extraordinary size. On it are painted the plans of the division of the Holy Land, and of the Holy Temple according to the description of the Prophet Ezekiel. The painter and writer was Ḥakham Sason Mordecai Shindookh of whom more has been said in a previous chapter. It was customary to exhibit it yearly on the day of the Rejoicing of the Law. Adjoining the Great Synagogue there is a large courtyard which is used as a summer synagogue for Divine worship during the hot season. This synagogue is styled by the Baghdadians Ṣlat Berraniyyi li-Kbiri (Outer Synagogue of the Great). This division of the synagogue into a winter and summer place of worship was known to the Babylonian Jews of the Talmudic period.[1]

Another synagogue is the Ṣlat Zghayri (Small Synagogue). This place of Divine worship is also of great antiquity, although no details of origin and history are preserved. Here a fifteenth century Pentateuch (now MS. Sassoon 916) written by Jacob ha-Sofer b. Moses ha-Sofer on behalf of Don Abraham b. Joseph ibn Krispin in the year 1487, was kept and used on the occasions of Berith Milah, placing it on the Chair

[1] Bab Bath. 3b, Rashi, s.v. בסיתווא.

of Elijah. It may be mentioned here in passing that a similar MS. of the same age (now MS. Sassoon 199) was used for the same purpose in the Great Synagogue. This synagogue too, provides for services to be held in the summer in the open.

Next I mention the New Synagogue (Ṣlat li-Jdidi). It is called by this name owing to its comparatively recent date. According to information gathered from a poem composed by Ḥakham Nissim, the son of Ḥakham Ṣaleh Maṣliyyaḥ, I gather that it was rebuilt and reopened in the month of Iyyar, 1797. The poet names Sason the Nasi, 'Abdallah b. Joseph, and Joseph Nissim b. Sliman as the principal benefactors who contributed towards the restoration of this ancient house of prayer by their munificence and piety. It is interesting that the rhymester gratefully mentions Suleiman Pasha, the Wali of Baghdad, for graciously permitting them to rebuild their synagogue.

I pass on now to synagogues named after certain founders or benefactors. Hereto belong: (1) Midrash Abu Mnashshi, built about 1839 by Ezekiel b. Reuben b. Manasseh; (2) Midrash Bet Zilkhah, called after Zilkhah, the wife of Ezra ha-Kohen, on whose property the synagogue and Midrash were erected; (3) Midrash Jacob Ṣemaḥ, originally a Talmudic college, now a synagogue; erected with the money left by Jacob Ṣemaḥ of Bombay to the charities of his native place, Baghdad; (4) Midrash Ḥakham Shim'on, called after Simeon, the son of Ḥakham Sason Mordecai Shindookh, about 1854; (5) Ṣlat Ḥakham Ḥazkel (Ezekiel b. Solomon b. David, the father of the first Jewish member of the Turkish Parliament, Sason, who represented Baghdad, and is now a member of the Government of Irak); (6) Ṣlat Sheikh Yiṣḥak, in memory of Isaac Gaon, whose tomb is close to it; (7) Ṣlat Bet Ghawi, named after the family of Ghawi; (8) Midrash Reuben Hazkel Yehuda; (9) Ṣlat Bet Daniel, given by a member of the well-known Daniel family; (10) Ṣlat Bet Barukh Karkukli, which has, however, not the appearance of a synagogue owing to the fact that the founder could not obtain permission from the government of Sultan 'Abd el-Ḥamid II in Constantinople; (11) Ṣlat Farḥah bint el-Dabbi; (12) Ṣlat Reuben Shukur Isaac; (13) Ṣlat Moshi Sofer; (14) Ṣlat Shaul Yosef Moshi; (15) Ṣlat Dinah, called after Dinah, the daughter of Reuben Nissim and the wife of Elijah, the son of Moses Joseph Ezra Goorji, who died without issue. The expenses of erection of this synagogue were defrayed out of the proceeds of her jewellery, and built at the approach to the desert; (16) Ṣlat Farḥah also called after its beadle, Malkah, where the old liturgy of the 'Akedath Yisḥaḳ described further on, is still in vogue on the eve of the second day of New Year; (17) Ṣlat Reemah; (18) Ṣlat Yisḥaḳ Shalom Obadiah; (19) Ṣlat Bet Mkammal; (20) Ṣlat Bet el-Masri; (21) Ṣlat 'Ajmiyyee; (22) Ṣlat Moshi ibn Dahhan, and (23) Ṣlat Na'sa.[1] Besides the name Ṣlat, which means place of prayer, the Baghdadians designate their synagogue also by the name Kodesh, i.e. sanctuary. Some of the synagogues are known by the name Midrash, a designation for the more usual Beth ha-Midrash among European Jews. Most of the colleges have likewise places of worship. They may, therefore, rightly be included among the synagogues.

A few words should be said here about the history of the Ṣlat Sheikh Yiṣḥaḳ mentioned in the preceding list of synagogues. According to an ancient tradition one of the earliest Geonim, Rab Isaac Gaon, who is called by the Jews of Baghdad up to the present day Sheikh Yiṣḥaḳ Gaon, and by the Moslems, Sheikh Iṣḥaḳ Ṣarraf 'Ali, lived and died in Baghdad. The present epitaph which was composed about 1860 by the Baghdadian poet and scholar, 'Abdallah b. Khḍeir, bears the date of the Gaon's death as having occurred in the year 688 C.E. The shrine of this Gaon is a place of

[1] For such lists of synagogues in Baghdad and surroundings, see *Paerah* Calcutta (1882), No. 33; ibid., vol. 10 (1887), No. 22; *Maggid Mesharim* Calcutta, 7 (1896), No. 40; *Shoshannah*, Calcutta (1901), No. 19, where some of the synagogues are named after persons who are not known to me from other sources; v. also the reference to the *Lebanon* quoted previously in footnote No. 2 on p. 165.

pilgrimage for Jews and Moslems alike. The Yeshibah situated in close proximity of the shrine is called Ṣlat Sheikh Yiṣḥaḳ Gaon. The members of this college, who are all poor and unfortunate cripples, recite there Psalms, Idras and Zohar the whole day, for which they receive their sustenance from the local communal authorities. People in bereavement mourning the death of some near relative gather at this place of worship for prayers. On such an occasion food is provided for the poor members of this synagogue. Less mournful are the Friday afternoon gatherings which take place here. It is customary that unmarried Jewish women repair to this shrine and pray to their patron saint for a good husband. This patron is called by them Sheikh Yiṣḥaḳ Abu el-Bnat. The Gaon shares this distinction of figuring as a local saint with an earlier authority of the Tannaitic period, R. Jose the Galilean, whose alleged resting place is identified with the tomb of 'Abd el-Ḳader el-Jilani in Baghdad, similarly a place of worship and pilgrimage, but not for Jews.[1] One may recall in connection with this tradition the outburst of an old Karaite writer, who reproaches the Rabbanites by saying: "How could I keep quiet when idolatry is spreading in Israel? They are sitting on the graves, spending nights in caves, inquiring of the dead, and shouting 'Ya R. Jose ha-Galili, heal me and bless me with child!' They light candles on the graves of the pious, burn incense before them and tie knots on the date tree of the saint", etc.[2] It is not impossible that the Baghdadian tradition and the Karaite report have more than one point in common. Of course the selection of R. Jose ha-Galili for invocation by suffering and distressed people may have been influenced by a certain passage in an earlier source.[3]

A report issued by the "Jewish Schools Committee on the Jewish Schools in Baghdad", 1930, throws light on the present-

[1] I. Yahuda, *Doar Hayyom*, Elul, 17, 5681.
[2] S. Pinsker, *Likkute Kadmoniyyoth*, Vienna, 1860, pt. 2, p. 32.
[3] *Yer. Berakoth*, ch. V., Hal. 2.

day educational institutions in Baghdad. There are ten educational establishments, some of them going back to the early nineteenth century, others are of a more recent date, 1928. The oldest is the Midrash Talmud Torah, founded in 1833, with twenty-seven classes and 2,049 students. This institution is essentially a school for religious instruction with elementary teaching in Arabic. Next to this is the David Sassoon school which was handed over by his son Sir Albert Sassoon to the Alliance Israelite Universelle in the year 1874, having been founded in 1865.

This transference aroused some opposition by 'Akiba Joseph Schlesinger of Jerusalem, who protested against the interference in educational matters on the part of the Alliance. This school now contains 475 boys. Here are twelve classes, and in addition to Hebrew and Arabic, French and English are taught. The teaching in French includes arithmetic, algebra, geometry, geography, history, science, object lessons, Jewish history and literature, while Hebrew is limited to language, moral and religious studies. This school is provided with a library of French and English books. A report of an examination held in the year 1872, is printed in a letter from the director of the institution, M. Max, addressed to the central committee in Paris.[1] A similar school for girls was established by Sir Eliezer S. Kadoorie of Hong Kong and Shanghai, bearing the name of the donor's wife, Laura Kadoorie. In this institution 1,177 girls receive tuition in the subjects mentioned in connection with the other Alliance school. Other girls' schools are the Haron Ṣaleḥ, and Gan Manehem Daniel, known as Gan Yeladim (Kindergarten), with 649 and 325 girls respectively. The first was founded in 1902, the second in 1910. Of more recent dates are the boys' schools: Raḥel Shaḥmoon, Wataniyyah, Kerem and Shammash, with several hundred pupils. The latter group follows the government syllabus, with the exception of the Shammash School, which is entirely

[1] See *Zikhronoth min Ḥebrath Kol Yisrael Ḥaberim*, 1871-72, Paris.

English. Altogether these ten schools provide education for 7,182 boys and girls, out of which there are only 2,595 paying pupils; the rest enjoy free instruction. The curriculum of the Talmud Torah consists of Bible studies and selected passages from anthologies, Ḥoḳ le-Yisrael and Leḳaḥ Ṭob. All subjects are taught in Arabic. Besides these elementary schools there are colleges for advanced studies of different grades, and colleges for adult education. Finally, the Atelier Ezra Sassoon, where girls are taught needlework, and Midrash Nuriel for boys, which was founded by Rebecca Nuriel, have to be mentioned.

With the rapid changes that are taking place in the method of teaching, it might not be out of place to record here the quaint manner in which the alphabet was taught to the young. This was the way of picturing each letter.

אבו ארבעה רוס א	That which has four heads—*Alef.*
ראזונה ב	A Window—*Be.*
אבו גנח ג	That which has a wing—*Gimal.*
נגר ד	A hatchet—*Dal.*
רגלהא מקטועה ה	She that has her leg cut off—*He.*
אברי ו	A needle—*Waw.*
דנבוס ז	A pin—*Zan.*
אם רגלתין צאג ח	She that has both her legs sound—*Ḅeth.*
רגלהא בבטנהא ט	She that has her leg in her inside—*Ṭeth.*
אכתך אל זגירה י	Your younger sister—*Yod.*
ראזונה מדוורה כ	A round window—*Kaf.*
אל גמל ל	The camel—*Lamad.*
ראסהא זביבאיי מ	She whose head is a raisin—*Mim.*
נגנאל נ	A hook—*Noon.*
מדוור ס	A circle—*Simmakh.*

אבו ראסין ע	That which has two heads—*An.*
בתמהא זביבאיי פ	She that has a raisin in her mouth —*Peh.*
ראסין ומחני צ	Two heads and is bent—*Ṣad.*
רנלהו טוילי ק	He that has a long leg.—*Ḳof.*
מגרוך ר	That which is curved—*Rosh.*
אבו תלת רוס ש	He that has three heads—*Shin.*
רנלהא מערונה ת	She that has a crooked leg—*Ta.*
אלף לאם סלאם ﻻ	The joined letters *Alef* and *Lamad*—goodbye!

There was a society for promoting religious life in Baghdad. The name of the society was Shomre Miṣwah, established in the summer of 1868. The statutes of this society throw light on the aims of the founders as well as on the religious conditions prevailing among the Baghdad Jews in that period. They aim first of all at improving the education, especially that of the poor. This should be achieved by better organization, by appointing God-fearing and learned teachers, by proper supervision, examination of students in due season, encouragement by prizes and advancement of successful pupils and by rebuke to the lazy ones. Presents have to be allotted to successful teachers. Secondly, the founders intended to organize the different charities in the city and unite and co-ordinate them. The wealthy members of the community had to be appealed to on behalf of the poor who would rather suffer than partake of public charity. Order had to be introduced into the administration of charities and synagogues. Trustworthy men should be chosen for the management of charitable and communal affairs. Their work had to be discharged with the utmost care and circumspection. Their endeavour would extend to providing male and female orphans and poor children with their needs in case of marriage. Charity was not limited to the local poor, but included strangers and travellers from afar, especially the poor of the Holy Land. In order to improve piety and religious life, scholarly and devout men were elected and selected to visit the synagogues and examine the fringes and phylacteries at least once a year. Once in three years they should examine the little scrolls encased and fixed on the doorposts—Mezuzoth. Their supervision and inspection included the tabernacles, the ritual baths, the baking of the Passover cakes, the cutting of wheat for the same purpose, and finally the supervision over the cheese-makers. Particular care had to be taken in assessing different taxes. All guilds of artisans had to elect trustworthy men for the assessment of taxes. The collection should be done by reliable and God-fearing men who should not be paid for their work. Members of the community were appointed for the festivals in order to watch public gardens, orchards and the banks of the river, that people should not gather there for food, drink and merriment, which might lead to sin. The leaders of the community were instructed to look after the work of the communal servants so that they should discharge their duties in the right way. The membership of this society could be gained either by application for it or by recommendation through an elected member. The members undertook to pay a yearly contribution. Gifts, in money as well as in kind, e.g. books, Tefillin, etc., were accepted. The annual meeting was held on the 26th of Elul. The officers were elected by lots. Only respectable, trustworthy, observant and God-fearing men who truly loved their people, could be elected for office. Their number was not to be less than seven or more than ten. Two or three of the most worthy of them were to be leaders of the committee, who in turn were to allot the presidency to the worthiest among themselves. Certain privileges and powers were placed in the hands of the president, for which he had to discharge such very important duties as the supervision of the society and its members. The society had a treasurer as well as a secretary who discharged special functions.[1]

[1] The material about this society is derived from the statute dated 26th Elul, 1868, and signed by the founders, e.g. Sason b. Ezekiel Reuben

A few words will suffice for the charitable institutions in Baghdad. There is a society for the upkeep of a Jewish hospital, known as Ḥebrath Meyassede Beth ha-Refuah, which is connected with the hospitals called after Meir Eliyyahoo, and Reemah Khḍoory. The income of this society was in 1925-26 about 80,000 Rupees. This income was derived from various sources, such as voluntary contributions from local members on one side, and Baghdadians in India, etc., on the other. The expenses amounted to about 66,000 Rupees. Independent from the hospital is the already mentioned society which provides medicine for the poor members of the community. It is called Ajzakhana (dispensary). A society for providing relief for the Jewish poor exists under the name 'Ozere Dallim. During the Great War[1] this committee was "authorized and controlled by His Britannic Majesty's Government". According to a report of the year 1925-26, the income of the committee was about 20,000 Rupees, expenditure about 17,000 Rupees. There is also a society called Zekhuth ha-Rabbim, and another named Hebrath Tomkhe Tora. The aim of the former is the care of the blind; the latter supports poor scholars so that they may be enabled to devote all their time to study.

Manasseh, president, David b. Ezekiel Khḍoory, treasurer, Solomon b. Joshua David Bekhor Ṣadḳah Ḥuṣein, vice-president, and others. A full report about the activities of this society is given in a letter from Baghdad, published in the Lebanon, VI (1869), No. 11 ff.

[1] [1914-1918.]

CHAPTER XXIX

THE LITURGY OF THE BAGHDAD JEWS

THE liturgy used by the Jews of Baghdad shows so many peculiarities that it fully deserves a special chapter in this monograph. The lost prayer book of Ibn el-Jasus, who lived before the time of Maimonides, might have offered valuable material for this chapter.[1] We have seen further that before and during the Geonate of Hai b. David the Baghdadian liturgy differed from all other rites in so far as they recited a composition of the 'Abodah, not only in the additional service of the Day of Atonement but also during the morning service.[2] It was further pointed out that there are striking parallels between the Baghdad ritual on the one side and the Minhagh of Yemen on the other.[3] These parallels are most remarkable in the additional pieces inserted into the Passover Haggadah which are characteristic of the Yemenite Haggadah and of the rite of Aleppo as well. Further, some liturgical pieces in the prayers for Dew and Rain are unique in the Baghdadian and Aleppo rites. I availed myself of a tradition current among the Jews of Baghdad that this insertion beginning with the word Midkar 'Abdekhon Kodamekhon was copied by Ḥakham Sason from the Aleppo rite, and was introduced into the Baghdad rite. Now, however, I learn from an old Persian prayer book written in the year 1599, that this liturgical piece was in use among the Persian Jews. It would lead us too far to ventilate the question whether this prayer book, although written in Persia, does not originally represent the old rite of Geonic

[1] See above, p. 14.
[2] See above, p. 11.
[3] See my article "Boi Teman", in *Hazofeh*, vol. VIII (1924), pp. 307-316, especially p. 314 f.

Baghdad. The investigation, in case this question should or could be answered in the affirmative, will be extended to the interdependence of the rites of Aleppo and Yemen respectively on the Minhag of old Baghdad. Here it must suffice to draw attention to these parallels. Unique are the rituals which are to be found in Baghdad in connection with the prayers used by members of a certain synagogue there for the second night of the New Year, called 'Aḳedath Yiṣḥaḳ,[1] and the special liturgical compositions in vogue among the Baghdadian pilgrims to the Tombs of Ezekiel the Prophet in Kifil, Joshua the High Priest in Baghdad, and Ezra the Scribe at el-Ozeir.[2]

Here reference may be made to the local Purims—first of all the Nes Tahmasp, which is celebrated on the eleventh of Ab and sixteenth of Tebeth, on which days Tahanun is omitted. These days are in memory of the relief of the city of Baghdad in the years 1638 and 1733 respectively. These two dates commemorate memorable episodes in the history of Baghdad. The first event took place in the year 1638 when Shah' Abbas II held sway over the city and country. The population suffered a great deal under Persian rule. Thanks to a Jewish inhabitant of Baghdad who evinced great courage in carrying a confidential letter from the Baghdadians to the Sultan of Turkey, the city was relieved of the Persian rule. Tradition tells that the Jew disguised himself as a Moslem and appeared before Sultan Murad IV. When he entered the Diwan the Viziers rose before him and the king accorded him a very friendly reception. Then the messenger disclosed his Jewish origin, and handed the letter to the Sultan. On reading it, the Sultan became very angry, and made up his mind to collect an army and march on Baghdad. He entered the city first in the disguise of a dervish, then publicly at the

[1] This liturgy was printed for the first time in 5691 (1931), in Baghdad by Elisha Shoḥeṭ, under the title *Seder 'Aḳedath Yiṣḥaḳ*. Up to this time the order of service used was in manuscript.

[2] See above, p. 150.

head of his troops by the Bab el-Ṭilsam, and broke the power of the Persian Shahs. This delivery of the city of Baghdad is commemorated up to this day in a ballad sung at weddings. The second Purim celebrates the victory of the army sent by Sultan Maḥmud against Shah Tehmasp, king of Persia in the year 1733, when Baghdad was again under the power of the Persians. More recently Ḥakham Ezra Dangoor instituted a Purim for the 17th of Adar, commemorating the entry of the armies of Great Britain into Baghdad on the 11th March, 1917.

The present day Baghdad ritual, apart from the peculiarities just pointed out, is under the influence of the Spanish rite. Owing to the predilection for Kabbalistic studies in Baghdad, it is not surprising that Kabbalistic authors exercised their influence and that Kabbalistic additions have been inserted. As such the Pethihath Eliahoo and various Tikkunim may be pointed out. Some liturgical compositions like those for the 15th of Shebat give evidence of liturgical activities among local poets in Baghdad. This occupation of many Baghdadian scholars with poetry is amply evidenced by the numerous poems and poets of Baghdadian origin represented in the liturgical and poetical collections extant in manuscripts and in printed or lithographed works. Some of these poets were already mentioned on previous occasions, such as Sliman b. David Ma'tuḳ, Ṣaleḥ Maṣliaḥ, Nissim b. Ṣaleḥ Maṣliaḥ, Joseph Ḥayyim and others. It is noteworthy that the Haftaroth for sections Shemoth and Bo differ from the usual rites, and especially printed little booklets in Baghdad and Bombay supply the needs of readers in this respect. The Haftarah for Shemoth is Ezekiel, Ch. XVI, 1-13, and for Bo, Isaiah, Ch. XVIII, v. 7, to the end of Ch. XIX. These booklets contain other peculiarities of the Baghdad rite.[1] First of all, in one of them

[1] There are several prints containing these Haftaroth with a lectionary for the Sabbaths of the year from the *Prophets and the Hagiographa and Mishnah*, referred to in the text. They are Baghdad prints without indication of place and year, with the exception of the booklet under the title *Simane Pisḳe Nebiim wu-Khethubim*, Baghdad, 1930, Elisha Shohet.

are added the verses from the Prophet Isaiah which are read when the bridegroom takes part in the service on the Sabbath after his wedding. Secondly, the Baghdad rite has a special lectionary for the Sabbaths from the Prophets, Hagiographa and the Mishnah. For instance, on the first Sabbath of the year they read Joshua, Chaps. I-XI, Psalms, Chaps. I-XI, and Tractate Ḥaghigha. In this connection it may be pointed out that the Baghdad liturgy, like other rites, for instance that of Maghreb, knows no Haftarah for the afternoon reading on the 9th of Ab. It is true that a late print of 1905 has the remark that *some* are accustomed to read the Haftarah Shubah (Hosea, XIV, 2 ff.). It is interesting to notice that there is a coincidence in this point between the North African and the Baghdadian rites. The former may be based on the Sefaradi custom, while the Baghdad liturgy may have preserved the Talmudic or Geonic rule. The Baghdadian ritual on many occasions uses Arabic translations of liturgical pieces, called Sharḥ. Such are the Arabic translations of the Passover Haggadah, and further the Arabic translation of the Aramaic paraphrase of the Canticles, the Arabic translation of the Haftarah for the morning service on the 9th of Ab, and the Arabic translation of Judah ha-Levy's well-known poem for Sabbath Zakhor beginning Mi Khamokhah, of which, however, only the last section, Ikhloo Re'im, is read in Arabic as well as in Hebrew. Baghdad printers provided the community with special booklets of these translations. Here may be mentioned the collection of poems under the name of Sefer Pizmonim, printed in Baghdad, which furnish songs and hymns for various days including weddings, festivities and special occasions.

Finally, some peculiarities of the Baghdad ritual shall conclude this chapter. In Baghdad, at the conclusion of the morning service ('Amidah), whether on Sabbath or week days, the Kohanim pronounce the prescribed blessing (Numbers VI, 24-27). On New Moon days and on festivals when the short,

THE GRAVE OF JOSHUA THE HIGH PRIEST OF BAGHDAD

[Facing page 180

Hallel is read, the Baghdadians omit the usual benediction. Similarly the benedictions to be said before and after the reading of the Scroll of Esther are not customary at the reading of the Meghillah on the second day of Purim, which is observed by the Jews of Baghdad. Five elegies in memory of the destruction of the Second Temple are recited one at a time between the afternoon and evening service on the first days of Ab, as from the 1st to the 9th of Ab, excepting Fridays, Saturdays and the eve of the Fast. A little booklet printed in Calcutta in 1889, contains this order of service under the title Seder ha-Ḳinoth Shesimanam Nebiah. In the afternoon of Shemini Asereth the whole Pentateuch is read by the congregation.

CATAFALQ OF EZEKIEL THE PROPHET AT EL-KIFIL

For the wording of the inscriptions on the walls see Ohel Dawid, pp. 568–9. The cover over the tomb is seen here rolled up over one corner to show underlying writings.

[*Facing page* 181

CHAPTER XXX

CUSTOMS AND USAGES

JUST as the liturgical rites of Baghdad have shown many differences from other rites, so have the customs of the Baghdad Jews generally shown their own differences. Their religious rites up to this day preserve the custom of redeeming the first-born of the ass (Pidyon Peṭer Ḥamor.)[1] This ceremony is celebrated with great festivities. The owner arranges a big banquet to which relatives and friends are invited. Such invitations are announced in the synagogues, and in more recent days issued in print. In one such printed invitation in my possession, Moses, of the family of Ṣadḳah Ḥuṣein, invites a friend of his to such a celebration. Among the Baghdadians it is customary on the Passover nights for the father to ask his son some questions as to whence he came, his destination and his provisions for the journey, in order that the child should take an interest in the Passover celebration. Mention has already been made of the fact that the Scrolls of the Law are kept in cases (Tiḳ) as in the time of the Talmud, and bear the donor's name and dedication. The Baghdad Jews make pilgrimage on special days of the year to the graves of the pious and the saints buried around Baghdad. Every New Moon day one may see crowds of people going to the grave of Joshua the High Priest. The Tombs of Ezekiel the Prophet in Kifil and of Ezra the Scribe, respectively, are visited by large numbers of people on Pentecost. The anniversaries of the death of famous sages like R. 'Aḳiba and his disciples, R. Meir or R. Simeon b. Yoḥai, are kept and celebrated. Invitations are issued to these celebrations.

Usages connected with births, weddings and deaths are too

[1] Based on Exodus, XIII, 13.

numerous to be detailed here in full. Some of them, which are of special interest from the point of view of the social, economic, religious and intellectual conditions of the Baghdad Jews, may be pointed out in this chapter. Childbirth is still connected with many superstitious fears and protections. The general belief that mother and child have to be protected from demons and evil spirits is still prevalent. Many magic rites are performed. I mention first of all the rite connected with the custom, called "Shashshah". Some of these rites remind us of prescriptions familiar to the reader of the Talmud, which naturally suggest that the present day Baghdadians kept these beliefs and rites since hoary antiquity. Thus, hanging some of these apotropaic articles by the bedside of the child or mother, or tying them to the head of the mother and the child, are to be found in Jewish as well as in general folklore. Of interest is the superstition called "Dusan el'Atbah", i.e. the stepping over the threshold. It is believed that for the first forty days after childbirth demons and spirits are particularly dangerous. Therefore it is not allowed to visit two places where childbirth occurred, without breaking the journey before entering one of them. This is called "Stepping over the Threshold", which means that the person has to step on the threshold of the half-way house. Next in importance are the nights of the sixth day and the evening before the eighth day. The first is called "Leilt el-Sitti" and the other "Leilt 'Aḳd el Yas". During these nights the child must be borne on the lap and must not be in the cradle. A ceremony with saffron and water is performed on the night of the sixth. All the little boys of the neighbourhood approach the house with pieces of water melon peels or potsherd in their hands, over which the prepared liquid is poured out, whereupon the boys repeatedly shout the word "Shashshah", casting away their peels or earthenware. When returning they are rewarded with sweets or roasted water melon seeds. The ceremony is called "Shashshah". The birth of boys is more favoured than that of girls. The name of the latter is pronounced by the midwife on the Shashshah night. The congratulation accorded at the naming of the girl is Mazzal Ṭob, while at the birth of the boy the bilingual greeting Siman Ṭob Wuḳadum el-Khair (i.e. a good sign and the forerunner of bounty) is uttered.

The festivities connected with the circumcision require a fuller description. On the evening preceding the eighth day the Chair of Elijah the Prophet is removed from its place in the synagogue and brought to the house of childbirth. Here a Pentateuch[1] is placed on it and covered with rich brocade, and decorated with flowers and with twigs of fresh myrtle and rue. A pair of bells from the Scroll of the Law is also fixed to the chair. The Baghdadians give a popular explanation for the use of myrtle on this occasion by identifying the name of the Prophet Khiḍr Elyas, and the Arabic name for myrtle, el-Yas. However ingenious this etymology is, we know that the use of myrtle in burial, wedding, and birth ceremonies goes back to Talmudic times and serves the purpose of protecting from demoniac powers. The father of the child prepares a feast on this night, at which Hebrew and Arabic songs are sung. It may be mentioned here that there are special singers called "Mezammerim" belonging to the M'aṭoo family who for many generations past entertained the guests on such and similar occasions with their musical and artistic performances. In the morning the father of the child attends service in the synagogue, where the child is brought by the mother, who is accompanied by another lady. The special service for this occasion with a number of rules and customs may be found in the booklet "Ṣorkhe Ḥuppah wu-Milah", Baghdad, 1892.

We turn now to the wedding ceremonies of the Baghdadians. In olden days marriages took place between girls of nine years and boys of fifteen. The Rabbis found it necessary to abolish

[1] See above, p. 167.

this abuse and ordered that no marriage ceremony should be performed unless the bride reached the age of thirteen. The interval between the betrothal (Erusin) and actual marriage (Nissuin) is sometimes a very long one. According to the Baghdadian custom, the former has the character of actual marriage (Ḳiddushin) and in case of default ritual divorce is necessary. The expenses for the wedding festivities are defrayed by the father of the bridegroom. Some expenses, however, are incurred by the father of the bride. They became so heavy and unbearable that the spiritual and lay leaders of the community had to abolish gifts and presents customary on these occasions. The bride's father used to supply his son-in-law for the first year after the wedding with presents of various kinds, on Hanukkah and Purim, travelling expenses to the Tomb of Ezekiel the Prophet, called "Ziyarah", outfit for the first-born son (Ḥwas Walad el-Bekhor), and the festivities arranged at the first visit of the newly-married couple, which takes place on a Sabbath about twenty to thirty days after the wedding ceremony which is called "Fatḥ el-Wujh", i.e. uncovering the face. There is a custom called "Hleehel". The women in the galleries call out "Kili-lili-lili-lili . . ." when the bridegroom is called up to read the lesson in the synagogue on the Sabbath before and after his wedding. On the same occasion pistachio nut dragées are thrown at the bridegroom. Special attention is paid by the Jews of Baghdad to the ceremonies on the "Leilt el-Ḥinni" or "Leilt el-Khaḍbah". The ceremony takes place on the eve of the wedding. The bridegroom sends some Henna, sweets, gloves, wax candles and shoes to the house of the bride where the nails of the bridal couple and those of the Shushbin, male and female, the latter being called Shbinnimat, are painted, in order to protect them from the evil power of the demon. It may be mentioned by the way, that this custom is also at home among the Jews of North Africa. In a French wedding invitation before me, the invited party is entreated "de bien vouloir les honorer de votre présence le Mardi 16 Septembre, 1930, a 4 heures de l'après-midi *à la Cérémonie de Hené*". A similar protection is afforded by the rue leaves sent from the house of the bridegroom to the bridal house on a circular tray full of sugar candy weighing about 50 to 100 pounds. This precedes the Ḳiddushe Erusin, or the first marriage, which is celebrated in the home of the bride, accompanied by music and singing of Hebrew and Arabic songs. The lack of music on such an occasion is regarded as a bad omen. The invitations to the wedding are sent through the beadle of the synagogue at the request of the bridegroom. Some women attend without invitation. In these cases, however, the women do not appear in their usual attire but under disguise, called "Tabdil". A second marriage ceremony is performed within a year of the first, according to the economic position of the couple. This ceremony also takes place in the bride's house where no nuptial canopy (Ḥuppah) is used, but two men hold a piece of cloth in front of the bride. Also of interest are the ceremonies in connection with the entry of the bride into her future home. When she leaves her parents' house in the company of female friends and relatives, a loaf of bread, a cock and a hen are sent to her future home. Then the bridegroom, followed by relatives and friends, to the sound of drummers and pipers, accompanied by lamps and torches borne by Moslems, walks with great dignity to his home, where he is received by his bride and her female friends. Here the loaf of bread is broken over the heads of the bridegroom and his best man. A banquet, at which the bride's people may not be present, concludes the festivities of the day. The Baghdad Jews still keep the seven days of festivities with the usual benedictions prescribed by the Talmud. A special feature of these festivities is the custom of the singing of Hebrew and Arabic songs by professional singers. Songs sung by women on this occasion accompanied by music are called "Jalwah",[1]

[1] See MS. Sassoon 485, p. 117.

and the singers, "Daḳḳaḳat". The bridal couple are not allowed to remain during the wedding week without companions, nor do they leave their home, except to attend divine service in the synagogue. There is a special custom to be mentioned in this connection: on Friday afternoon within the wedding week, before the bridegroom leaves the house, the cook employed for this week sticks three spits into the ground in the courtyard, and when leaving he pulls them out and throws them behind him. This symbolic act serves the purpose of counteracting the influence of the evil spirits. The Sabbath after the wedding is called "Sabt el-Niswan", i.e. Sabbath of the Women, because crowds of veiled women, invited and uninvited, visit the house of the newly-married couple and peep at the bride. There are a number of broadsheets preserved containing regulations and orders by the leaders of the community, showing changes and alterations to which some of the marriage customs were subjected in the course of the centuries.

I turn now to the funeral and burial customs of the Baghdad Jews. First of all, in case of death, the women of the house loosen their hair. Death is announced by proclamation in the synagogues, and by placing the bier in front of the house. While the ritual washing "Taharah", takes place in the house, the wailing women, called in Hebrew "Meḳonenoth" or in Arabic "Ma'addedat", chant Arabic elegies. Before leaving the house the mourners rend their garments and the Ṣidduḳ ha-Din is read. When the bier leaves the house Psalm 78, verse 38 is recited and the mourners say the short Ḳaddish. The bier is carried on the shoulders. In the streets Solomon ibn Gabirol's poem "Shokhene Bate Homer" is chanted. This office is vested in a member of Ḥakham Sason Mordecai's family, who is the leader of the procession by right of heredity. This poem, it may be mentioned here, is similarly used in the burial service of the Yemenite Jews. The Baghdad rite preserves the custom of the seven circuits with the corresponding

Ḳaddish after each circuit. When the body is taken from the bier, the latter is overturned. After the burial a cloth is laid over the grave, and all present throw coins on it. A peculiarity of the Baghdad rite is that a son mourning the loss of his parents ties a handkerchief round his neck. The special Ḳaddish usual after burial is not known in the Baghdad rite. Funeral orations and services in the synagogue are permitted only in the cases of a qualified and recognized Rabbi. In such a case women are permitted to attend a funeral which otherwise they would be strictly prohibited to do. For the details of the liturgy of the burial service, the booklets הנהגת הח"ק, Baghdad, 1893, and עילוי הנשמות Baghdad, 1888-89, have to be consulted. Parts of the former were edited and translated for the use of the Baghdad Jews in Shanghai by Rabbi W. Hirsch, B.A. (Shanghai, 1923). The seven days of mourning are held in the house where death occurred. Services are arranged in the house of mourning during the first year in the afternoons on Thursdays and Saturdays, on the twenty-second day after death, called "Shahr el-Naḳiṣ" (i.e. the incomplete month), further on the thirtieth day after death, called "Shahr el-Tamam" (i.e. the complete month), similarly on the afternoon preceding the last day of the completion of the eleventh month, called "Sant el-Naḳiṣ" (i.e. the incomplete year), and finally on the day of the first anniversary, called "Yom el-Sanah" (i.e. anniversary). After these services biscuits made of flour and oil, fruit and black coffee are served. The biscuits are shaped in the form of large thick rings, and are called "Ka'ak", mentioned already in the Talmud.[1] During the week of mourning a tray of food and fruit is sent to the Ḥazzan of the synagogue of which the deceased was a member. These meals are called "'Ashwiyyit el-Mayyit" (i.e. the dinner of the dead). During the year of mourning this meal is provided for the Ḥazzan on the evenings of Thursday and Saturday. Further there is a custom to distribute a food called

[1] v. *Berakhoth*, 38a and 42a.

"Kaleicha", which consists of flour mixed with butter and sugar, and baked into flat cakes, flavoured with saffron, among the relatives and friends with whom the deceased had business dealings. This distribution is made in the first year after the death, in the days of Ab before the fast. The remainder, if any, is sent to the poor members of the community and to the attendants of the Yeshibah named after Sheikh Isaac Gaon. This food is regarded as a kind of conscience money to absolve the departed from any obligation which he may not have discharged during his lifetime. Then there is the תמר״י, pronounced "Timghiyyee", which is distributed on the Hannukah following the death. It consists of a sweetmeat made of fine flour and sugar, and serves the same purpose as the "Kaleicha". The recipients of these cakes say the "Hashkabah", or "I have forgiven X the son of Y". These customs have to be carried out even by the poorest of the poor.

The mourners were accustomed to wear black during the twelve months of mourning, even on New Year's days and the Day of Atonement. Since the death of Ḥakham Elijah b. Moses Ḥayyim in 1859, this usage has been discarded. It may be mentioned here that mourners in the same period abstain from eating roasted water-melon seeds. The cracking of these little seeds with the teeth is regarded as an amusement, and therefore forbidden. This amusement is called by the Baghdadians "Ḳa'ed Yikassir Ḥab". Hence developed a figure of speech in the Arabic of the Baghdad Jews "Ḳa'ed Tikassir Ḥab 'Alayyi?" which means "art thou cracking seeds over me?" meaning "are you making fun of me?" or "do you want to amuse yourself at my expense?" The tombstone is set on the eighth day after the funeral. Since there are no stones in Baghdad, it has to be built of bricks and mortar, and is provided with a short epitaph on paper covered with glass. The graveyard requires watching owing to the Arabs who break the tombs and carry away the bricks. It is further customary every day during the week of mourning and on every Friday during the first year to visit the grave where the "Hashakabah" is recited. This custom throws light on a hitherto not clearly understood saying of Samuel ha-Naghid, who mentions in one of his elegies the usage of visiting the grave during the week of mourning.[1] A mourner visiting the synagogue in his vicinity carries a bottle of rosewater with him on Sabbaths and festivals and passes it round to the worshippers who proclaim the prescribed benediction.

In memory of the departed many articles of sacred worship are dedicated. First of all many Scrolls of the Law owe their origin to this custom. The dedication is celebrated with great solemnity. The Scroll is carried in a procession to the synagogue on a Saturday morning when the hymn "Simḥoo Na Simḥoo Na be-Simḥath ha-Torah" is sung. Similar dedications are preserved on the scrolls used for the pilgrimages which are undertaken to the shrines of the saints. They are to be found on the little booklets comprising the order of service for the afternoon and evening prayer, called "Minḥah we-'Arbith". Some buildings like synagogues or Karavanserais owe their erection to this pious feeling of desiring to commemorate the memory of the deceased.

[1] See Sassoon, *Diwan of Shemuel Hannaghid*, p. 31 and reference thereto in the Introduction, p. XIV.

CHAPTER XXXI

SUPERSTITIONS AND PROVERBS

This chapter will be devoted to the description of superstitious beliefs and practices which I gathered and wrote down from the lips of Ḥakham Sason Smooha in the year 1910. Since there is no other literary document preserving these rites and usages, they surely will not be out of place in this monograph. Here a short description may be attempted, and the comparison with the folklore of other peoples or other countries must be left to students of folklore. My collection consists of twenty-eight paragraphs, some shorter, others longer, all of some interest to the student of popular beliefs.

Here may follow some of the more interesting and instructive items of my collection:

1. *Ḥaṣbah. Against Measles.* A merchant who generally carries with him his writer's inkhorn must not enter a house where a person with this malady lies. This person is carried on the third day of his illness to the synagogue, either for a very short visit or for a circuit round the "Tebah". Care must be taken that two sufferers of this malady should not visit the synagogue simultaneously.

2. *Charm against Death of Children.* To avert the death of children in their infancy, parents who have already suffered such a loss must not incur any expenses at the time of the birth of their next child. The small outfit necessary must be, even in cases of well-to-do parents, begged from strangers. When visitors come to the house of the new-born child, they are induced to put money into the hand of the baby. A woman carries the baby on Purim to the synagogue where strangers put coins in a box which the infant holds in his hand. She also goes

with the child from house to house for this purpose. This child is called "Ibn el-Darb", i.e. "Child of the Street". In the case of a girl they provide her with a nose-ring, whilst the boy receives an ear-ring. This charm, according to tradition, was applied to an infant child born to Se'adyah Ḥuṣein, father of Ḥakham Ṣadḳah, whose other children had died whilst infants, in order to assure the life of his youngest son. Hence the name "Ṣadḳah", meaning charity.

3. *Nashrah.* The act of averting evil by magic. Before 1909, an Arab woman was reputed to have the power of performing magical rites. After her death a Jew called Jacob ibn Leilah, teacher in the Talmud Torah, an old man who reached the age of one hundred years, was said to be able to perform the same rites. He appeared in the houses of the bridal couple, of childbirth, etc., in order to exercise his magic art. He took a piece of lead, encircled with it the heads of the bridal couple, of the newly-born children, etc., while uttering his incantation. Afterwards he melted the lead and pronounced his verdict from the bubbles caused by the melting which look like eyes.

4 *Dusan el-'Atbah.* The ceremony and belief connected with it is described above, page 182.

5. *Dwarat el Kbiri wu-Dwarat el-Zghayri.* The Big and the Small Circuits. These circuits are applied in case of fever without perspiration. In the first case, the patient is carried to the three chief synagogues, where he has to go around, or is carried around, twice round the "Tebah", hence to various smaller synagogues, a number of places of different character, among them to the tomb of Sheikh Isaac Gaon, and that of Sheikh 'Abd el-Kader el-Jilani, supposed to be the grave of R. Jose the Galilean, and several other places, so that when he arrives home he is perspiring.

6. *Against Barrenness.* The ceremony of the "Dwarat el-Kbeeghi" is applied, with the addition that the woman is led to the Baghdad Bridge of Boats where she steps into a "guffa"

(a circular boat), which meanders between the boats. This last ceremony is repeated seven times.

7. *Mafrak el-Droob.* Crossways. Jewish women anxious for their absent husbands or sons sit on the cross roads on Saturday, Thursday and New Moon nights and guess from the talk of the passers-by the whereabouts and fate of their relatives.

8. *Mṣaḥbah.* Appeasement of Demons. The Baghdad Jews, before moving into a new house or lodging, send on the eve of removal into the empty house or lodgings a basket containing a looking-glass, rue, a new pitcher with water, and sweets. These serve to make friendship with the demons or spirits in the house. It will not be out of place to make here a passing reference to Manasseh Sittehon's work "Kenesiyyah Leshem Shamayim", Jerusalem, 1874, where such practices are strongly objected to. From a quotation by R. David ibn Zimra we learn that this practice is called "el-Mandel" in Arabic. It is called "Indulḳa" by the Ladino-speaking Jews, as described by A. M. Luncz in the first volume of his Jerusalem, Vienna, 1882, pages 21 ff.

9. *Mṣalḥa.* Prolonged illness is due, according to popular belief, to the influence of the harmful demons. They avenge themselves for some hurt inflicted on them by the sick person. A professional woman is called who empties the house of the sick person, prepares a table with food (especially sweets), stays overnight with the sick person, and by magic formulas appeases the demons. I may refer here again to Sittehon's work, mentioned above, which supplies a wealth of material about the spread of this custom among Eastern Jews, and contributes a good deal of information as to the history of this magic performance among Jews of various ages and different countries.

10. *Bizzoonah.* Cat. Jews in Baghdad do not keep cats or dogs. A black cat with shining eyes is regarded as demoniac, and therefore must not be beaten, but is driven away by knocking on the floor.

11. *Mai Ḥar.* Hot water should not be poured on the ground. In case a pot or a vessel containing hot water has to be emptied, the following saying, addressed to the demons has to be uttered: "Put your bowls on your heads, hot water is coming on you", i.e. a warning to the demons to be careful lest they get scalded.

12. *Dheeb.* Wolf. In a house where children die in infancy, a wolf is kept in order to keep away demons. The belief is current among the Baghdad Jews that the wolf keeps away spirits and demons. In the dark they exclaim in their fear of demons: "Dheeb Ḥaḍer", i.e. the wolf is present. If the wolf scratches the ground, they believe that he is pulling out and consuming the fingers of the approaching demons.

13. *Mai wu-Milḥ. Water and Salt.* To cure a person from his illness, he is taken to the river by a professional woman on Saturdays, or Tuesdays, or Thursdays, a quarter of an hour before sunset, and she throws water and salt into the river in order to appease the demons who cause this illness. The Rabbis of Baghdad endeavoured to stop this magic performance but without any result.

14. *Digdig.* A boy suffering from a stye on the eyelid has to visit three houses, knock at the door and when asked "who is it?" he has to reply: "Digdig min 'eini l'einkum yizbeḳ", i.e. "the boil from my eye shall enter your eye."

15. *Against Evil Eye.* Shells and imitation turquoises are connected by a gall-nut. The gall-nut it is believed would split in case a person with evil eye beheld it. Therefore by wearing them children are protected against the effect of the evil eye. The elements of which this charm consists are difficult to describe. An example of such an amulet before me enables me to furnish the following description. On a small triangular velvet pillow is fastened a row of three imitation turquoises, called in Arabic Dehhash, to which are joined three shells, in Arabic: Wada'. The gall-nut which is suspended from the pillow is connected with a bigger piece of imitation turquoise,

which has seven holes. A similar amulet is used for a woman in childbirth. They take seven garlics and thread them together with seven imitation turquoises with two holes in each, one shell, and a root which is called in Arabic Sa'd (*Cyperus esculentus*, in commerce Chuda nut). With these is connected a piece of allum, in Arabic Shabb, from which is suspended an imitation turquoise also with seven holes.

16. *Talzim el-Ḥayyi.* A strange snake is considered as an angel, or the angel of death in disguise. Jews therefore would not touch or hurt it. A Moslem who has drunk from the same water as the snake is asked to catch it.

17. *'Ein. Evil Eye.* A person suspecting the effect of an evil eye takes the eye of a fish, treads on it, and says: "The eye which cast its spell on me shall be smashed as I smash this eye". Then he must take it and bury it near the outer gate of his house.

18. *To Raise the Intelligence of the Child.* Take the first egg laid by a hen and write Divine Names on the shell. On the first day of Pentecost it should be broken and its contents swallowed by the child.

19. The remnant of the wicks of the Hanukkah lights are collected and burnt. To pass through the smoke of the burning wicks three or four times is considered a charm for many purposes.

20. *Ṭarkah.* Charm against Fright. Take a horseshoe, heat it till it gets red hot, then pour water over it and drink the water.

These few specimens will suffice to give some clear idea of the popular mentality of the Baghdad Jews, which is greatly dependent on the mentality of their surroundings. For centuries these customs and beliefs, practices and conceptions have clung to the soil of Babylonia, and in spite of the agitation of the better informed Rabbis it is impossible to eradicate them. The historian has no right to condemn or to praise them, but merely to record these prevailing usages which are not without parallels among other, civilized as well as primitive, nations. They may have had a sound foundation in their origin, which has been lost in the process of time.

Another test for the mentality and cultural development of the Baghdad Jews is to be found in their proverbs. A collection of fifty such proverbs was presented in 1906 by A. S. Yahuda.[1] Another collection of general Arabic proverbs is being edited by Isaac B. S. E. Yahuda.[2] Others are printed in a little booklet under the title "Ḳiṣṣat Ahl Mathal", of which three different editions are known to me. Unfortunately none indicates the date or place of printing, but undoubtedly Baghdad is the place of their origin. There is further a Bombay edition, dated 1886. I will offer here a few proverbs from my collection made during a visit to Baghdad in the year 1910. The transcription of the Arabic words is according to the pronounciation of the Baghdad Jews, which ought to be borne in mind, when compared with other dialects or with classical Arabic. They are:

1. *Min 'ammud il'ammud yifrija rabb il ma'bud.* From pillar to pillar the Worshipped God will deliver, i.e. while the condemned was having his gallow changed the messenger of the king arrived with amnesty; cf. the Talmudic saying "even if the sharpest sword touches the neck of a man, he should not refrain from asking God's mercy."[3]

2. *Lihudi ittali yijinul 'aḳel 'iḳeb ma yinnahib yishawwik ilḥayit.* To the Jew comes wisdom at the end; after he is plundered he puts brambles on his wall, i.e. to protect his property against robbers.

3. *Il 'indu jeeji yidainonu beiḍi.* To him who has a hen, an egg is lent, i.e. he who has property can ask for a loan.

4. *Khidh lieṣil wulo 'aliḥṣeer.* Take a man of good family even if he be on matting. This is an advice to a father with a

[1] Baghdadische Sprichwörter. *Orientalische Studien*, Giessen, 1906, 18 pp.

[2] *Mishle 'Arab* (or Proverbia Arabica), Jerusalem, I, 1932, II, 1934.

[3] *Berakhoth*, 10a.

marriageable daughter to choose a man of good descent, even if very poor.

5. *Shaher il ma 'indak beenu ḥseeb lat 'idd iyyamu.* A month in which you have no account to settle, do not count its days, i.e. do not meddle in people's affairs which do not concern you.[1]

6. *Min yiflas lihudi yidawwur idfatir il 'ittaḳ.* A bankrupt Jew searches his old account books, i.e. hopes to recover old forgotten or overlooked claims.

7. *'Aṣfur kafal zirzur wuthneinhum ṭiyyar.* The sparrow stood surety for the starling, and they are both flyers, i.e. both equally unreliable.

8 *Mithḳal samm wula ḥibbayi hamm.* Better twenty-four grains of poison than one grain of grief, i.e. death is to be preferred to grief.

9. *Il yimshi 'al rikhṣu yirmi biddarb niṣṣu.* He who goes after cheapness leaves half on the way, i.e. cheap things are more expensive than dear ones in the long run.

10. *Il me shibberakh mai rabbi frakh.* Mi Shebberakh will not feed the little ones. It is customary in the East that the poor attend festivities and earn small sums by reciting certain blessings, "Mi Shebberakh", in honour of the individual guests. The proverb conveys the idea of the uncertainty and paucity of such income.

11. *Waiḥid shayyil liḥyitu illakhi leish yitthḳḳal minna.* If a man is carrying his beard, why should another feel the burden of it? Needless to trouble about other people's worries.

12. *Ḳallib bilirṭal wula biṭṭal.* Turn the weights about, but do not be idle. Advice against laziness.

13. *Kan takil wiyalla'ami kil bilinṣaf.* If you eat with a blind man, eat moderately. Advice against those who take advantage of a person's ignorance or inability.

14. *Yiṣum irrasha' yomil ma yinḳabil ṣomu.* The wicked fasts on the day that his fast will not be accepted, i.e. the good done by bad people is done at the wrong time and on a wrong occasion.

[1] For a similar proverb, see A. S. Yahuda, p. 14, No. 33.

15. *Ḥjara ilma tirḍaha tifshikh.* The stone which you despise can cause a fracture. The smallest thing can be of great consequence. (Cf. Targum to Proverbs 13, 13.)

16. *Beiḍi min beiḍi tifsad.* An egg can be spoilt by another egg. Bad society spoils good manners. One scabbed sheep infects the whole flock.

17. *Id ilme'yuba ḳiṣṣa.* Cut off a defective hand. A man should not allow bad habits to grow on him.

18. *Iladmi min ramza wulihmar rafsa.*[1] The man with a wink, the donkey with a kick, i.e. a hint is sufficient for a wise man, a fool must be pushed to a thing.

19. *Ilyisawwi ruhu nekkhala tilḳeṭu ejjeeji.* He who reduces himself to grain will be pecked by the hen. A man without self respect will not be respected by others.

20. *Ḳirsh ilabyaḍ yinfa' yomil aswad.* A white ḳirsh (i.e. a Turkish coin worth about twopence) will come useful on a black day. Even the smallest thing may be useful in time of need.

21. *Khallil kaskeen yikser kirrabetu.* Strong vinegar will break its jar. A bad tempered person does the greatest harm to himself.

22. *Ash yakhedh ilejreidi min dekkan ilḥeddad.* What can the mouse take away from a blacksmith's shop? None will look for help in a miser's house. Another version of this proverb is given by Yahuda (No. 5): *Ash yakhidh illiḥrami min iggeme.'* What shall a thief take from the mosque? According to Yahuda it means you do not risk danger where nothing is to be expected. I noted another variant: *Ash yakhedh ilejreidi min ijjame'*. What can a mouse take from a mosque? This accounts for the designation of the mosque as the empty one (Reḳ), while in opposition to this Judah ha-Levy in his poem addressed to R. Barukh b. Isaac calls the synagogue "the holy house which is filled with wisdom".[2]

[1] Cf. Midrash Proverbs, Ch. 22.

[2] *Diwan des Abu-el-Hasan Jehuda ha-Levi, ed.* Brody, Berlin, 1894; *Gibeath Saul*, Vienna, 1923, p. 9; S. Krauss, *Bate Kenesiyyoth 'Attikim*, in the volume *Jerusalem*, p. 249, footnote.

23. *Ḥerem innaḳdi wula brakha biddein.* A ban in cash (hand) and not a blessing on loan, i.e. better the worse thing at present than the good thing delayed.

24. *Rizk libzazeen 'anniswan lim'ethrat.* The livelihood of cats depends upon untidy women. Untidiness is the blessing of cats.

25. *Ijjamal ja yisawwi ḳrun ḳeṣṣolu adhanu.* The camel desired horns and his ears were cut off. Grasp all, lose all. This proverb is mentioned in an apocryphal Midrash known to the Yemenite Jews,[1] where the proverb is in Hebrew. In the Talmud it is rendered in Aramaic.[2]

26. *Jibnanul akka' yiwunnesna kashaf rasu wukherr'ana.* We brought the bald-headed to amuse us, he uncovered his head and frightened us. Expectations are often disappointed.

27. *Ilbard min ṣad ilweiḳef liṣad ilkei'ed.* The cold lasts from the standing to the sitting *Ṣad.* By the term "standing Ṣad" the Baghdadians mean the final *Sad* (Zaddik) in the word Mikkes (Gen. 41), by the "sitting Ṣad" they mean the ordinary Ṣad in the word *Teṣawweh* (Exodus, 27, 20). The period of winter begins with Mikkes and ends with Tesawweh. Hereto belongs the proverb *Bitsawweh mabḳalu lilbaghd ḳuwwei*, meaning at *Teṣawweh* there is no severity left in the cold. A similar saying is current about the meaning of section *wa-Yaḳhel* for the popular calendar.

28. *Bkhi Thissa il'aḳruḳa yiṭla' ḥissa.* The voice of the frog is heard in *Ki Thissa.* When Exodus XXX, 2 is read on the Sabbath in the synagogues, then the river Tigris begins to rise and the frogs approach.

29. *Bifḳudei ḥiṭṭ 'mametak 'al 'udei.* In *Peḳude* put your turban on the staff, that means the rainy season is over and the summer arrived, so that one can leave one's turban outside, in the courtyard.

30. *Ja libḳe' yimshi mashwet ilbekhtiyyi ḍayya' ilmishewtein min*

[1] See my article *Aggadoth 'Attikoth mi-Teman, Jahrbuch der Juedisch-Literarischen Gesellschaft*, Frankfort/M., 1925, p. 19.
[2] See *Sanhedrin*, 106a.

idu. The raven tried to imitate the dove and lost its own and the dove's way of walking, i.e. the vulgar cannot imitate the ways of the nobility (see Yahuda, No. 9). The raven is so despised and hated by the Baghdad Jews that they call a fool (also Haman) "the son of the raven". In an old list of names of Biblical women, Haman's mother is called "Amthelai-bath 'Orbetha", which rests on the same tradition.[1]

[1] See *Kissat Haman wu-Mordekhai*, Calcutta, 1896; *Ohel Dawid*, p. 7, note, and *B. Bathra* 91a.

CHAPTER XXXII

PRINTERS

An important factor in the communal life, religious as well as intellectual, was the activity of the Hebrew printing press. Till the middle of the nineteenth century the requirements of the Baghdad Jews were supplied by printers of Livorno. A number of works printed in Baghdad indicate neither the date nor place of printing, nor the name of the printer. The first dated book, as far as I know, bears the year of printing 5626, i.e. 1855-56. The books printed in this year comprise Hadrath Zekenim, collectanae from the Zohar, Idra, etc., as arranged by Kabbalistic masters for Pentecost, the night of Hosha'ana Rabba and the 33rd of 'Omer. The printer was Raḥamim b. Reuben b. Mordecai. The same printer published in the same year a Sefer Ḥezyonoth, containing the well-known biographical notes on Isaac Luria's life, compiled by Ḥayyim Viṭal). In the same year Barukh b. Moses Mizraḥi edited after the Ferrara edition the Travels of R. Benjamin of Tudela. This edition appeared in lithographed form, with poems in honour of the Prophets Ezekiel and Elijah at the end of the book. Mizraḥi was the editor of a Hebrew periodical (ha-Dober) which appeared in Baghdad between 1868 and 1870. There are only a few stray numbers preserved in my collection, so that I am unable to furnish more details about this periodical. There is another short-lived weekly periodical of a more recent date which appeared under the name of Jeshurun. It is partly in Hebrew and partly in Arabic, and lasted from Kislew 5681 to Tebeth of the same year, altogether five numbers. This weekly contains among others, poems, essays on the Baghdadian Jews and their customs, a biography of Maimonides in Arabic, communal news and Zionist propaganda. Of the more important publications issued by Raḥamim's press are: (1) Ḥoḳ le-Yisrael (1868), which was printed at the expense of Sir Albert David Sassoon and his brothers for the school children of the David Sassoon Benevolent Institution in Bombay; (2) Sefer ha-Ma'asiyyoth, a collection of 112 stories, probably a reprint of the Calcutta edition, published by Eleazar 'Iraki, Calcutta, 1842; and (3) Sefer ha-Yashar, comprising the well-known popular Bible stories. The Baghdad Jews have always been very fond of this kind of literature as shown by the different editions of Ma'asiyyoth, printed and published by various printers at different times. Apart from the previous collections of stories there are to be mentioned the Ma'asim Mefoarim, containing fifty-three stories with a specially long novel under the title Sullam ha-Haṣlaha (The Ladder of Success), giving the biography of a particularly wealthy man, David Barney of London; Ma'aseh Nissim, a similar collection of fifty-nine numbers; and finally a reprint of the Ma'asiyyoth, all of them by Solomon Bekhor Ḥusein, another Baghdad printer. His printing activities can be traced to the eighties and nineties of last century, and were continued by his son Joshua. Earlier than both of them was Ftayyah, who flourished in the seventies and later than them were Dangoor and Shohet. At present there are only two printing offices. Besides the Shohet press, there functions the Maṭeb'at el-Waṭaniyyah el-Asrailiyyah. The products of these are mostly of a popular nature, or of a liturgical character. Altogether about 245 books and booklets are known to me as having been printed in Baghdad. They are partly in Hebrew and partly in Arabic. It is characteristic that scholarly works of authors and Rabbis, who lived and taught in Baghdad, were printed abroad, for instance, in Jerusalem. The only exception is the work of Ḥakham 'Abdallah Somekh, which appeared under the title of Zibḥe Ṣedeḳ in two volumes (1904). The market for the products of the Baghdad press is not limited to the community in Baghdad but finds an outlet among all communities in India, the Straits Settlements and the Diaspora of China, which look upon Baghdad as their mother community. This will be made clearer by the next chapter, in which I shall endeavour to relate in brief the settlements and developments of the new communities in India and other countries in the Far East, hailing from Baghdad.

CHAPTER XXXIII

SETTLEMENTS OF BAGHDAD JEWS IN THE FAR EAST

THIS final chapter shall be devoted to the history of the Baghdad Jews who left the mother community for far away countries where they founded new branches of religious activity and Jewish life. Though removed from the original soil, and so many thousands of miles away they continued to live under the holy shadow of the life-giving tree of their native place. Spiritually and religiously they remained dependent on the teaching and tradition of Baghdad, although politically and economically they became independent. Yet the wealth gathered and the good fortune experienced in the new countries did not make them forget the "Rivers of Babylon", the sanctuaries and shrines, the colleges and schools, the scholars and the poor, the ailing and the needy, in their old homestead on the Tigris and the Euphrates. It is therefore appropriate that a final chapter shall be added to this history of the Baghdad Jews, depicting the fate and life of their descendants in the Diaspora. We turn first of all to the Jewish communities which were organized, mainly through the influx and devotion of the Baghdad Jews, in Surat, Calcutta, Bombay, Poona and Rangoon. Then we shall turn to the descendants of the Baghdad Jews who settled in Singapore, Hong Kong and Shanghai and last, but not least, to the members of the Baghdad colony, called 'Ole Babel, in Jerusalem.

India was known to the Jews of antiquity as well as to those of the Middle Ages. Many reminiscences of India fill the writings of medieval authors. Modern scholars seriously discuss the question whether or not one of the great luminaries of Jewish learning and poetry, Abraham b. Meir ibn Ezra, visited the land of the Ganges. Whatever the answer to this enquiry may be, whether in the affirmative or in the negative, for our purpose it suffices to say that, with the exceptions about to be noted, there were no extensive settlements of Jews in India before the end of the eighteenth century. However, it may be that from time to time small groups of Jews settled in various towns in India for reasons of commerce even before the eighteenth century. For instance there was a colony of Jewish merchants in Madras in the seventeenth century. They appear to have had some communal life for they acquired a separate burial ground which is still to be seen, and for the preservation of which, steps were being considered in 1944.[1]

Two branches of the house of Israel spread in India before the new settlement which is the subject of this chapter, and therefore have to be mentioned, however briefly, in this connection. The first branch is that of the Bene Israel in Bombay. Their tradition, which is not based on documents, knows of a history going back many centuries.[2] The existing evidence, however, for their communal and religious activity is of a more recent date. Their oldest synagogue, called Sha'ar ha-Shamayim, was built by Samuel Ezekiel Diveker Cammodan Moocadum, in Samuel Street, Bombay, in 1796. Their customs and ceremonies are reputed to be of great antiquity, yet not free from outside influences. Their liturgy and religious conduct show many peculiarities which, however, it would be out of place to describe here.[3] The Bene Israel were early in close connection with the other branch of Jews in India, the Cochin Jews. The latter are much richer as far as historical documents and literary evidence go. Their tradition is dated from hoary

[1] *Jewish Advocate*, Vol. XIII, No. 10 (June, 1944), p. 11.
[2] See Additional Notes on p. 218.
[3] For further details, v. an article by Mrs. Selina Sassoon, "de Bene Israel", in the *Joodsche Gids*, vol. I (1929), p. 362 ff.

antiquity, but is substantiated by archæological remains and historical proofs. The copper plates speak of a Jewish kingdom and ruling house. Their poets and historiographers, as well as gentile travellers and officials, offer interesting accounts of their Jewish life and spiritual endeavours. Yet both groups are actually outside the line of my investigation, and would form a subject of historical treatment by themselves.[1] Here they interest us only as neighbours of the founders of the new communities in India. It was impossible to avoid contact being established between the old settlers and the newcomers. A certain influence was exercised mutually between them.

SURAT. The first place, in which the Jewish immigrants from Syria and Mesopotamia founded a Jewish community was Surat, then the most important port in Western India, and a great commercial centre. It was not surprising that the newcomers selected this place as their future home. In the year 1769 Moses Ṭobi, who is styled ha-Nasi ha-Zaken, died. He must have been a Yemenite by birth who settled in Surat. Another Moses Ṭobi is mentioned in a letter written by Aaron b. Rahamim Barzani of Surat to Sliman Ḳaṣar at Cochin in 1786. Barzani, as the family name indicates, hailed from Mosul. Later on, after 1790, we find members of Baghdad families in Surat. Such are Isaac b. David Jacob of Baghdad, who died 1790, and a member of the Gabbai family, namely Sason b. Ezekiel Mordecai Gabbai, who copied the Idra in Surat in the year 1848.

BOMBAY. The second station of the newcomers was Bombay. The first Baghdad Jew who settled in Bombay was Sliman b. Jacob Sliman. The traveller David d'Beth Hillel says about him: "I arrived at Bombay in October, 1828, and remained there forty days in great inconvenience. I found there few Jews from Arabia and they are domineered over by Solomon Yakob a rich man and the first Arabian Jew who established himself in Bombay." Whether the rest of the

[1] See Additional Notes on p. 218.

traveller's description about the first settler's "bad disposition", "notorious character", the habit of his fellow Jews, "who speak their mind freely enough of him in his absence", and "are careful to assent to all his saying", is based on truth or is the result of some disappointment, cannot be discussed here. According to the writer, the trouble arose out of the fact, as he puts it, that he "had not been accustomed to dishonourable subterfuges" and was "a man who worship only my Creator". On no account would he conform "to their unlawful usages which they have learnt from the Arabs and the Hindus".[1] Our documents present him in a different light altogether. There he appears as a benefactor of his native city and the educational and charitable institutions in its midst. In 1828 he bought some houses in which Ḥakham Moses Ḥayyim and his sons were lodged free of charge and expense. The houses remained in the trust of the community. Simḥah, the wife of Ezekiel b. Sason b. Mordecai, which is now in the Maghen Shalom Synagogue in Karachi, and belongs to the Bene Israel. Another early settler in Bombay was Jacob b. Ṣemaḥ Nissim, who also came from Baghdad and figures as a great benefactor of the Baghdad community generally, and institutions particularly. His charities which he left gave rise to many acrimonious disputes between the heirs to the estate and the trustees of the charities. As we saw previously, one of the colleges and a synagogue was named after Jacob Ṣemaḥ. Among the later settlers in Bombay was David Sassoon (born in Baghdad, 1792, died in Poona, 1864). His father, Sheikh Sason, bore, as we have seen, the dignity of a Nasi. He was born in 1750, and died in 1830 in Bushire. His pedigree may be traced to five generations of ancestors, Ṣaleḥ, David, Jacob, Ṣaleḥ, David. The residence of this family is known as Bet Abu Rubein. As leaders of the community, both father and son were subjected on the part of the Turkish authorities to oppression and persecutions at any time when

[1] *The Travels of Rabbi David d'Beth Hillel*, Madras, 1832, p. 116.

the Pasha intended to extort money from the Jews. In a document dated in the early winter of 1772, it is stated that Sheikh Sason is unable to appear in public, owing to the terror of the local governor. The same fate befell his son David, who had to flee to Bushire where he was joined later by his father, Sheikh Sason, who died there. His son continued his journey and settled in Bombay. Here he began his prosperous commercial activities, and with his growing influence he endeavoured to improve the spiritual and religious life of the community. This was done by building the Maghen David Synagogue in Bombay (1861), the Ohel David Synagogue in Poona (1863), the David Sassoon General Hospital in Poona (1863), the David Sassoon Industrial Reformatory Institution, and the school, called the David Sassoon Benevolent Institution, both in Bombay. For the use of this school several educational works were provided at the expense of David Sassoon. Through the agency and under the editorship of the famous bibliographer, Moritz Steinschneider of Berlin, several moralist writings, in verse and in prose, by earlier and later writers were re-edited and furnished with English glossaries for these schools. Further, he provided the Sassoon Mechanics' Institute with a technical library.[1] He also dedicated a statue to the Prince Consort in the Victoria and Albert Museum, Bombay. The statue, which was erected in 1864, in the twenty-seventh year of the reign of Queen Victoria, has an inscription in English and Hebrew.

Another Baghdadian immigrant was David Ḥai b. Ezekiel Abraham Maṣliaḥ, who was an owner of a considerable library, consisting of manuscripts and valuable printed books. An account of this collection is preserved by another traveller and visitor to Bombay, Jacob Saphir, the author of Eben Saphir.[2] Among the Baghdadians in Bombay Saphir found Moses b. Mordecai Gabbai, his son-in-law David Ḥai,

[1] See the Sassoon Mechanics' Institute, Bombay. Bombay, 1914.
[2] Eben Saphir, II, Mainz, 1874, p. 41.

Ezekiel b. Joshua Gabbai the son-in-law of Sir Albert Sassoon and others. About David Ḥai he says: "In his house I found many and valuable books, ancient and modern, among them a considerable Diwan in an old manuscript containing poems of the classical period, by Solomon ibn Gabirol, Judah ha-Levy, Moses and Abraham ibn Ezra, and the work of Tadros ha-Levy, Solomon Bonfid, Naḥmias, and other Spanish poets". Besides Baghdadians, the Bombay community consisted of Jews coming from Basra and others who escaped religious persecutions in Persia in those days. Among them was Mulla Ibrahim b. Nathan, a native of Meshed in Persia. He and his friend, Mulla Musa, rendered valuable services to the British government and the British armies during the Afghan War, for which they were rewarded by the Government of India.[1] David Sassoon, also rendered great services to the British Government during the Indian Mutiny, which were duly acknowledged by the Governor of Bombay, Lord Elphinstone who, at a banquet given by David Sassoon on Monday, 28th February, 1859, said in a speech: "We must not forget that at the time of the mutiny, amongst all those who offered us help, the Jews were the first to send me a memorial, signed and headed by Mr. David Sassoon, and it gave us great pleasure."[2]

As soon as the Baghdad Jews took root in the new country they endeavoured to transplant their old longing for spiritual wealth and traditional Judaism to their new homes. In the years of struggle for life many of them had to go without their learning and books. Before they could afford to establish a printing press of their own the necessary books had to be imported from Europe. Then they availed themselves of the device of lithographing books for their ordinary needs; for example, the Sefer ha-Pizmonim, a book of songs providing

[1] *A Review of the Career of the Late Mulla Ibrahim Nathan*, Bombay, 1910.
[2] See my article "A Unique Jewish Newspaper", *The Jewish Chronicle*, 3rd July, 1908.

more than 250 songs and hymns without which a Baghdad Jew could not celebrate his festivals or enjoy his festivities. The first collector and lithographer of these Pizmonim was David b. Ḥayyim. David who was also the editor of the Bombay Jewish-Arabic periodical called Doresh Ṭob le-'Ammo.[1] A number of the first Jewish-Arabic works appeared both in lithographed form and in type. For more general purposes Ezekiel b. Nisan rendered a part of the Thousand and One Nights into Hebrew characters, and Aaron b. Jacob Samuel printed it in Bombay in 1888. Of peculiar interest is a work by Ezekiel b. Jacob Raḥamim, a part of which appeared under the title Sefer Ya'rath Debash, in Bombay in 1890. It purports to offer a Hebrew dictionary to the Holy Scriptures, Talmud, Targum and Midrash, and a vocabulary to the Zohar with Arabic and English renderings. An interesting work of late Jewish-Arabic literature! Another specimen of this literature is the "Ma'aseh Nissim, containing prayers, daily and Sabbath, with an Arabic translation by the Rev. Nissim Elisha Eliyahoo Zechariah, Minister to the congregation of Keneseth Eliyahoo Synagogue, Bombay, 1888".

At present the Jewish community in Bombay consists of about 1,400 souls. The immigration from Baghdad at present is not so strong as it was in the last century. There are two synagogues providing for the spiritual needs of the Baghdad Jews in Bombay. The one, Maghen David, already mentioned, is situated in Byculla, in the city, and the other, the "Keneseth Eliyahoo", built in 1888 by Sir Jacob Sassoon in memory of his father Elias, is in the Fort of Bombay. The officials of the community, readers and teachers are natives of Baghdad.

CALCUTTA. The earliest Jewish settler in Calcutta was Shalom b. Aaron Obadiah ha-Kohen (b. 1762, d. 1836), who hailed from Aleppo. His diary reveals a chequered career and a romantic life, details of which can be found in an article by

[1] Ibid.

Sir David Ezra, which appeared in the "South African Jewish Chronicle", Rosh ha-Shanah Number, 1929, pp. 13-15. Another diarist, Moses b. Simeon Dwek ha-Kohen (b. 1785, d. 1861), also a native of Aleppo, preserved in his Kaneh Middah, some valuable material for the history of the Jews in Calcutta. A third diarist, who came from Yemen and settled in Calcutta, Eleazar b. Aaron Se'adyah 'Iraki ha-Kohen (d. 1861), furnishes us with further material for our purpose. These chroniclers and diarists supply us with material about the Baghdadians in Calcutta. Soon the latter became the most prominent element in the community. Among the first Baghdadian settlers in Calcutta, although only for a short time, was Jacob b. Ṣemah Nissim. Probably owing to business disagreements with his brother-in-law, the aforementioned diarist, Dwek ha-Kohen, which cost Jacob Ṣemah 60,000 Rupees, he left Calcutta and returned to Bombay. The Baghdad immigration into Calcutta became strong in the twenties of the nineteenth century, when the misrule of Daud Pasha compelled many members of the community to seek residence abroad. Among these were the members of the Ezra (first Khleif, later Baher) and the Yehudah (or Judah) families the Yehudahs being descendants of Sliman David Ma'tuk. Among the signatories to a document containing the Constitution of the Calcutta Jews, dated 15th Elul, 1825, the majority belongs to the Baghdad Jews, the minority consisting of Aleppo and Yemenite Jews. It was about that date that Ezekiel Yehudah arrived in Calcutta. Among them two Baghdad Jews, Ezekiel b. Elijah Maṣliah and Benjamin b. Abraham Solomon David, were instrumental in buying the site for the synagogue called Neweh Shalom. The place was bought in 1825 from an Englishman, John Bowers, for 16,000 Rupees. The sum of 6,000 Rupees was paid at once from the funds of the community, the balance was borrowed from the firm of Mackintosh & Company. It speaks well for the material well-being of the community that in 1831 the entire sum, with the accrued interest of 8 per cent. per annum, was paid. The whole community, including the Aleppo and Yemenite Jews, looked to Baghdad as their spiritual centre and turned to the Rabbis of Baghdad for advice in religious and communal matters. The activities of the Calcutta Jews include religious life in other places as well, such as Chinsura and Chandernagore, two places connected with, but outside Calcutta. The former was under Dutch rule, the centre of trade in Bengal; the latter is still under French authority. Further away, Madras in India and Mulmein and Rangoon in Burma, and Singapore in the Straits Settlements depended in their religious life on Calcutta. In these places again the majority of Jews consisted of Baghdadians, with a small minority of Aleppo and Yemenite settlers.

About the inner life of the Jews in Calcutta, as well as in other places in India, some features may be pointed out. The Jews kept slaves. These were bought mostly from among Arabic-speaking tribes. Males and females of this class observed during their servitude certain religious laws and enactments as ordered by the Talmud. Some of them received their freedom from the hand of their masters. Such a document still exists in which David Sassoon signs in the presence of witnesses in Bombay, on the 24th of Siwan, 5603 (1843), a Letter of Release to his late slave Salem, using a formulary familiar to students of the Talmud. A similar document is preserved for a female slave, Ruḥanah, who was released by her master, Ezra b. Ezekiel Maṣliah, on the 22nd of Ab, 5604 (1844), in Calcutta. In passing it may be mentioned that the same conditions prevailed among the Cochin Jews. Thus I have in my possession a similar document issued by Isaac b. Judah Mizrahi of Cochin, who releases his slave Samuel in Bombay. In this case the slave is designated as a Yelid Bayith (a house-born). A second point which has to be raised here is the relation of the newcomers from Baghdad, Aleppo, etc., to the older Jewish residents in India. Baghdad

Jews often ventilated the question whether the black Jews of Cochin in India have the status of proper Jews or not. A number of Responsa and newspaper articles deal with this problem. Theory as well as practice decided in their favour, and they enjoy the privileges of the Jewish law. At the time of writing there is still a dispute over the status of the Bene Israel. Thirdly, the three groups of Jews in India are divided linguistically. The Baghdad Jews as well as those coming from Aleppo or Yemen use Arabic as their vernacular. The Bene Israel speak and write Marathi. They developed a considerable literature, religious and secular in this language and script. Their printing presses produced besides a number of periodical publications, also Hebrew and Marathi Haggadahs with illustrations, prayer books in Hebrew and Marathi, and finally a number of Marathi books like "Children in the Wood", etc. The Black Jews of Cochin use Malabari as their vernacular for their daily intercourse and liturgy.

The loyalty of the newcomers in their Indian settlements to England can be seen from many small as well as great deeds. No wonder, for we have the testimony of a traveller, Jacob Saphir, who was in Calcutta in 1860. He writes: "From the time when Great Britain fixed the peg of her rule in this town, it has become an emporium for nations and a city of freedom and security to all those who enter its gates without bribe or discrimination between people and people."[1] What greater tribute could be given! Thus we see that in a marriage document, a bridegroom, Ezekiel Ḥayyim b. Salem ha-Levy promises to treat his wife decently, and to consider this document as if it were an Act of Parliament at Westminster. A travelling Rabbi, R. David d'Beth Hillel from Jerusalem, who journeyed through Arabia, Kurdistan, Persia and India, published an account of his travels in English. The book appeared in Madras in 1832. David d'Beth Hillel was accompanied by

[1] Eben Saphir, II, p. 98.

Raphael Moses Zalkind, who married in Calcutta in the presence of David d'Beth Hillel. A chronicler of Calcutta, Eleazar 'Iraki, does not omit to record the patriotic celebrations arranged in the two synagogues of Calcutta on the occasion of Queen Victoria's birthday. A number of liturgical pamphlets, containing orders of service for prayer and thanksgiving, used on such occasions as the celebration of the Sixtieth Anniversary of Queen Victoria's Accession to the Throne, the Coronation Day of King Edward VII, and the Coronation Day of Their Majesties King George and Queen Mary, all testify to the loyalty of the Jews in India. During the Great War an Intercession Service was held for the success of His Majesty's Armies. I may here remind the reader again (see page 178) that in Baghdad itself the Jews celebrate yearly the occasion of the entry of the British Army into Baghdad with prayers and thanksgiving.

Among the interesting visitors to Calcutta we hear of Solomon Zalman, a messenger of Jerusalem, and Jacob Saphir. The latter mentions 'Iraki, who showed him hospitality, and informs us, that there were two synagogues in Calcutta at the time. Besides the first, mentioned already, there was a second synagogue built more recently by Ezekiel Judah, who is praised by Jacob Saphir as an influential and successful communal worker, as a scholar and learned man. He was the son-in-law of the Baghdadian Ḥakham, Moses Ḥayyim, and lived for more than thirty-five years in Calcutta. Among other Baghdadians whom Saphir met were David b. Joseph Ezra, the leader of the community, his son Elijah (Elias), and members of the Gabbai family. He praises their mind and their faithful adherence to their Baghdadian customs. The second synagogue mentioned by Saphir was called Beth El.

The intellectual life of the community was provided with literature coming from the press of Eleazar b. Aaron Se'adyah Iraḳi. This printer produced twenty-seven publications between 1840 and 1857. Among them are the 'Ein Ya'akob, Sefer ha-Ma'asiyyoth, the Pizmonim (two editions), Eldad ha-Dani, Ben Sira, Laws of Shehitah, Polemics, Josippon and Sefer ha-Yashar, and Kabbalistic writings, like the Book of Raziel the Angel, and Interpretations of Dreams. Calcutta provided weekly newspapers for the Arabic-speaking Jews in India. Such are: "Mebasser: The Jewish Gazette" (1873-77), edited by Ezekiel b. Solomon; "Paeraḥ: The Jewish Gazette (1878-89), edited up to January, 1888, by Moses b. Mordecai Meyoḥas and Elijah b. Solomon and afterwards by E. M. D. Cohen; Maggid Mesharim (1889-1900), and Shoshannah, or the Jewish Gazette (1901), both edited by Solomon b. 'Abed Twena. All these periodicals are in Jewish-Arabic. Solomon Twena was one of the most prolific and versatile Hebrew writers of modern times. In the approbation of Ḥakham Elijah b. Joshua Obadiah in Twena's book of Ruth with Arabic translation, the titles of sixty-seven works by our author are enumerated. This was in the year 1889. Twena died in the year 1913, when the number of his writings may have considerably increased. Some of his printed books are not listed in the usual bibliographical compilations. One of these is Twena's Ḳunṭres Kothbenu le-Ḥayyim, a Ḥalakhic compendium for the New Year's day, Baghdad, 1878. Twena translated into Arabic from the Hebrew some of Dr. Markus Lehmann's historical novels, like Suss Oppenheim (Calcutta, 1897), Bustanai (reprinted from the "Maggid Mesharim", Vols. VI-VII, 1895), Hathan ha-Melekh, a history based on the events which occurred during the Chmielniscki persecutions in the Ukraine in 1648-49 (Calcutta, 1897) and the Story of the Sar of Coucy (Calcutta, 1898). A number of works remained in manuscript; others went through the press but were never published. It is especially regrettable that his Ma'aseh Ḥiyya, a collection of stories and legends collected from many sources, of which only twenty leaves, sixty-five numbers, were printed in Livorno in 1887, remained a *torso*.

The whole work, which was planned in many parts might have offered the richest collection of this type. A similar fate fell to the lot of his edition of the Psalms, with an elaborate commentary, under the title Shir Yediduth, of which only 248 leaves were printed, covering fifty-one chapters of the Psalms. Twena's books were diligently read and greatly enjoyed by his fellow countrymen. He held no official position in the community, but had his own synagogue where he worshipped and taught.

In 1856 the first synagogue called Neweh Shalom sufficed no longer for the increased Jewish population. At the expense of the aforenamed Ezekiel Judah and David Joseph Ezra, a new synagogue was erected under the name of Beth El. Both synagogues served their purpose till the eighties, when alterations and renovations became necessary. The same David Ezra's son, Elias Ezra, erected in the years 1883-84 a synagogue adjoining the ground of the Neweh Shalom synagogue, a new place of worship which was called "Maghen David". The latter actually took the place of the Neweh Shalom Synagogue. Here for the time being no services were held; later on a Yeshibah with a library was placed in it, and gradually it turned again into a house of worship. Finally a new synagogue was established in the same building, under the old name Neweh Shalom. These changes and proceedings gave rise to a protracted lawsuit which cannot be reported here in detail. In short, the plaintiffs claimed that the Maghen David took the place of the Neweh Shalom, and the defendants insisted that the Neweh Shalom synagogue had its own right of existence and name. Naturally minor or major financial questions were also involved in it. Ultimately all the three synagogues remained open for worship.[1]

[1] The following legal documents and newspaper articles refer to this case: (1) Judgment in the Synagogue Case. Suit No. 489 of 1916, D. E. D. Ezra and Others *v.* E. S. Levy and Others, and Suit No. 507 of 1914, E. S. Levy and Others *v.* D. E. D. Ezra and Others. Delivered by the Honourable Mr. Justice Chaudhuri on the 16th day of May, 1917; (2) Appeal from Original

Besides synagogues there are educational and charitable institutions established by Baghdad Jews in Calcutta. There is first of all the Jewish Free School Talmud Torah,[1] which is now known as the Elias Meyer Free School Talmud Torah. Then there is the Jewish Boys' and Girls' School which changed later on into the Jewish Girls' School.[2] Lastly, the Jewish Free School Ḳehillath Jeshurun, a kindergarten, belongs to this group. Of charitable institutions the following may be mentioned: the Ezra Hospital founded, by Mrs. Mozelle Ezra, the Jewish Charitable Fund, and the Jewish Women's League.

POONA. This was the fourth place in India where Baghdad Jews settled and established communal life. A synagogue, a school and a hospital were erected here by David Sassoon, who found his resting place in the grounds of the synagogue. For some time there was also a printing press active, producing Hebrew prints and Jewish books. To the first group belongs the edition of the Idra text with Arabic translation, which gave rise to much opposition and strife; to the latter group belongs an introduction to the Ḳabbalah by Abraham David Ezekiel, F.T.S., Poona, 1888.

CHINA. Jews, of Baghdad origin, emigrated to the Far East and founded communities in Canton, Hong Kong, Shanghai and Tientsin. Some of their descendants are to-day British subjects, others enjoy the protection of Great Britain or France.

[1] Annual Reports with Syllabus and Class and Prize Lists appeared regularly for the years 1907 till 1929.

[2] Reports for the former were issued regularly from 1886 till 1894, for the latter, from 1897 till 1917.

Decree No. 71 of 1917. In the High Court of Judicature at Fort William in Bengal. Calcutta, 1917; (3) Notice. *The Calcutta Exchange Gazette*, 7th May, 1914; (4) Rival Synagogues, in *The India Daily News*, Calcutta, 5th December, 1916; (5) Rival Synagogues, in *The Statesman*, Calcutta, 8th December, 1916; (6) The Jewish Synagogue Case, ibid., 22nd December, 1916; (7) The Jewish Synagogue Case, ibid., 10th February, 1917; (8) Jewish Synagogue Case, ibid., 17th May, 1917; (19) Jewish Synagogue Case, in *The Indian Daily News*, Calcutta, 17th May, 1917; (10) Rival Synagogues, in *The Empire*, Calcutta, 4th September, 1917; and (11) Jewish Synagogue Case, ibid., 17th September, 1917.

They come either direct from Baghdad or from India. Here they founded Jewish communities, erected places of worship, established schools and founded charitable institutions. Owing to economic conditions they left Canton and Tientsin, but flourished and prospered in Hong Kong and Shanghai, where Jewish life grew stronger and stronger. Now there are considerable Jewish communities in these places, with remarkable Jewish activities. As a sign of flourishing Jewish life may be mentioned the "Israel's Messenger", an irregular periodical which endeavours to strengthen the cause of Zionism. It has been appearing for the past twenty-eight years (with an interval of six years) under the editorship of N. E. B. Ezra.

JERUSALEM. Quite a considerable number of Baghdad Jews settled in Jerusalem, where they formed a special community and worshipped in their own synagogue, called Shoshannim le-David. It has been pointed out already that in the time of Ḥakham Joseph Ḥayyim a great longing for visiting and dwelling in the Holy Land took hold of the pious among the Baghdad Jews. Many of them left their native city for Palestine. Nowadays they are known under the name of Wa'ad 'Adath ha-Bablim, and form a separate group among the Jews of Jerusalem.

In latter years Baghdad Jews have spread to other parts of Israel and to-day they have a Synagogue and an Organization in Tel-Aviv also. They are fully integrated into the general life of the country and the National Organizations have granted them facilities, of which they have taken good advantage, for founding agricultural settlements on the land.

ADDITIONAL NOTES

It is much regretted that as the printing of the book had advanced too far when these notes were added, they could not be inserted at the foot of the pages to which they refer.

Page 204:

[1] The reference of Maimonides, (thirteenth century) however, to the "Jews of India who do not have the oral law but only keep the Sabbath and Circumcision" may very well refer to the ancestors of the present Bene Israel. See Kobeṣ Teshuboth Harambam Leipzig, 1859, Part III, folio 44, col. 2.

Page 205:

[1] Since this was written there has appeared on the Bene Israel a work entitled *The History of the Bene Israel of India* by Haeem Samuel Kehimkar, Tel-Aviv, 1937 (290 pp. + 28 pp. illustrations) and on the Jews of Cochin an article which includes a history of their community, entitled "The Jewish Way of Life in Cochin" by David G. Mandelhaum (*Jewish Social Studies*, New York, Vol. I, No. 4, 1949, pp. 423-460).

INDEX

Aaron, 55
Aaron b. Abraham b. Aaron, 29
Aaron b. Amram, 28–29, 33–34, 36
Aaron b. Jacob Samuel, 209
Aaron b. Joseph ibn Sarjadah, 22–23, 26, 29
Aaron b. Meraioth, 61
Aaron (b. Samuel b. Daniel ha-Kohen), 81
Ab Beth Din, 10, 13n, 51, 56, 72, 138
Abba Arikha, 4
Abbamari, 43
Abbas Judah Samuel, 80
'Abbas II, Shah, 177
'Abbas Mirza, 155
'Abbasid, 15, 30, 92
Abbasid Caliph, 39, 91
'Abbasid Empire, 8, 16, 90
'Abd el-Hamid II, Sultan, 169
'Abd el-Kader, 134
'Abd el-Kadir el-Jilani, Sheikh, 170, 191
'Abd el-Khalik, Obadiah Kemal el-Dawlah, 100
'Abdallah b. Ezra b. Jacob, 139
Abdallah b. Joseph, 131, 168
'Abdallah Khdeir b. Sliman, 139–140, 169
Abdallah b. Moses b. Hayyim, etc., 136
'Abdallah Pasha, 129
'Abeidi, 137
Abhar, 92
Abi 'Ali Hasan el-Bagdadi, 7
'Abodah, 11, 176
'Abodath ha-Sedakah, 116
Aboth see Pirke Aboth
Abraham, 60
Abraham (brother of Isaac Pasha), 121
Abraham, R., b. Halafton, 96
Abraham b. Hayyim, 107
Abraham b. Isaac Aṣlan, 139
Abraham b. Moshe Hillel, 160
Abraham b. Moses ibn Jami of Kabes, 53
Abraham the Nagid, 76
Abraham, R., b. Nathan of Lunel, 11
Abraham b. Sahl b. Sagri, 41
Abraham b. Shalom, see Ibn Yayi
Abraham Gaon, R., b. R. Sherira, 10–11, 17
Abraham David Ezekiel, 216
Abraham Ibn Daud, see Ibn Daud
Abu el-Baka b. 'Abbas el-Maghrebi, 83, 85, 88
Abu Bakr, 6
Abu el-Barakat Hibbat Allah (also see Nethanel Abu el-Barakat), 61, 77, 82–83, 86–88
Abu el-Fatḥ b. el-Baṣri, 83
Abu el-Hasan, 75, 97
Abu 'l Hasan 'Ali b. 'Isa, 36
Abu Mansur, 75, 97
Abu el-Mazaffar, 83
Abu Nasr el-Dawudi, 83
Abu Sa'd, see Ibn Ezra, Isaac
Abu Sifain, 134
Abu l-Tayyib b. Faḍlan, 79
Acre, 43, 80
Adarbizan, 84
Adereth Eliyahoo, 149, 153
Adler, M. N. 62n–63n
'Adud el-Dawlah, 44
Afghan War, 208
Africa, 11, 40–41, 55n
Aha, R., 14
Ahikar, 123
Ahl el-Dimmah, 84
Ahwaz, 36–37
'Akeda, 80
'Akedath Yishak, 169, 177
'Akiba, R., 48, 150, 181
Akkad, 6
Al Majisti, 39
Albrecht, K., 86n
Aleppo, 32, 68, 70, 72, 75, 106, 113, 115, 124–125, 129, 137–138, 163, 176–177, 209, 211–212
Alexandria, 125

Alfasi, 68
'Ali, 31, 79
Ali b. David el-Shami, 41
'Ali b. 'Isa, Vizier, 36
'Ali, son of Sahl, 40
'Ali, Caliph, 7
'Ali, Gaon, 62
'Ali, Gaon II, 80
'Ali Pasha, 126
'Alim le-Terufah, 152
Alliance Israelite Universelle, 171
Alluf, 33
Alluf ha-Yeshibah, 19, 61
Alluf Ṭob, 29
Alroy, David, 62
Amora, 95
Amoraim, 47
'Amram, R., Gaon, 14
'Ana, 128, 130, 163
'Ananites, 32
Anilai, 4
Arab, 16, 84, 90, 92, 102, 142, 206
Arabia, 127n, 205, 212
Arabic, 106, 119, 151, 170–172, 179, 185, 195, 200, 205, 209, 214, 216
Aramaic, 111, 198
Arbela, 32
Arbil, 95–96, 42
Argun Khan, 92
Armenia, 90
'Arughath ha-Bosem, 145
'Arukh, 5, 52
Asad, 117–118
'Asarah Nibharim, 105
Asher b. Yehiel, 152
Ashkenazi, 148
Ashur-bani-pal, 2
Ashwiyyit el-Mayyit, 187
'Askariyyi, 143, 157
Aslan b. Ezekiel, 114
Assaf, S., 9, 56n, 60–61, 70, 96n
Assi, R., Gaon, 76, 141
Assyria, 6
Astrolabe, 112
Atelier, Ezra Sassoon, 172
Auerbach, 48n
Australia, 122
Avicenna, 66
Awhad el-Zaman, 79, 87
Awran, 128
'Azariah, 61n, 70, 72, 78
Azariah (Biblical), 96
Azariah, the Prince, 98, 100
Azariah b. Yahalalel b. Azariah b. David, 100
Azulai, Hayyim Joseph David, 146

Ba'albek, 41, 66
el-Bab, 66
Bab el-Tilsam, 178
Baba de Merwatha, 13
Babel, 5
Babla Rabbathi, 10n,
Babylon, 4, 6, 101, 165
Babylonia (and Babylonian), 1, 6, 7, 9, 16, 32, 61, 72, 77, 79, 98
Babylonian Academies, 35, 48, 54
Babylonian Jewry, 9, 19, 21, 29, 31, 33, 38, 42, 50, 153
Babylonian pilgrims, 4
Babylonian Scholars, 32
Baethgen, F., 31n
Bagadaonia, 5
Bagdath, 5
Baghdad, 1–2, 5–8, 10–17, 25–29, 31–32, 39–42, 46, 49–50, 52–56, 60–63, 65–69, 74–77, 79–83, 85–86, 88–96, 98, 100–104, 106, 108–116, 118, 120–121, 123–128, 130–132, 134–137, 139, 141, 145–146, 150–155, 157, 160, 162, 164, 167–169, 173, 176, 178–181, 187, 194, 199–203, 206, 209–213, 216–217
Baghdadian merchant bankers, 33
Bahbood bar Nater, 13
Baher, family of, 210
Balad, 87
Bamberger, 11n
Bankers, 33
Bar Satia, see Joseph b. Jacob
Baradan, 42
Barbun, 40
Barwagard, 119
Barsauma, 95
Basliyyah, 96
Barcelona, 35
Barna Shala, 10
Barney, David (of London), 201
Barukh, R., b. Isaac, 197
Barzani family, 107
Barzani, Aaron b David, 107
Barzani, Aaron b. Rahamin, 108, 205
Barzani, David b. Mordecai, 107, 129
Barzani Isaac, 108

Barzani, Joseph, 108
Barzani, Moses b. David, 107
Barzani, R. Samuel, 108
Barzani, Samuel b. Nethanel, 107
Barzani, Sason b. Mordecai, 107
Barzani, Yahya b. Reuben, 108
Basoos, Abraham, 159
Baṣrah, 15, 75, 83, 87, 95, 97, 101, 124–125, 129, 130, 208
Beirut, 146
Ben Aaron el-Bagdadi, 29
Ben 'Athira, 97–98
Ben el-Awani, 77
Ben Ish Hai, 150
Ben Ish Hayil, 151
Ben Jacob, Abraham, 144n
Ben Sion Mordecai Hazzan, 133
Ben Meir, 32–33
Ben Sira, 214
Ben Yehoyada, 151
Bene Aaron, 29
Bene Israel, 136, 204, 206, 212
Bene Natira, see Natira
Bene Yeshibah, 142
Benevolent Institution, David Sassoon, 207
Bengal, 211, 216n
Benisch, 64n
Benjamin b. Abraham Solomon David, 210
Benjamin of Tudela, 62–63, 67, 89–90, 95, 97, 98, 102, 165
Benjamin, J. J., 134
Benayahu, 151
Bet Abu Rubein, 206
Beth Din, 105, 115
Beth Din ha-Gadol, 41
Beth ha-Midrash, 169
Beth ha-Midrash in Baghdad, 137, 154
Beth Ya'aḳob, see Synagogue
Bialik, 59n
Bills of Exchange, 35
bin el-Furat, 34–37
Birkath Aboth, 149
Birkath Erusin, 143
Birkath ha-lebanah, 143
Bisher b. 'Ali el-Salubi, 98
Bishop of Baghdad, 16
Bishr b. Aaron b. 'Amram, 25, 29
Blessing of the Kohanim, 179
Bokhara (also Bokharian), 147, 148
Bombay, 125, 136–137, 143, 146, 148, 168, 195, 203–211
Bonfid, Solomon, 208
Book of Precepts, 68
Bornstein, 33n
Bowers, John, 210
British, 161, 164, 208, 216
Brody, H., 86, 96, 101n, 197n
Browne, Edward G., 93
Budge, Sir E. A. W., 2
Burial customs, 186
Burma, 152, 211
Bushire, 125, 128–129, 206, 207
Bustanai, 214
Buza'ah, 66
Byzantine Empire, 42
Byzantium, 38, 46

Cairo, 147
Calcutta, 104n, 120, 122, 136–137, 142, 144n, 148, 153n, 159, 161–162, 163n, 169n, 180, 199, 201, 203, 209–214, 216
Calendar, 106
Caliph, 11, 16, 38, 60, 67, 73, 74, 89, 90, 92 and under respective names
Canaan, 61
Canton, 216–217
Catholic, 17, 95
Caucasus, 90
Central Europe, 61
Chair of Elijah, 167, 183
Chancellor of the Empire, 92
Chandernagore, 211
Chaudhuri, Mr. Justice, 215
Childbirth, 182
China, 142–143, 149, 202, 216
Chinsura, 211
Christians, 16, 52, 87, 94, 130
Christianity, 138
Church, 138
Circumcision, 143
Cochin, 108, 204, 205, 211, 212
ha-Cohen, R. Abraham, 69
Cohen, E. M. D., 214
Confession, 141
Constantine, 148
Constantinople, 110–112, 123, 126, 137–138, 147, 158–160, 163, 169
Cordova, 54, 65, 88
Coronel, 106n
"Court Bankers", 33
Crypto-Jews, 118
Cyrus, 3

Da'ath wu-Thebunah, 152
Dabar be-'Itto, 133
Daiches, S., 3
Daḳḳakat, 185
Daḳuḳa, 95, 96
Damascus, 54, 60, 64, 80, 106, 124–125, 129, 130, 138, 142, 146
Dangoor, Elisha b. Nissim, 158–160, 162–164, 166
Dangoor, Ezra Reuben, 108, 164, 178, 201
Daniel (Biblical), 96, 98
Daniel, 66, 75
Daniel, family of, 168
Daniel, Alluf ha-Yeshibah, Gaon, 61, 62
Daniel ('Aziz) Resh Methibta, 74
Daniel b. Abi el-Rabi' ha-Kohen, 78, 80
Daniel, Gaon, ben Elcazar Hasid, 97
Daniel b. Elcazar b. Nethanel (Hibbat Allah), 73, 75
Daniel b. Hisdai, 90, 91
Daniel b. Judah, the son of the Exilarch, 10, 17
Darkhe Noam, 106
Daud Pasha, 123–126, 210
Daud, Sayyidna bin, 90
Daughter of Samuel b. Ali, 83
Daughter of Samuel b. Hofui, 56
David, ancestor of Sheikh Sason, 206
David, grandfather of Sheikh Sason, 206
David, King, 10, 16
David (the Naghid), 80
David, R., D'Beth Hillel see D'-Beth Hillel
David b. Hayyim, 209
David, b. Hodayah, 101
David b. Joseph b. Elijah Baba, 98
David b. Judah, the son of the Exilarch, 10, 17–18
David b. Mordecai Kohen, 116, 121
David, R. (of Mosul), 91
David (son of Sheikh Sason), see Sassoon, David
David Sassoon School, 171
David Sassoon Benevolent Institution in Bombay, 201
David b. Zakkai the Exilarch, 10–11, 13–14, 17–19, 21–22, 25–28, 32, 33, 56–57, 97
Davidic origin, 46, 67
Davidson, 42, 52, 53n, 75
Day of Atonement, 11, 141
Dayyan (also Dayyanim), 11, 56, 80, 138, 139, 164
Dayyana di Baba, 13n
D'Beth Hillel, R. David, 127, 205, 212, 213
De Lacy O'Leary, 40n
De Lisbona, Rephael, 128
Deir el-Gharbi, 130
Denia, 60
Derekh ha-Hayyim, 138
Diarbekr, 90, 124, 142
Diaspora, 46, 59, 69, 122, 203
Digdig, 193
Diwan of Elcazar habbabli, 70, 73, 79
Diwan of Isaac Ibn Ezra, 60, 86
Diwan of Saleḥ b. Joseph Maṣliah, 120
Diwan, Judah, 108
Damayin, 103
Dim'ath 'Ashukim, 148n
Dinah, daughter of Reuben Nissim, 169
Doresh Tob le 'Ammo, 209
Dosa, 51
Dukes, L., 88n
"Dusan el 'Atbah", 182, 191
Dutch, 211
Dwarat el Kbiri, 191
Dwek ha-Kohen, family of, 210
Dyers, 33

Eastern communities, 31
Eastern Jewry, 25, 155, 192
Eben Saphir, 207
Eben Shelema, 150
Ebiathar, 107
Ebiathar Kohen Sedek, R., 54
Edessa, 66
Effendi, 123
Egypt, 7, 33, 38, 46, 61, 142, 146
'Ein Ya'akob, 151, 214
el-Abbasi, el-Muminin, 89
el-Atir, 85
el-Baghdadi, Samuel b. Joseph, see Samuel b. Joseph
el-Birah, 66
el-Dahri, 96, 101
el-Daskari, Sheikh Abu el-Hasan, 83
Eldad ha-Dani, 5n, 214

Elam, 61
Elias Meyer Free School Talmud Torah, 216
Eleazar b. Hilal ibn Fahd, 73–74
Eleazar b. Jacob ha-Babli, 70, 76
Eleazar b. Phinchas, 78
Eleazar, son of Samuel b. 'Ali, 77
Elḥanan b. Shemariah of Fusṭaṭ, 53
Elḥanan of Alexandria, 41
El-Harizi, Judah b. Solomon, 76, 91, 95–97
El-Kahir, 23
"el-Mandel", 192
"el-Moser", 124
el-Ozeir, 84, 97, 110, 112, 115, 155
Eliezer Ashkenazi, 45
Eliezer ben Pedath, 1
Elyashar, Jacob b. Joseph, 120, 129
Elyashar, R. Yeruham, 164
Elijah, 30, 55, 99, 108, 183, 200
Elijah b. Joshua b. Obadiah, 137–139, 214
Elijah b. Moses b. Hayyim, etc., 136, 140, 146, 188
Elijah of Nisibis, 31
Elijah b. Sliman Mani, see Mani
Elijah b. Solomon, 214
Elijah b. Solomon Kohen, 137
Eliot, George, 94
el-Kal'ah, 66, 95
el-Kifil, see Kifil
el-Kifti, 86
el-Maghrebi, see Abu el-Baka, 85
El-Mas'udi, 30
el-Moser, Mulla Muḥammad, 124, 126
'El-Mu'addilin, 15
el-Muktadir, Caliph, 23, 34, 36
el-Muminin el-Abbasi, 89
el-Musta'sim-billah, 91
El-Mu'tamid, 34
El-Mutawakkil, Caliph, 34
el-Nasir bidin-Allah, 73, 91
el-Rahbah, 66
el-Rakah, 66
el-Zagani, 86
Elphinstone, Lord, 208
Em ha-Melekh, 106, 150
Emir, 89
Emir of Baghdad, 90
England, 212
English, 171, 172
Epstein, A., 13, 31n, 65
'Erub, 166
Esther, 97
Ethrogim, 143
Euclid, 84
Euphrates, 4, 8, 80
Europe, 51, 162, 208
Evil Eye, 193
Exilarch, 8–12, 14, 16, 18–28, 42, 46–47, 66–67, 69, 80, 90–101, 105
Exilarch-Gaon, 27
Exilarch's Court, 13
Exilarchate, 10, 13, 17, 18, 21
Ezekiel (the prophet), 98, 101, 104, 140, 150, 154, 156, 167, 181, 184, 200
Ezekiel b. Hakham 'Abdallah Hanein, 161
Ezekiel b. Jacob Rahamim, 209
Ezekiel called Khawajah Shams el-Din b. Ithamar, 78
Ezekiel b. Nisan, 209
Ezekiel b Rahel (also see Gabbai), 123–125
Ezekiel b. Reuben b. Manasseh, 136, 168
Ezekiel b. Sason b. Mordecai, 206
Ezekiel b. Solomon, 214
Ezekiel b. Solomon b. David, 168
Ezekiel b. Mordecai Kohen, 116, 121
Ezobi, Joseph, 152
Ezra family, 210
Ezra, the Scribe, 75, 84, 97, 101, 104, 110, 112, 115, 150, 154, 181
Ezra, Sir David, 210
Ezra, David b. Joseph, 213, 215
Ezra, Elijah, 213, 215
Ezra b. Ezekiel ha-Babli, 111
Ezra b. Joseph (the Nasi), 139
Ezra ha-Kohen, 168
Ezra, Mrs. Mozelle, 216
Ezra, N. E. B., 217
Ezra b. Rahel (also see Gabbai), 123–125
Ezra b. Sason b. Ezra, 140
Ezra, R., el-Sheikh Sadakah b. R. Israel, 97–98

Fano, 112
Far East, 202, 216
Faraj Hayyim b. Solomon b. Ezekiel Judah, 135
"Fath el Wujh", 184
Fatimid Caliph, 39

Ferrara, 200
Firdaws al-Hikhma, 40
Fischel, Dr. W., 33–36
France, 44, 80, 216
French, 43, 155, 171
Friedlander Israel, 5n
Fright, 194
Ftayyah, 201
Fulda Jacob b. Mordecai of, 108
Funeral customs, 186
Fustat, 7, 68, 70

Gabbai family, 213
Gabbai, Aaron b. Saleh b. Joseph, 129, 130
Gabbai, Abraham b. Ezekiel, 141
Gabbai, Ezekiel b. Joseph b. Nissim b. Menahem, 123
Gabbai, Ezekiel b. Joshua, 146, 208
Gabbai, Hayyim b. Moses, 129
Gabbai, Isaac b. David b. Jeshu'ah, 120
Gabbai, Joseph b. Ezra b. Abraham 158
Gabbai, Joseph b. Nissim, 110
Gabbai, Joshuah, 141
Gabbai, Michael b. David b. Jeshuah, 116
Gabbai, Moses b. Mordecai, 208
Gabbai, Rachel, 123
Gabbai, Saleh b. Aaron, 116
Gabbai, Sason b. Ezekiel Mordecai, 205
Gabriel b. Jacob b. Elisha, 140
Gagin, R. Shalom Moses Hai, 147
Gan Yeladim, 171
Gaon (or Geonim or Geonate), 7, 9–11, 15, 18, 20–22, 35, 42, 45–51, 53, 54, 60–61, 69, 72–74, 76–78, 80, 81, 87–90, 104–105, 141, 179
Gaon of Palestine, 32, 41
Gaon of Wilna, 136, 152
Garden of Eden, 57
Garch, Isaac, 126
Genghis Khan, 91
Genizah, 7, 9, 12, 17, 28, 32, 48, 55, 57, 63–64, 70, 73–75, 100
Geonic period, 5
Geonim, see Gaon
Georgia, 90, 123
German, 93, 118, 155
Germany, 99
Gerondi, Jonah, 112
Ghawi family, 168
Gikitilia, Joseph, 134
Ginzberg, L., 15n, 28, 42n
Goldziher, 73
Goorji, Elijah b. Moses Joseph Ezra, 169
Goorji, Joseph, 159–163
Graetz, 17, 43
Great Baghdad, see Babla Rabbathi
Great Britain, 175, 178
Greek medicine, 40
Greek science and philosophy, 39

Hab, 188
Haber, 80
Ḥabib b. Isma'il, 41
Hadrath Zekenim, 200
ha-Dober (periodical), 200
Hadrakh, 60
ha-Emunoth weha-De'oth, 23
Haftaroth (according to Baghdad rite), 178
Haggadah, 141, 176
Haggadah Shel Pesah, 145, 179
ha-Kanah, 112
ha-Sepharadi, Abraham b. Hayyeem, 112
Hai, R., Gaon, 12, 15, 26–27, 41–44, 45n, 46, 48, 50–56, 59, 60
Hai b. David, Gaon, 11–13, 176
Hakham Bashi, see also Wakil Hakham Bashi, 103–105, 107, 138, 157–164
Hakhamim, 157, 160–161, 166
Hakkafoth, 54
Hakkafoth le-Simhath ha-Torah, 150
Halakhoth Gedoloth, 41
Halat Effendi, 123
Halper B., 68n
Hamadan, 95, 97, 119, 139
ha-Maggid, 153
Hamai Gaon, 106
Haman, 29, 199
Hamath, 66
Hamid bin 'Abbas, 37
Hamwi, Abraham b. Raphael, 163
Hana, R. – Bagdethaa, 4, 5
Hananel, R., b. Hushiel, 51, 53
Hananel (b. Samuel b. Daniel ha-Kohen), 81

Hananiah (Biblical), 96
Hananiah (the nephew of R. Joshua b. Hananiah), 4
Hanaiah b. Ali ha-Levy, 63
Hananiah Gaon, 46
Hanilai, 4
Hanina b. Hamma, 1
Hanokh b. Moses, 53
Hanukkah, 184, 194
Hanuth Abu Sifain, 134
Haran, 66
Hariri family, 109
Hariri, Moses b. Abraham, 109
Hariri, Phinehas b. Isaac, 106, 109
Harizi, 75, 77, 85
Harkavy, A., 13n, 29, 30, 36n, 53, 58n, 66, 88n
Harun ar-Rashid, 40
Hasan bar Barikhan, 13
Hasan b. Fadlan, 98
Hasde Aboth, 152
Hasba, 115
Hashim, 31
Hashkabah, 188
Hasid, 75
Hathan ha-Melekh, 214
Hayyim b. Amram, 128
Hayyim Jacob ha-Kohen, 142
Hazoorayat wa-Tafsirhum, 151–152
Hazzan, 80, 99, 133, 148, 187
Hazzan, Ben Sion Mordecai, 133, 151–152
Hazzan Joseph, 99
Hazzan, Saleh, see Masliah
Hazzanim, 67, 72
Head of the Captivity, 62, 90
Heads of the Exile, see Exilarchs
Hebar, 84
Hebrath Meyassede Beth ha-Refuah see Society
Hebrath Tomke Torah, see Society
Hebrew, 106, 111, 138
Hebron, 118, 120, 129, 146, 148n, 171
Hefes, R., b. Yasliah, 68
Hekhal, 166
Henna, 184
Hezekiah b. David, 60, 95
Hezekiah, Khawaja Bazur Jamhar, 100
Hibbat Allah, see Abu el-Barakat and see Daniel b. Eleazar b. Nethaniel
Hibbat Allah b. Malka, 86–87
High Festival, 14
Hildesheimer, 13n, 45n
Hilkhoth Niddah, 66
Hilkhoth Tefillin of Nahmanides, 74
Hillah, 61, 95–98, 128–129
Hillel, 4
Hillula Rabba, 150
Hirsch, Rabbi W., 187
Hisdai, Head of the Captivity, 62
Hisdai b. Naṭronai, 13
Hit, 4
Hiyya, R., 1
Hizana, 84
"Hlechel", 184
Hoil Mosheh, 110
Hok le-Yisrael, 201
Homs, 66
Hong Kong, 143, 171 203, 216, 217
Hormuz (Persia), 101
Hosha'na Rabbah, 54, 55
Hospital, David Sassoon General, 207
Hospital, Ezra, 216
Hospital, Meir Eliyyahoo, 175
Hospital, Reemah Khdoory, 175
Hulago Khan, 91
Huppah, 185
Huzai, 37

Ibn Abi el-Baghl, 29, 30
Ibn Aflah, 86
Ibn 'Aknin, R. Joseph b. Judah, 67
Ibn el-Darb, 191
Ibn el-Dastur, 63
Ibn el-Jasus, 14, 176
Ibn el-Sa'i, 73
Ibn Daud, Abraham, 26–27, 60
Ibn Ezra Abraham b. Meir, 5n, 61, 85–86, 204, 208
Ibn Ezra, Isaac (Abu Sa'd), 60–61, 85–86, 88
Ibn Ezra, Moses, 208
Ibn Gabirol, Solomon, 59, 186, 208
Ibn Janah, R. Jonah, 14
Ibn Kemmune, 98
Ibn Krispin, Don Abraham b. Joseph, 167
Ibn Nayim, Simeon Ben Sion, 148
Ibn Sa'id, Israel b. Joseph, 129
Ibn Sakni, 60
Ibn Satanas, see Joseph b. Isaac ibn Satanas

Ibn Yahya, David, 112
Ibn Yayi, Abraham b. Shalom, 124, 126
Ibn Zimra, R., David, 192
Idra, 205, 216
Ifham el-Yahud, 82
"Iggereth Araḥith", 64
"Iggereth Dikar", 64
Iggereth Maggid Mesarim, 139
Iggereth Rab Sherira Gaon, 47
Ihi Dekara, 4
Ikhloo Re'im, 179
Imdi, 99
Imre Binah, 152
Imre Sason, 133
Imre Shabbath, 142
India, 126, 127n, 131, 135–136, 142, 146, 149, 162, 175, 202, 204–205, 208, 211–212, 216–217
India, Western, 205
Indian, 83
Indulka, 192
Installation service, 10
Interpretations of Dreams, 214
Iraki ha-Kohen, Eleazer b. Aaron Se'adyah, 201, 210, 213
'Iraq, 7, 84, 168
Isaac R., Gaon, 7, 77–78, 96, 168–169, 191
Isaac the Nasi, 116
Isaac el-Awani, 77
Isaac of Acre, 43
Isaac b. David Jacob, 205
Isaac, R. b. Israel, 75, 77
Isaac b. Mordecai b. Sason, 133, 145
Isaac b. Moses, 60
Isaac b. Natira, 30, 31
Isaac Nissim b. Rahamim, 113, 148n
Isaac Pasha, 120, 122
Isaac b. Reuben of Barcelona, 52
Isaac, R., Sar Shalom, 96
Isaac b. Sheshath, 43
Isaac, R., Shohet, 164
Isaac ibn Shweikh, 75, 77
Isaiah b. Josef of Tiflis, 78
Isaiah R., ha-Levy b. Rab Abba, 8
Ishak b. Ibrahim el-Basri el-Hawi, 83
Ishaq, ibn Amran al-Israeli, 40
Ishmael, R., 48
Islam, 83–85, 87, 89
Ispahan, 139, 152
Israel, 51, 74, 217
Israel b. Joseph, see Ibn Sa'id
Israel b. Samuel of Sklow, 136
Israel b. Sason Israel, 159
Israel R., b. Shalom, 163
Israel Kohen, R., Gaon, 58
Israel's Messenger, 217
Issi R., Gaon, 141
Italian Schools, 52
Italy, 42, 46

Jacob b. Fathi b. 'Abayyid, 137
Jacob, great grandfather of Sheikh Sason, 206
Jacob ha-Sopher b. Moses ha-Sofer, 167
Jacob b. R. Joseph Hayyim, 152
Jacob b. Joseph b. Jacob ha-Rofe, 137, 144
Jacob ibn Leilah, 191
Jacob b. Nissim of Kairuwan, 53
Jacob Semah, 137, 154, 168, 206, 210
"Jalwah", 185
Jamal el-Dawlat Yehizkiah (Hezekiah), 97
Jamal Satem, 97
Japheth b. 'Ali 5n, 70
Jedid el-Islam, 119
Jehoiachin, (King), 165
Jelal, 99
Jemuel, 97
Jerba, 152
Jerusalem, 1, 3–4, 54, 85, 110–111, 120, 127n, 129, 133, 137, 142, 146–147, 150–152, 156, 163n, 164, 171, 201, 212, 217
Jeshu'ah, 97
Jeshu'ah b. Joseph of Tlemcen, 112
Jeshurum (periodical), 200
Jewish Boys' and Girls' School, 216
Jewish Charitable Fund, 216
Jewish Free School Kehillath Jeshurun, 216
Jewish Free School Talmud Torah, 216
Jewish Girls' School, 216
Jewish Schools Committee, 170
Jewish Women's League, 216
Jew's Bridge, 7
Jezira, 142
Jihan, Barukh, 147
John bar Maserjoye, 39
Jonah of Mardin, 98, 100

Jose, R., the Galilean, 170, 191
Joseph, R., of Pumbaditha, 11
Joseph b. 'Ali ha-Kohen, 95
Joseph descendant of Sliman b. David Ma'tuk, 131
Joseph b. 'Amram of Sajelmasa, 53
Joseph R., b. Berakhyah, 45
Joseph R., bar Mar Rab Hiyyah, 10
Joseph el-Baradani, 42
Joseph el-Basir, 58
Joseph ibn Satanas, see Joseph b. Isaac ibn Satanas
Joseph Hayyim, Hakham, 134n, 137, 149–155, 157, 158, 167, 178, 217
Joseph b. Isaac ibn Satanas, 53–54
Joseph b. Jaber, 14
Joseph b. Jacob, 21, 26
Joseph b. Jacob b. 'Ubal, 35
Joseph b. Moses, 125
Joseph Nissim b. Sliman, 168
Joseph b. Phineas, 30, 33, 36–39
Joseph Rahamim, 124
Joseph b. Sliman Ma'tuk, 112
Joseph b. Taber, 66
Josephus, 4n
Joshiah, 100
Joshiah Hasan, 21, 23
Joshua, also see Safi el-Dawla 80,
Joshua b. Solomon Bekhor Husein, 201
Joshua the High Priest, 144, 150, 155, 181
Josippon, 214
Judah family, 210
Judah Rab, 166
Judah b. Abun, 83
Judah b. Bethera, 4
Judah b. David b. Zakkai, 20, 47
Judah, Ezekiel, 213, 215
Judah bar Ezekiel, 5
Judeo-Spanish, 139

Ka'ak, 187
Kaarath Kesef, 152
Kabbala, 48, 52–53, 106–107, 110–111, 134, 146, 152–153, 155, 178, 200, 214, 216
"Kabsah", 143
Kaddish, 186–187
Kadoorie, Sir Eliezer S., 171
Kadoorie, Laura, 171
Kairuwan, 35, 39–40, 45, 47, 51, 68
"Kaleicha", 187, 188
Kallah, 10
Kalon, 84
Kalwadi, 8
Kaminka, 86n
Kaneh Middah, 210
Kanfe Yona, 106
Kanisat el-'Irakiyyin, 7
Kantarah, 142
Kantarah-el-Yahud, 7
Kanun el-Nisa, 151
Kapparoth, 153
Karachi, 206
Karaite, 22, 32, 48, 85, 170
Kark, 89
Karmisin, 11, 38
Karo, R., Joseph, 139, 141
Kasar, Sliman, 108, 205
Kasin family, 139n
Kasin, Elijah, 138
Kasin, Raphael b. Elijah, 138, 157
Kasini, 138
Kasr, 11
Kauffmann, Dr. D., 45
Kayserling, M., 97n
Keeper of the Seal, 123
Kehillath Ya'akob, 106
Kehimkar, Haeem Samuel, 218
Kemmune's Tanḳiḥ el Bahath, 98
Kenesiyyah Leshem Shamayim, 192
Keren Yeshu'ah, 150
Kether Malkuth, 150
Khalaf, 62, 130
Khalid (the general), 6
Khalkol, 88
Khans, 91, 94
Khawaja Badi' el Zaman, 100
Khawaja Bazur Jamhar, see Hezekiah
Khawaja Khalifah, 100
Khawajah Shams el-Din b. Ithamar see Ezekiel
Khleif, 210
Khorasan, 18, 23, 38–39, 90, 139
Khuzistan, 37
Kifil, 98, 155
Kings of Judah, 16
Kirkuk, 95–96, 98, 142
Kirsh Rayich, 134, 158
Kirsh Rumi, 134
Kissat Ahl Mathal, 195
Kitab al-Bawl, 40
Kitab el-Iman, 52
Kitab el-Imanat wul-I'tikadat, 23

Kitab el-Madkhal ila el-Talmud, 57
Kitab el-Shara wul-Bai', 52
Kitab el-Sharayi', 57
Kitab Mu'taber, 87
Kitab Nuskh el-Shar' wa-Usul el-Din wa-Faru'ah, 58
"Kodesh", 169
Kohanim, 54
Kohen, David b. Mordecai, 116
Kohen Ṣedek, Gaon, 11, 17–21, 28, 32, 38–39, 56
Kohen, Shabbethai, 139
Kol Sason, 132
Kohut, 5
Koldeway, Dr., 2
Kolmar, Joseph b. Saul, 129
Koordistan, 127n
Koran, 58, 84
Krauss, S., 99, 197
Kufah, 31, 95
Kuhistan, 84
Kuntres Kothbenu le-Hayyim, 214
Kuntris Maroth Yehezkel, 152
Kurd, 129
Kurdistan, 212
Kut, 142

Labourt, 95
Ladino-speaking Jews, 192
Lahba, Nissim, 147
Laniyado, David b. Solomon, 151
Laniyado, Isaac, 119
Laniyado, Raphael Solomon, 108
Laniyado, Samuel, 113
Laniyado, Saul, 126
Laniyado, Solomon, 113
Laws of Shehitah, 214
Lazarus, Felix, 16n, 17n
Le Strange G., 2n, 5, 6n, 7n
Lebanon, 41
Legal recognition, 36
Lehmann, Dr. Markus, 214
"Leilt 'Akd el-Yas", 182
"Leilt el-Himmi", 184
"Leilt el-Khadbah", 184
"Leilt el-Sitti", 182
Leshon Hakhamim, 151
Leshon Limmudim, 112
Letters of credit, 35
Levy, E. S., 215n
ha-Levy, Eleazar b. Hillel, 73
ha-Levy, Ezekiel Hayyim b. Salem, 212
ha-Levy, Ezekiel b. Ezra b. Joshua, 145
ha-Levy, Hananaiah, see Hananaiah
ha-Levy, Jacob b. Joseph, 99
ha-Levy, Judah, 112, 179, 197, 208
ha-Levy, R., Moses, 158
ha-Levy, Obadiah b. Abraham, 138, 157
ha-Levy, Raphael, 147
ha-Levy, Samuel, see Samuel
ha-Levy, Todros, 268
Lewin, B. M., 7n, 51n
Likkute Amarim, 139
Livorno, 132, 140, 149, 150, 200, 214
London, 143
Luah La-Tekufoth, 106
Luncz, A. M., 192
Luria, Isaac, 150, 152, 154, 200

Ma'aseh Eliyyahoo, 148
Ma'aseh Hiyya, 214
Ma'aseh Nissim, 201, 209
Maaseh Rab, 110–111
Ma'asim Mefoarim, 201
Madras, 127n, 204, 211
Maggid Mesharim, 214
Maghreb, 76
Maghreb liturgy, 179
Magi, 16
Mahazor Aleppo, 75
Mahazor for the Festivals, 108
Mahmud, 86
Mahmud II, Sultan, 123, 178
Maḥmudiyyah, 96
Mai wu-Milh, 193
Maimonides, 14, 43, 63, 65–69, 72, 76, 80–81, 85, 88, 95, 98, 107, 176, 200
Malabar, 143
Malabari, 212
Malaga, 27, 43
Malkah, the beadle, 169
Malkisedek, 100
Malter, H., 26n, 31n
Mamlekheth Kohanim, 150
Manasseh b. Ezekiel Reuben, 154, 165
Manbagh, 66, 95
Mandelbaum, David G. 218
Manhig ha-Rofeim, 40
Mani, Abraham Barukh, 148n
Mani, Elijah b. Sliman, 145–148

Mani, Menasseh, 148n
Mani, Sliman Menahem, 145
Mann el-Sama, 144
Mann, J., 10, 29, 35n
Mansur-Caliph, 7, 8
Marabut, 134
Marathi, 212
Mardin, 95, 98–100, 142
Margoliuth, 5n
Market of Baghdad, 6
Marmorstein, A., 50n
Marranos in Persia, 119
Marranos, Eastern, 119
Marriage law, 136
Marw, 39
Mashal we-Nimshal, 152
Masliah of Sicily, 53
Masliah, David Hai b. Ezekiel Abraham, 207
Masliah, Ezra b. Elijah, 210–211
Masliah, Nissim, 115, 136, 168, 178
Masliah, Saleh b. Joseph, 107, 128, 130–131, 133–134, 178
Masliyyaḥ, Hakham Saleh, 168
Mateb'at el-Wataniyyah el-Asrailyyah, 201
Matloob b. Rahamim b. Mordecai, 129
M'atoo family, 183
Matteh Mosheh, 110
Matthews, 5n
Ma'tuk family, 112
Ma'tuk, Sliman b. David, 112, 120, 178, 210
Max M., 171
Mazidiyyah, 61
Measles, 190
"Mebasser: *The Jewish Gazette*," 214
Mebasser Kahana, 32
Mebo ha-Talmud, 57
Meborakh, R., b. R. David, 14
Media, 64
Medians, 6
Medical school, 39
Meghillah, 25
Meghillath ha-Nabi Daniel Wa-Haberaw, 98
Meghillath Paras, 129
Meir ha-Kohen, 99
Meghillath Setharim, 68
Meir R., 150, 181
Meir Bath 'Ayin, 150
Meirath 'Enayim, 43
Mejlis in Baghdad, 158
Mekah u-Memkar, 52
"Mekonenoth", 186
Menahem b. Saleh b. Daniel, 159
Menahem b. Suliman ibn el Rukhi, 85
Merchant bankers, 33
Meshed, 208
Meshullam b. Ḳalonymos of Lucca, 53
Mesopotamia, 1, 16, 51, 61, 70, 74, 76, 90–92, 94, 142, 205
Messiah (Messianic), 55, 63
Meyohas, Moses b. Mordecai, 214
"Mezammerim", 183
Mi Khamokha, 112, 179
Michael (brother of Isaac Pasha), 121
Michael Nasi, 129
Midkar 'Abdekhon Kodamekhon, 176
Midrash, 121, 169
Midrash Aaron Saleh, 152
Midrash Abu Mnashshi, 136, 168
Midrash Bet Zilkha, 168
Midrash Eliyyahu, 140, 146
Midrash Hakham Shim'on, 168
Midrash Jacob Ṣemaḥ, 137, 168
Midrash ha-Mishnah, 49
Midrash Nuriel, 152, 172
Midrash Reuben Hazkel Yehuda, 168
Midrash Talmud Torah, 171
Midrash Tannaim, 49
Milah, 167, 183
Military Tax, 103, 143
"Minha we-Arbith", 189
Minhag of old Baghdad, 177
Minhag of Yemen, 176
Minhag Kirsh Rumi, 134
Minhath Kenaoth Mazkereth 'Awon 148
Mishael (Biblical), 96
Mi Shebberakh, 103, 196
Mishmereth ha-Hodesh, 150
Mishpete ha-Shebu'oth, 52
Mismor le-Asaf, 132
Mizrahi Family, 106
Mizrahi, Barukh b. Moses, 200
Mizrahi, Isaac b. Judah, 211
Mizrahi, Jacob b. Jonah b. Benjamin b. Abraham, 106
Mizrahi, Simeon b. Jona, 106–108, 112

Mizrahi, Solomon b. Simeon, 112, 113
Moda'ah we-Gillui Da'ath, 152
Money changers, 33
Mongol Khans, 91–92
Mongols (Mongolian), 91–94
Montefiori, Sir Moses, 137, 163
Mordecai, 77, 97
Mordecai b. Moses, 99
Mosciri family, 147
Mosciri, Nissim, 147
Moses, 27, 69, 150, 154
Moses (brother of Isaac Pasha), 121
Moses b. Abraham b. Aaron, 29
Moses b. Abraham b. Saleh, 98, 129
Moses b. Benjamin, 110
Moses Hayyim, R., 127, 137, 141, 206, 213
Moses Sadkah, 181
Moses b. Simeon b. Moses b. Sason, 133
Moses, R., of Kief, 65
Moses b. Isaac of Maghreb, 53
Moslem, 6, 8, 16, 31, 44, 52, 58, 61, 82, 84, 87–88, 90–91, 94, 114, 119, 130, 134, 139, 161, 169–170, 177, 185
Mosul (Ashur), 32, 64, 67, 80, 87, 91, 95, 107–108, 114, 124–125, 128–129, 142, 205
Mount of Olives, 54–55
Msahbah, 192
Msalha, 192
Muhaddib el-Dawla, 92
Muhammad, 84
Muhammad bin 'Ubaidallah bin Yahya, 34
Muhammadan, 89
Muhammadan law, 34
Muhammedans, New, 119
Muhassin b. al-Furat, 36
Muktadir, 30
Muller, D. H., 5n
Muktafi, 30, 82, 87
Mulla Ibrahim b. Nathan, 208
Mulla Muhammad, see el-Moser
Mulla Musa, 208
Mulmain, 211
Musar Haskel, 53
Murashu, 2
Murad IV, Sultan, 177
Musar ha-Rofeim, 39
Mussafia, 48n
Mustadi, Caliph, 82
Mustafa Beg ibn Muhammad Beg Arbi'i, 123, 124
Mutanjid billah Yusuf, 89
Mu'tadid, Caliph, 29
Mutakallim, 45, 66

ha-Naghid, Joseph, 123
ha-Naghid, see Samuel ha-Naghid, 26
Nahalath Shib'ah, 148
Naharwan, 14
Nahmanides, 43, 74, 152
Nahmias, 208
Nahr Malka, 4
Nahr Sura, 4
Nahum (the prophet), 108
Nahum b. Haroon el-Ba'albeki, 41
Nahum ha-Hazzan el-Baradani, 42
Nahum, ha Madi, 4
Nashra, 191
Nasi (also Nesiim), 100–101, 105, 113–116, 120–121, 123–124, 127–129, 131–132, 136, 139, 166, 206
Nathan ha Babli, 4, 9, 11–12, 28–30, 38–39, 97
Nathan R., b. Yehiel, 52
Natira, 10, 12, 28, 30, 32–33, 38
Natira b. Sahl, 31
Natronai R., Kahana b. Rab Amunah (Ahnai), 7
Nawah Tehillah, 137
Nawi Reuben b. David, 136
Nazarite, 119
Nebuchadnezzar, 2
Neharde'a, 4, 8, 15, 111, 166
Neharde'a, Jewish Academy, 4
Nehemiah b. Abraham, 41
Nes Tahmasp, 177
Nestorian monks, 7
Nestorians, 95
Ner Tamid, 167
Nethanel, R., Abu el-Barakat, 85, 88
Nethiboth 'Olam, 138
Neubauer A., 11n, 12n, 17n, 26n, 54n, 59n, 95n, 96n
New Moon, 150, 155, 179, 189
New South Wales, 122
Neweh Saddikim, 151
Niflaim Ma'asekhah, 152
Ninth of Ab, 154
Nippur, 2
Nisibis, 32, 142

Nissi, R., of Naharwan Resh Kallah 14, 19
Nissi, R., b. R. Samuel, 14
Nissim, R., contemporary of R. Meborakh, 14
Nissim R., Rosh Yeshibah, 14, 76, 141
Nissim b. Jacob of Kairuwan, 35, 51, 53, 68
Nissim b. Shalom Huṣein, 139
Nissim Hazzan, see Masliah Nissim
Nissim, R., of the family Hazzan Joseph, 99
Nofeth Sufim, 140
North Africa, 38, 46, 51–52, 83, 179, 184
Nuriel, Rebecca, 172

Obadia Kamal el-Dawlah 'Abd el Khalik, 98
Obermayer, Jacob, 2n, 5, 37, 79n, 95, 153–156
"Oheb Emeth", 162
'Okbara, 89
Old Market of Baghdad, 41
'Ole Babel, 203
Or Zarua' 74, 150
Orhoth Hayyim, 152
Oriental Jews, 138,
'Ozere Dallim, see Society

"Paerah: *The Jewish Gazette*", 159, 161, 214
Paitanim, 42
Palestine, 1, 3–4, 32, 38, 55, 59, 99, 101, 118–119, 129, 146, 149, 155, 165, 167, 173, 217
Palestinian, 41
Palestinian Gaon, see Gaon of Palestine
Palestinian Jewry, 31–32
Palestinian scholars, 4, 32
Palmyra, 66, 130
Papu, R. David, 164
Panigel, R. Raphael Meir, 151
Parise Yisrael, 43
Parma, 75
Parokheth, 167
Parthians, 6
Pasha, 122–123, 125, 129–130, 146–147, 157
Passover, 153
Pasul, 84
Peath ha-Shulhan, 136
Penso, Abraham Hayyim, 148n
Pereira, Moses, 146
Peroz—Shabur, 7
Persia (also Persian), 2, 3, 5, 6, 13, 38–39, 61, 64, 70, 77–78, 84, 90, 92–94, 101, 107, 118, 127n, 129, 139, 142, 153, 155, 176, 208, 212
Pethahiah of Ratisbon, 63–64, 70, 91, 102, 165
Pethihath Eliahoo, 178
Phinehas, 100
Pidyon Peter Hamor, 181
Pinsker, S., 170
Piri Shabur, 13
Pirke Aboth, 152
Pithe Teshubah, 145
Pithron Holomoth, 53
Pizmonim, 145, 214
Plague, 127
Plague, the Great, 113, 121
Poets Baghdadian, 178
Polemic, 214
Poona, 205, 207, 216
Porte, see Sublime Porte
Poznanski, S., 31n, 41n, 60–61, 65n, 67–68, 71n, 72n, 73n, 75, 77n, 80, 81n, 86n, 87n, 101n
Prince of Baghdad, 98
Prince of the Captivity, 126
Prince Consort, 207
Proverbs, 196–199
Pseudo-Messiah, 85
Ptolemy, 39
Pumbaditha, 5, 8, 10, 12, 15, 19–22, 26, 28–29, 50–51, 56
Punishment, corporal, 120
Purim, 25, 178, 180, 184, 190
Pyrenees, 76

Rab, 4
Rab Berakhoth, 149
Rab Pealim, 151
Raba, 77
Rabba Bar Abbahu, 46
Rabbah bar bar Hannah, 110
Rabbanites, 32
Rabbinate, Baghdad, 130, 136–137
Rabnitzki, 59
Rahamim 'Abdallah, 108

Rahamim b. Reuben b. Mordecai, 200
Rakkah, 95
Rakuk, 96
Rangoon, 153, 203, 211
Rapoport, 13n, 43, 95n
Rashe Galuyyoth, 16
Rashi, 5
Rawlinson, Sir Henry, 2
Rayyis el-Ruhani, 164
Reformatory Institution, David Sasson Industrial, 207
Refuath ha-Nefesh, 150
Reifmann, 13n
Renaissance, 39
Rephael de Lisbona, see de Lisbona
Resh Methibta, 13n, 74, 76
Reuben B. Hakham Israel Sason, 161
Rhine, 74
Rhode, Erwin, 5n
Romano, Mercado, 147
Rosewater, 189
Rosh Be Rabbanan, 70
Rosh Kallah, 7
Rosh Yeshibah, 14, 76
Rosh Yeshibath Geon Ya'akob, 60, 70
Rupee, 119, 161
Ruhamah, 211
Russia, 93

Sa'arti, 99
Sabbath, 8
Sabbath Kallah, 151
Sabbath Zakhor, 179
Sabt el-Niswan, 186
Saburaim, 47
Sa'd el-Dawlah, 79, 92–93, 97, 100, 102, 123
Sadakah, see Sheikh S.
Sadid el-Dawlah Abu Mansur, 78
Sadkah Husein, 114–116, 118–121, 128, 132, 191
Safed, 106, 108, 136, 138, 142
Safi el-Dawlah, 92
Safi el-Dawla Joshua, 79
Sahl b. Natira, 30, 33
Sahl ibn Rabban al-Tabari, 39
Sa'id b. Hibbat Allah, 87
Saleh, father of Sheikh Sason, 206
Sedeh Laban, 133
Saleh b. Daniel, 159
Saleh b. David b. Jacob, 120
Saleh, ancestor of Sheikh Sason, 206
Salem, 211
Samaria, 1
Samuel, the Exilarch, 69
Samuel, R. (of Mosul), 91
Samuel, 67, 211
Samuel, the prophet, 64, 84
Samuel (Mar), 5, 166
Samuel, son of Gaon Solomon, 61
Samuel b. Abi el-Rabi', 78
Samuel b. Abraham of Tahart, 53
Samuel b. Ali, ha-Levy Gaon, 17–18, 62, 64–65, 70–74, 87, 95–97
Samuel b. Azariah, 82
Samuel b. Daniel ha-Kohen Gaon, 80, 81
Samuel R., Ben Hofni, 46, 51, 56–58
Samuel Ezekiel Diveker Cammodan Moocadum, 204
Samuel b. Joseph el-Baghdadi, 60
Samuel b. Joseph Resh Kallah, 42, 47
Samuel b. Judah ibn Abun, 82
Samuel b. Meir, 5
Samuel ha-Naghid, 26, 42–44, 53, 57, 59–60, 188
Samuel, Mar, Rosh Kallah, I, 7, II, 14
Samuel of Schlettstadt, 101
Samuel b. Yahya el-Maghrebi, 82, 85
Sant el-Nakis, 187
Saphir, Jacob, 207, 212–213
Sar of Coucy, 214
Sar Shalom b. Phinehas the Nasi, 100
Sarajevo, 146
Sarat Point, 6
Sardanapalus, 2
Sarjadah, see Aaron b. Joseph ibn Sarjadah
Sarraf Bashi, 123
Sason, the Nasi, 168
Sason b. Ezekiel Reuben Manasseh, 175
Sason b. Ezekiel b. Solomon b. David, 168
Sason b. Saleh (the Nasi), 131
Sason 'Abdallah, 108
Sassanides, 6
Sassoon, Sir Albert, 137, 171, 201, 208
Sassoon (D. S.), 27n, 42n, 50n, 64n, 74n, 75n, 78n, 79n, 96n, 99n,

100n, 101n, 128, 138, 139, 141, 153n, 167–168, 189n
Sassoon, David, 125, 140, 206–208, 211, 216
Sassoon, David, Benevolent Institution, 207
Sassoon, David, General Hospital, 207
Sassoon, David, Industrial Reformatory Institution, 207
Sassoon, Elias David, 137
Sassoon, Sir Jacob, 209
Sassoon Mechanics' Institute, 207
Sassoon, Mrs. Selina, 204n
Sassoon, Solomon David, 152
Satanas, see Joseph b. Isaac ibn Satanas
Saul b. Joseph Moses, 154
Sayyidna bin Daud, 90
Schechter, Dr. S., 32, 49n
Schlesinger, 'Akiba Joseph, 171
School, Gan Menahem Daniel, 171
School, Gan Yeladim, 171
School, Haron Saleh, 171
School, Kerem, 171
School, Rahel Shahmoon, 171
School, Shammash, 171
School, Wataniyyah, 171
Schreiner, Martin, 82
Schwarz, 78n
Scribe, 143
Scroll of Ezekiel, 98
Se'adyah, Gaon, 12–13, 17–25, 28–29, 31–33, 46, 51, 57
Se'adyah, the poet, 53
Se'adyah Husein, 191
Seadyah, Son of Samuel b. 'Ali, 77
Se'adya b. Shalom, 41
Se'adyah Sirbani, see Sheherbani
Sedakah wu-Mishpaṭ, 113
Seder 'Akedath Yishak, 177n
Seder ha-Kinoth Shesimanam Nebiah, 180
Seder ha-Yom, 150
Seder Rab Amram Gaon, 35
Sefarad, 61
Sefardi, 75, 83, 147, 179
Sefer ha-Galui, 22
Sefer ha-Kawwanoth, 134
Sefer Hakkabod, 78
Sefer ha-Ma'asiyyoth, 201, 214
Sefer Hasidim, 54
Sefer Hezyonoth, 200
Sefer ha-Meassef, 52
Sefer Pizmonim, 179, 209
Sefer Raziel, 214
Sefer ha-Yashar, 201 214
Seine, 80
Selim Pasha, 130
Seljuk Sultan, 86
Semah Jacob, see Jacob Semah
Semah b. Shahin, 19
Semah b. Solomon, 13
Serugh, 66, 95
Seruj, see Serugh
Sha'ar ha-Shamayim, 204
Sha'are Sedek, 133
Sha'are Teshubah, 112
Sha'are Yerushalyim, 110
Shabbatta de Righla, 8, 14, 18
Shabbethai, 107
Shaf we-Yathib, 166
Shah, 178
Shahis, 119
Shahr el-Nakis, 187
Shahr el-Tamam, 187
Shalom b. Aaron Obadiah ha-Kohen, 209
Shammash, R., Moses, 164
Shams el-Dawlah Abu el-Hasan b. Abu el-Rabia', 78
Shanghai, 171, 187, 203, 216–217
Shapira Moses, 120
Shasha, Mordecai, 127
"Shashsha", 182
Shbinnimat, 184
Sheherbani, Se'adyah, 107
Shealtiel Khalaf b. David ha-Melamed, 61
Sheikh Ishak Sarraf 'Ali, 169
Sheikh Sadakah, 97
Sheikh Sason, 122–123, 166, 206, 209
Sheikh Yishak, 155
Sheikh Yishak Abu el-Bnat, 170
Shem Tob ibn Gaon, 78
Shem Tob Bible, 100
Shem Ya'akob, 140
Shemaryah b. Elhanan, 41
Shene Eliyyahoo, 151
Sher'abi, Shalom, 150
Sherira, R., Gaon, 7, 10, 12–14, 17–18, 39, 41, 43, 45n, 46–51, 56–57
Shib'ah be-Adar, 150
Shibbale ha-Leket, 74
Shin'ar, 61, 90
Shindookh family, 114, 186
Shindookh, Aaron b. Samuel, 134

Shindookh, Moses b. Mordecai, 110, 113, 122, 132
Shindookh, Sason, b. Mordecai b. Moses, 132–134, 167, 176
Shindookh, Simeon b. Hakham Sason, 168
Shir Hadash, 137
Shir Yediduth, 133, 215
Shira Hadashah, 150
Shiraz, 128–129, 139
Shi'ur Komah, 48
Shohet, Elisha, 177n, 178n, 201
Shokhene Bate Homer, 186
"Shoshanna", see the *Jewish Gazette*, 214
Shomre Miswah, see Society
Shulhan 'Arukh, 141
Shushbin, 184
Siah Yishak, 145–146
Siddur Rab 'Amram, 14
Sidney, 122, 125
Sidon, Moses, 129
Siege, 126
Simeon b. Moses, 134
Simeon b. Rahamim Shohet, 139
Simeon, R., b. Yohai, 96, 181
Simhah daughter of Sliman b. Jacob, 205
Simhath Yom Tob, 145
Simhoo-Na, 189
Singapore, 203, 211
Sittehon, Menasseh, 192
Slat 'Ajimiyyee, 169
Slat Berraniyyi li-Kbiri, 167
Slat Bet Barukh Karkukli, 168
Slat Bet Daniel, 168
Slat Bet el-Masri, 169
Slat Bet Ghawi, 168
Slat Bet Mkammal, 169
Slat Dinah, 169
Slat Farha, 169
Slat Farhah bint el-Dabbi, 169
Slat Hakham Hazkel, 168
Slat li-Jdidi, 168
Slat el-Kbiri, 133, 149, 165, 167
Slat Malkah, 169
Slat Moshi ibn Dahhan, 169
Slat Moshi Sofer, 169
Slat Na'sa, 169
Slat Reemah, 169
Slat Reuben Shukur Isaac, 169
Slat Shaul Yosef Moshi, 169
Slat Sheikh Yishak, 168–170
Slat Yishak Shalom Obadiah, 169
Slat Zghayri, 167
Slaves, 211
Sliman b. David Ma'tuk, 111
Sliman b. Jacob b. Sliman, 136–137, 208
Smooha, Sason b. Elijah, 157–159, 163–164, 190
Smyrna, 137, 139
Snake, 194
So'an (Egypt), 61
Society, Hebrath Meyassede Beth ha-Refuah, 175
Society, Hebrath Tomkhe Torah, 175
Society, 'Ozere Dallim, 175
Society, Shomre Miswah, 173
Society, Zekhuth ha-Rabbim, 175
Sofer, 105
Sofer, Moses b. Sadkah 161
Solomon ibn Addereth, 43
Solomon b. 'Ali b. Tabnai, 29
Solomon Bekhor Husein, 133, 165n, 201
Solomon b. Isaac b. Hayyim, 141
Solomon b. Joshua David Bekhor Sadkah Husein, 174n
Solomon b. Judah, 41, 55
Solomon b. Samuel Gaon, 61–63
Solomon b. Samuel Petit, 80–81
Solomon Yakob, 205
Somekh, R. Abdallah b. Abraham, 141–144, 149, 151, 157, 160, 162–163, 201
Somekh family, 141
"Sorkhe Huppah wu-Milah", 183
South African *Jewish Chronicle*, 210
Spain (Spanish), 27, 38, 40, 46, 52–54, 60–61, 76, 89, 107, 123, 138, 178, 208
Spanish Schools, 52
Steinschneider, M., 96, 207
Stone from Palestine, 167
Straits Settlements, 202, 211
Sublime Porte, 123, 130, 147, 158
Sufis, 30
Suk Baghdad, 6
Suleiman Pasha, 123, 168
Suleiman Pasha el-Kebir, 131
Sullam Haslaha, 201
Sultan of Turkey, 131, 158, 177
Sumer, 6
Superstitions, 157, 182, 190ff

Sura, 4, 7–8, 12, 14–15, 18, 21–24, 26, 45, 50–51, 56–57, 97
Surat, 108, 203, 205
Surganah, Jacob, 120
Susiana, 5
Suss Oppenheim, 214
Synagogues of Baghdad (also see under 'Slat'), 154, 165
Synagogue of Barna Shala, 10
Synagogue, Beth El, 213, 215
Synagogue, Beth Ya'akob, 146
Synagogue, Great, see Slat el-Kbiri
Synagogue, Keneseth Eliyaboo, 209
Synagogue Lawsuit, 215
Synagogue, Maghen David, 207, 215
Synagogue, Maghen Shalom, 206
Synagogue, Neweh Shalom, 210, 215
Synagogue, Ohel David, 207
Synagogue, Shoshanim le-David, 217
Syntagma of Aaron, 39
Syrian, 33, 41,39, 66, 70, 72, 84, 205
Syriac, 39, 106

"Tabdil", 185
Tabernacle, 135
Tabernacles, 8, 54
Tabriz, 78
Talmud, 4
Talmud Torah, 172, 191
Talmudic Age, 4, 9
Tanḥuma, 9
Tankih el-Behath, 99
Tannaim, 47
Tanners, 33
Tartars, 91
Teaching methods, 172
Tebah, 166, 190
Tehillab we-Tifereth, 145
Tehillah le David, 133
Tehmasp, Shah, 178
Tel-Aviv, 217
Temple of Jerusalem, 2–3, 167, 180
Tiber, 74
Tiberias, 17, 96
Tientsin, 216–217
Tigris, 2, 8, 30, 41, 69, 87, 89, 95–96, 101, 155
Tik, 166, 181
Tikkun Tefillah, 149
Tikkune ha-Zohar, 151
Timghiyyee, 188
Tiriyyat, 167
Tlemcen, 75, 122
Tobi, Moses, 205
Tokfo Kohen, 139
"Tokhahoth Muser", 111
Toledano Rephael Moses, 162
Tomb of Ezekiel the Prophet, see Ezekiel
Tomb of Ezra the Scribe, see Ezra
Tomb of Joshua the High Priest, see Joshua
Translation of Greek classics, 39
Travels of R. Benjamin of Tudela, 200
Tunis, 148
Turgeman, R. Abraham, 129
Turkey, 131
Turki, Abraham, 127
Turkish, 93, 138, 157, 161, 206
Turkish Empire, 123
Turkish law, 143
Tutira Bara, 7
Twena. Solomon b. 'Abed, 135, 140, 214–215

'Ubaidallah b. Yahya el-Hakani, see Vizier
'Ukba, Mar, Exilarch, 10, 17–18, 28, 38
Urfa, 130
Urim we-Thummim, 114
Urmia, 139

Vital Hayyim, 108, 134, 200
Vizier, 92
Vizier Ali bin 'Isa, 36
Vizier bin el-Furat, 34–37
Vizier Ibn Abi el-Baghl, 29
Vizier Muhammad bin 'Ubaidallah bin Yahya, 34
Vizier, Samuel ha-Naghid, see Samuel ha-Naghid
Vizier 'Ubaidallah b. Yahya el-Hakani, 33, 34

Waad Adath ha-Bablim, 217
Wakf, 103
Wakil (Acting), Hakham Bashi, 159
Wali, 122–123, 159, 161

Wali of Baghdad, 125, 168
wa-Tithpallel Hannah, 135
wa-Yibhar Moshe, 109
Wardiawa, 128
Wast, 75, 95–97
Wedding ceremonies, 183
Weiss, 13
Western communities, 31
Widduyim, 75
Wolf, 193
Wolff, Joseph, 126–127

Ya'arath Debash, 209
Yahalalel the Prince of Baghdad, 98
Yahid ha-Dor, 79, 88
Yahuda, A. S., 195–197, 199
Yahuda, Isaac B. S. E., 170n, 195
Yahya, 41
Yahya b. Elijah, 130
Yayin Harekah, 139
Yehizkiyyahu b. David, 27
Yehizkiyyahu b. Judah, 26
Yehoseph ha-Naghid, 27
Yehosef, Son of Samuel b. 'Ali, 77
Yehudah, Ezekiel, 210
Yehudah family, 210
Yehudai, R., Gaon, 32
Yemen (or Yemenite), 52, 65, 69, 85, 90, 95, 98, 176–177, 186, 198, 205, 210–212
Yeshibah, 70, 170, 215
Yeshibath Ma'aseh Nissim, 147
Yeshibath Sheikh Yishak, 195
Yohanan b. Nappaha, 1
Yohasin, 9
Yom el-Sanah, 187

Zacut, Abraham b. Samuel, 9, 106
Zaku, 142
Zalkind, Raphael Moses, 213
Zalman, Elijah b. Solomon, 152
Zalman, Solomon, 213
Zar el-Mahbub, 119
Zara Elji, 130
Zechariah b. 'Ali, 79–80
Zechariah b. Berakhel, 67
Zechariah b. Berakhiah, 70, 72
Zechariah, Rev. Nissim Elisha Eliyahoo, 209
Zechariah b. Se'adyah b. Jacob el-Dahri, 95
Zechariah b. Rahamim, 129
Zekhuth Aboth, 152
Zekhuth ha-Rabbim, see Society
Zerubbabel, 46
Zibhe Zedek, 141, 201
Zikhronoth Eliyyahoo, 148
Zilkha, 168
Zion, 2, 146
Zionist (or Zionism) 201, 217
Ziyadet Allah III, 40
"Ziyarah", 184
Zohar, 96, 155

www.ingramcontent.com/pod-product-compliance
Lightning Source LLC
Chambersburg PA
CBHW022011300426
44117CB00005B/131
* 9 7 8 1 8 4 3 5 6 0 0 2 9 *